Monarchy

THE ROYAL FAMILY
AT WORK

Robert Hardman

EBURY PRESS

This book is published to accompany the television series
Monarchy: The Royal Family At Work, produced by HTI and RDF
Television and first broadcast on BBC One in 2007

1 3 5 7 9 10 8 6 4 2
 Published in 2007 by Ebury Press.
Ebury Press is a division of the Random House Group Ltd.

The Random House Group Limited Reg. No. 954009.
Addresses for companies within the Random House Group can be found
at www.randomhouse.co.uk

A CIP catalogue record for this book is available from the British Library

ISBN 978 0 09191 842 2

The Random House Group Limited makes every effort to ensure that
the papers used in our books are made from trees that have been legally
sourced from well-managed and credibly certified forests. Our paper
procurement policy can be found at www.randomhouse.co.uk

Commissioning editor: Mathew Clayton
Project editor: Steve Tribe
Designed by Oil Often
Printed and bound by Firmengruppe APPL, aprinta Druck, Wemding,
Germany

To buy books by your favourite authors and register for offers,
visit www.rbooks.co.uk

Photo credits:
Ian Jones Photos 4, 6, 8, 12, 16, 18, 28, 29, 58, 66, 68, 78, 81, 84, 95,
97, 98, 105, 106, 108, 110, 113 (right), 116, 123, 129, 132, 136, 143,
147, 148, 153, 155, 161, 166, 174, 175, 179, 181, 183, 185, 186, 187,
188, 192, 197, 205, 216, 252 (top), 256, 260, 262, 264, 270
PA Photos 37, 40, 47, 76, 89, 246, 247, 249
All other images © HTI and RDF Television

CONTENTS

ACKNOWLEDGEMENTS

Inevitably, *Monarchy: The Royal Family At Work* dwells primarily on the Monarch. Our particular thanks, therefore, go to Her Majesty the Queen. By 'us', I mean those involved not just in this book but also in the accompanying BBC television series. We are, collectively, very grateful to HRH the Prince of Wales, HRH the Duke of York, HRH the Earl of Wessex, HRH the Princess Royal and HRH the Duke of Gloucester, all of whom gave us interviews while on their travels. Our thanks also go to HRH Prince Philip, Duke of Edinburgh, HRH Prince William, HRH Prince Harry, HRH the Duke of Kent, HRH the Duchess of Cornwall, HRH the Countess of Wessex, and HRH the Duchess of Gloucester, all of whom gave us special access to their schedules.

We would also like to acknowledge the contributions from the former Prime Minister, Tony Blair, his successor, Gordon Brown, and the Leader of Her Majesty's Opposition, David Cameron. Of the many people around the world who have also played their part, we would like to thank the Presidents and Governments of (in alphabetical order) Estonia, Ghana, Latvia, Lithuania and the United States of America – as well as the First Lady of the United States, Laura Bush.

So many members of the Royal Household gave us the benefit of their time and wisdom. Space prevents me from listing them all but none has spent longer or worked harder in fielding our demands than Penny Russell-Smith, former Press Secretary, and Stuart Neil, Assistant Press Secretary to the Queen. Particular thanks are also due to Sir Robin Janvrin, Edward Young, Samantha Cohen, Ailsa Anderson, Paddy Harverson, Patrick Harrison and their respective teams. Inevitably, our work has overlapped with that of the Armed Forces, whose members have always been unfailingly courteous and efficient, as have the many other public servants to whom we have turned.

This book covers the same territory as the television series. The series has been a joint effort led by executive producer Andy Goodsir, who has been the driving force behind this entire project since we first developed it in 2005. The talents of the director, Matt Reid, the producer, Freya Sampson, and cameramen, Charlie Russell and Dom Hill, have been instrumental in bringing this book to life. I am indebted to them all. Special thanks also go to RDF executive producer Stephen Lambert and his RDF team – Mark Lesbirel, James McGregor, Janne Read, Heather Milward and Cat O'Gorman – as well as to the editing team of Brett Irwin, Mark Knowles, Ann Lalic, Jake Roberts and Meg Townend.

My old Fleet Street colleague, Ian Jones, has excelled himself with the stunning photographs which accompany the superb camera work from the series. I would like to thank Mathew Clayton at Ebury, project editor Steve Tribe, and my agent, Charles Walker at PFD, for all their hard work and sound advice. Historians Simon Sebag Montefiore and Andrew Roberts have also been generous with their time. Finally, no one has been more supportive or patient in the creation of this book than my darling wife, Diana. Three hours after I wrote the final sentence, she gave birth to our beloved daughter, Matilda.

To my parents,
Richard and Dinah Hardman

INTRODUCTION

Even the most powerful man on earth admits that it will be rather a special occasion. In his six years at the White House, the President of the United States of America and the First Lady have entertained almost every world figure of note. But no visitor has warranted a fairy-tale white-tie banquet. Until now.

Thousands of miles away, in a tiny nation where democracy has only just reached its teens, another president is planning one of the biggest parties since his country attained freedom. It will be quite a fairy-tale occasion there, too.

On the lawn of Buckingham Palace, a woman arrives for a tea party which will change her life. Outside one of the Palace's many drawing rooms, a poet, a bishop and a colonel are sitting nervously on huge sofas, waiting to be summoned. In the Houses of Parliament, the most senior legal figure in the land is practising a ten-second ritual. It does not require him to utter a word but he is a bundle of nerves. On a dusty Iraqi airfield, a combat-weary battalion is in a state of high excitement. So, too, are 300 proud relatives, gathered in the Buckingham Palace Ballroom to see their loved ones honoured by the nation. These are just random snapshots plucked from random weeks in a random royal year. Some of these occasions will lead the news bulletins. Others will warrant no more than a paragraph in a local newspaper. But, in most cases, those on the receiving end will remember the moment for as long as they live. Few forget an encounter with the Monarchy.

There have been countless books and productions devoted to the Royal Family. One film recently won an Oscar. There will, of course, be many more. The first question they tend to address can usually be summed up as: 'What are they really like?' The answers vary but they have helped to define a cast of characters which the public feels it knows reasonably well.

I am not sure outsiders will ever know what members of the Royal Family

are 'really like', just as we will never know what it is 'really like' to be them. Many biographies, no doubt, will continue to address these questions but that is not the purpose of this book.

No family in history can have endured more personal scrutiny than the post-war House of Windsor but whatever the fact, fiction, conjecture and polemic, that scrutiny appears to have done little to alter the fundamental attachment which the British people have towards the Monarchy.

What do I mean by 'Monarchy'? If the Royal Family, led by the Sovereign, makes up the cast, then the Monarchy is the production. And it is a system which also produces the Head of State for fifteen other independent countries and a further fourteen overseas territories (not to mention the Monarch's role as Head of the Commonwealth, a post-imperial cousinhood spanning nearly a third of the world's population).

Another question, frequently asked but perhaps more pertinent, is: 'What are they for?' Former Prime Minister Tony Blair believes that most people have a pretty clear idea. 'The public has come to an acceptance that the Monarchy is the best form of constitutional authority and a good way of keeping the country together in a changing world,' he says. 'It is, I believe, completely secure both in the affections of the people and in their understanding that it's got a role to play.'

Generations of 'constitutional experts', historians, journalists and politicians from every part of the spectrum have attempted to define the role of the Monarchy. None, though, has surpassed a political journalist whose observations remain the standard work on the subject after 140 years.

Most countries have a conventional written constitution; Britain has a constitutional monarchy instead. Laws are made by Parliament and the Monarch governs within those laws. So perhaps the closest thing we have to

a written constitution is the brilliant piece of analysis by a nineteenth-century editor of *The Economist*. If monarchs have a manual, it is, surely, *The English Constitution* by Walter Bagehot. Originally a series of essays, it was published as a book in 1867. The British Empire was near its peak and yet its matriarchal figurehead, Queen Victoria, was starting to attract criticism for retreating into private grief following the death of Prince Albert six years earlier.

Bagehot's achievement was to explain the role of the Monarchy to its squabbling subjects. Everyone knew that the Sovereign was a human link with the past and the signatory to all Acts of Parliament. But what else was he or she for? Bagehot split the machinery of State into 'elements of the constitution' and divided them between the 'efficient' and the 'dignified'. The first, notably the Cabinet and the Commons, were the parts of the State which actually ran the country. The 'dignified' elements were those which lacked direct power but enjoyed influence and inspired reverence. Chief among these was the Monarchy.

Bagehot observed, rightly, that the 'dignified' bits had an absolutely crucial role in propping up the 'efficient' elements. It was the Sovereign, he explained, who gave the State and its Government a human persona. 'The use of the Queen, in a dignified capacity, is incalculable. Without her in England, the present English Government would fail and pass away,' he wrote. These were not the words of a toady. In the same paragraph, he described Queen Victoria and the then Prince of Wales as 'a retired widow and an unemployed youth', but he went on to explain their allure:

'Royalty is a government in which the attention of the nation is concentrated on one person doing interesting actions. A republic is a government in which that attention is divided between many, who are all doing uninteresting actions.'

As far as Bagehot was concerned, the Royal Family, supporting the Monarch, only further underlined that sense of family, hearth and home at the apex of the nation. Equally, the Monarchy's position as custodian of the Church gave the Government further respectability.

The Queen alone could appoint prime ministers and dissolve Parliament. Above all else, Bagehot defined the Monarch's greatest powers as follows: 'The Sovereign has, under a constitutional monarchy such as ours, three rights – the right to be consulted, the right to encourage, the right to warn. And a king of great sense and sagacity would want no others.'

Bagehot's conclusions have stood the test of time and today remain the most authoritative guide to the constitutional function of the Monarchy. But Bagehot was not right about everything. One of his sternest warnings concerned privacy: 'Above all things our royalty is to be reverenced, and if you begin to poke about it you cannot reverence it. When there is a select committee on the Queen, the charm of royalty will be gone. Its mystery is its life. We must not let in daylight upon magic.'

But Bagehot could not foresee television, mass media and the Internet, let alone the shape and values of twenty-first-century society. The Monarchy has been well and truly poked about. It has endured the probings of a select committee. Historians and everyone else can argue whether daylight came in with newsreels, the televising of the Queen's Coronation, the modern documentary or the tabloid press. But it is, surely, beyond question that if the curtains had stayed resolutely drawn, the Monarchy would be withering away, if indeed it was still around at all.

In the course of writing this book I have spoken to many, inside the Palace and out. All of them believe that the pace of royal change has actually gathered momentum in recent years. It might seem odd that an institution run by the same person for more than half a century should be busier, livelier and more proactive since the boss turned 80 than it was when she was 30. But it is undeniable that there have been more fundamental changes to the Monarchy since 1990 than at any stage since the Abdication Crisis of 1938.

Opening the doors to tourists, the gardens to pop concerts and the accounts to the taxman and the world would have been inconceivable as recently as the late 1980s. Having just retired after six momentous yeas as Lord Chamberlain, the Queen's top courtier, Lord Luce is well-placed to offer an overview: 'The Monarchy cannot just exist. It depends on popular support to survive, and that means adapting,' he says. He is fond of quoting the most famous line from Giuseppe di Lampedusa's classic novel, *The Leopard*: 'If we want things to stay the same, things will have to change.'

Left: The State Opening of Parliament.

To survive, the Monarchy has always had to adapt, evolve and modernise. The present Sovereign made that clear in 1997, some weeks after the death of Diana, Princess of Wales. There has been endless conjecture – in print and in film – of the Monarch's thinking during those turbulent months. This, though, is what the Queen said at the Prime Minister's luncheon to mark her Golden Wedding anniversary. Having acknowledged that both monarchies and governments depend on the support and consent of the people, she went on: 'That consent, or the lack of it, is expressed for you, Prime Minister, through the ballot box. It is a tough, even brutal, system but at least the message is a clear one for all to read. For us, a Royal Family, however, the message is often harder to read, obscured as it can be by deference, rhetoric or the conflicting currents of public opinion. But read it we must.'

And read it she has, according to the Prime Minister who was sitting alongside her that day. 'The most important thing to realise about the Queen,' says Tony Blair, 'is she has understood that the fundamental link in the modern world between the Monarchy and the people is around the concept of duty. She understands that, provided that there is a clear sense of duty for a Monarch, people then reciprocate with loyalty and affection.'

Today's Monarchy is mindful of other duties and responsibilities well beyond those laid down by Bagehot, who was writing long before the Commonwealth came into existence. These more modern duties are not codified or enshrined in some oath. They are simply the ways in which today's

Queen has come to define her own role. That is why she splits her duties into two distinct categories: Head of State and Head of Nation. If the former comprises her constitutional role, the latter is the more human stuff.

So, I will leave it to others to keep on asking, 'What are they really like?' And I feel that Bagehot, his successors and the Queen herself are better qualified to answer the question: 'What are they for?'

This book, like the BBC television series which accompanies it, does not attempt to judge the Monarchy. This is not a history book but a portrait of an entire year. It aims to answer another serious question: 'What do they do?'

During the year in question, the Sovereign and thirteen members of her family will perform some 4,000 engagements, ranging from, say, a visit to a mosque in Pakistan to a coffee morning in Hampshire. If you work on the very rough basis that every engagement involves either a handshake, a conversation, a simple 'hello' or a passing nod to 100 people, then, each year, nearly half a million individuals will have some sort of royal encounter.

Add to that the 40,000 people who receive an invitation to a royal party every year, the 2,500 people who receive an honour at an investiture every year (plus the 7,500 people who will accompany them), and you start to understand why one former private secretary describes the Monarchy as being in the 'feel good business'. How does it all happen? And what are the results?

Over the course of our year on the inside, I have sought to examine just what goes on in the working life of Britain's best-known family.

We know the big, televised rituals because they come round like the seasons – the State Opening of Parliament, Remembrance Sunday at the Cenotaph, the Christmas Broadcast. But we have little idea of what goes on behind the scenes, of all the planning which goes into even the most ritualistic of events. We may read that the Queen held a garden party. We will not read of her inspection of the medical facilities or the chocolate cake in advance. Nor will we read what happened to the guests.

Only the most assiduous readers of the Court Circular will note that an ambassador or a spiritual leader has had an audience of the Queen. And they certainly won't know what was said. They won't be aware of the detailed computer analysis which decides royal movements six months in advance. They will not see the frantic efforts being made to track down the appropriate retired admiral to represent the Queen at a particular memorial service or the dance of the furniture at Buckingham Palace as a state room switches from dinner mode to party mode and back again. They won't see the royal

Left: Former Prime Minister Tony Blair has an audience of the Queen at Balmoral.

chef travelling to meet the animals which will end up in his oven for the next
state banquet. And, crucially, they won't see the other side of the equation
either – the quiet pride of a ship's company after a visit from their Lord High
Admiral; the satisfaction of the headmistress whose years of patient, hard
graft have not passed unnoticed.

Fine, some will say, but that is the Monarchy's job and that is what we pay
for. Some, indeed, will argue that we pay too much or that these are tasks
which could be performed by an elected head of state. Cost aside, there will
always be those who argue for an alternative system on ideological grounds,
claiming that a Monarchy perpetuates the class system or that it is unfair
for the top job to reside with one family. But opinion poll after opinion poll
suggests that the vast majority of people in Britain are happy with a system
which is quintessentially British, ancient, colourful, familiar and immune to
tampering. No politician, however over-mighty, can take the Crown.

That is not a debate I intend to enter here. Just as one can write a book
about the work of the Church or the Army without veering off into a debate
about the existence of God or the ethics of killing, so one can examine the
work of the Monarchy without a lengthy discussion of the pros and cons of
alternative systems of government.

After more than fifteen years of reporting on the life and times of the
Royal Family all over the world, my own view is that the United Kingdom
has been fortunate to have a constitutional monarchy. Britain might take its
own stability, continuity and individuality for granted but, seen through the
eyes of the rest of the world, these are enviable strengths. And at their root
lies the Monarchy.

I do not vouch for the peoples of Australia, Canada, Jamaica, New
Zealand, Papua New Guinea or any of the other realms which share the same
Head of State but, inevitably, have a different relationship with a Sovereign
based overseas.

In Britain, we have a system which is certainly popular and benign. It
receives more scrutiny than almost any other public institution and, as a
result, regular doses of criticism. Sometimes this is fair, sometimes this is
exaggerated, sometimes this is wrong. But this institution has learned to take
the long view and move with the times rather than the headlines. In good
weather or bad, it has just got on with the job.

This book and the BBC series that goes with it will, I hope, help to explain
the job.

CHAPTER ONE

HEAD OF NATION

S hane Huggins is on a mission. Absolutely nothing is going to stop him marching across the classroom to present the Queen with a trio of plastic-wrapped tulips. 'They're red,' he says thrusting them into the Queen's hand. 'Thank you,' the Queen replies, scooping them up. 'Do you know what flowers they are?' 'They're red,' Shane replies, with faultless three-year-old logic. 'Yes, I suppose they are,' the Queen replies, catching the wide-eyed pride of Shane's mother, Maria.

Emerging from the classroom, the Queen shakes another fifty or so hands – everyone from managers to midwives – and walks out into the car park of the new children's centre in Whitehawk on the outskirts of Brighton. It's not the grand, Regency quarter of the raffish old South Coast town which grew into a handsome resort on the back of royal patronage. This is the rough end. 'Most of our clients come from round here,' whispers a police officer. Perhaps that is why the welcome is louder here than it was earlier in the city centre where this royal away-day began with a concert at the Theatre Royal and a bicycle ballet in the street. Whitehawk does not get much in the way of VIPs, let alone monarchs. The engines start and a small royal convoy – four motorbikes, one State Bentley, one minibus for officials and one police Range Rover – moves off slowly. Hundreds of children try to run alongside for as long as they can as the convoy cruises through the council estate up to the main road. It picks up pace and drives at a sedate speed for a few miles back to the local railway station.

Along the unmarked route, the reaction is so similar that, from inside the convoy, it almost seems a genetic impulse. A handful of bored students, waiting at a bus stop, do it. So do a group of paint-splattered builders waiting to cross the road. They are going about their business on a pleasant spring afternoon when they suddenly see the most famous woman in the world looking at them. Without even thinking about it, they all stop in their tracks and wave. And, once the car has passed, they all turn to the people around them and lower their jaws. No doubt, all these people have varying views on life and society. They are not manic monarchists – if they were, they would have gone to see the Queen at one of her designated engagements. These are just ordinary people who, while walking down the street, have bumped into that reassuringly familiar face which has been on every stamp, coin and Jubilee mug for as long as most people have been alive.

At Brighton station, the Queen boards the Royal Train. The Royal Class 67 diesel locomotive, 'Royal Sovereign', slowly heaves its claret-coloured carriages out onto the branch lines of southern England. The train will take a slow, roundabout route to Windsor, weaving in between the rush-hour schedules. The Queen's day will not make the national headlines, but it will be long remembered in East Sussex. The local paper is already clearing the decks for a twenty-eight-page souvenir supplement. The Queen has a souvenir of her own. Settling down into her small sofa, she starts to browse through the farewell gift which she received from Whitehawk: a book of children's hat designs for their Monarch. 'I was rather amused by that,' she says, smiling at a picture of herself sporting a huge green splodge. 'Very inventive children, aren't they. But there's always the usual thing of why wasn't I wearing a crown?'

She starts laughing at another picture of herself in a pirate's hat. But less lively reading material is on its way. Her Assistant Private Secretary, Edward Young, arrives with the afternoon's red box, a slightly battered leather-bound thing the size of a deposit box, which bursts open with folded state papers when unlocked. The Queen puts aside her book of hats and works her way through a pile of dreary-looking Government correspondence before settling down with a Foreign Office profile of the President of Ghana who is coming to stay at the Palace next week. There are also notes on her forthcoming state visit to the USA. The British Ambassador will not make any key decisions without her approval.

It has been an unremarkable day in the sense that this is the sort of thing monarchs have been doing for years: visit a region, shake hands, open something, commemorate something, salute various deserving causes and meet as many people as possible before heading off to meet a visiting head of state. This is the day job of royalty. It is not the constitutional, parchment-signing side of being Monarch; that might be termed Head

Above: On board the Royal Train, the Queen prepares to study the day's state papers.

of State. This is the human side which is just as important. This is the Queen as Head of Nation.

At an age when most people are stuck rigidly in their ways (she was born in 1926), the Queen is very conscious that the Monarchy has to move with the times. Few will be aware that today's programme has been planned with forensic analysis. And few will appreciate that if a tour like this had taken place just twenty years previously, there would have been outrage. Some would have suggested that Her Majesty's advisers had taken leave of their senses. How could she come to Royal Brighton and not visit the Royal Pavilion? Why was she taken to unlovely Whitehawk instead? Why was the civic reception full of ordinary charity workers instead of important local dignitaries? There will be no complaints after this visit, though. All the elements of today's programme were personally approved by the Queen (as they always are). After more than fifty years in the same job, a bit of change is a blessed relief. Today has been a simple lesson in the basic rule of Monarchy: just keep on doing the same thing – differently.

HEADQUARTERS

This is the Palace tour you do not get with a £15 summer ticket. Stand at the front of Buckingham Palace and look through the railings. There will usually be someone going in or out of the entrance on the right-hand side, the Privy Purse Door. This must be the smartest tradesmen's entrance in the land. Provided you are expected, you crunch across the gravel, past the sentries, and there is no chance to knock before the door is pulled open by a footman in the Palace livery of black tails and scarlet waistcoat. You are now inside royal headquarters, 650 rooms ranging from the grandest imperial state apartments to drab little basement cubicles. The Queen and Prince Philip occupy only one section of one floor of one wing, but the Monarch always has a pretty shrewd idea of what is going on everywhere – upstairs and downstairs. 'She really does take an interest in it all,' says Lord Luce who recently retired as Lord Chamberlain, the most senior non-royal figure in the Palace. 'It is always a mistake to assume that the Queen does not want to be bothered with minor details.' The Queen may not regard this as 'home' – Windsor Castle serves that function – but it is her headquarters, and it is from here that the Monarchy is run all year round. No one has spent more time in this place and no one knows its ways and its quirks better than the present boss.

EAST WING

Buckingham Palace is really a mish-mash of extensions and renovations bolted together over a couple of centuries. But think of it as a giant square. The best-known side is the East Front which looks out onto the crowds and up the Mall. It is this façade which the world recognises instantly. Beyond it, on the principal corridor above the arches, is a series of conference rooms and guest suites. Above these are royal apartments with staff accommodation on top. Immediately behind the famous balcony lies the ornate Centre

Room with its Chinese decorations. On either side, the royal housekeepers are dusting down the rooms for the forthcoming state visit by President Kufuor of Ghana. His senior staff will stay in this part of the Palace. (The US Secretary of State, Condoleezza Rice, stayed here during the American state visit of 2003.) They will enjoy a wonderful view up the Mall and some old-fashioned luxury in rooms with the feel of an elegant hotel circa 1950 – sheets and blankets, not duvets; baths, not showers. Beneath cream-flecked wallpaper and portraits of Alexandra Federova, Empress of Russia, and Queen Charlotte, the occupant of Suite 227 will be able to recline on a large, bronze-coloured sofa and stare out at the London skyline. The resident reading material might be a little dry for some tastes: bound volumes of the 1898 *Magazine of Art* and copies of the works of Virgil stamped 'Osborne Library'. But guests can request whatever they want.

Suite 227's bathroom, a huge expanse of green carpet with a big bath, basin and loo tucked into a corner, is nearly as big as the sitting room. This room was clearly designed before the shower had attained social respectability. There is a half-hearted shower apparatus protruding above the bath, but it appears to be more of a gesture than an instrument of hygiene.

On the floor above, three well-dressed women are sitting at desks covered with cards, letters and paintings. This is the office of the Ladies-in-Waiting, who act as companions-cum-assistants to the Queen wherever she goes. When they are not 'in waiting', they handle much of her correspondence up here in a small suite with the atmosphere of a girls' school common room. China corgis and old photos line the mantelpiece. Lady Susan Hussey, a Lady-in-Waiting for forty years, is writing a reply to a girl called Katie who has sent the Queen a beautifully decorated birthday poem which she reads out: ' I hope you receive cards galore/loving wishes by the score…' Lady Susan makes sure that Katie's card is logged on a computer and adds her own words to a pre-prepared thank-you letter. 'The trouble these children take!' she says. 'I hope they know the Queen sees it and appreciates it. These are her letters, after all.'

Lady Elton, a self-confessed 'new girl' having been in the job for only 20 years, says that the Queen has started receiving large amounts of post from young people in former Soviet republics. 'They probably don't expect to get a reply,' she says, 'but everybody gets one.' Every reply is by post, never email. Annabel Whitehead, previously a Lady-in-Waiting to Princess Margaret, says the Queen is also in great demand as a party guest: 'A lot of people invite her to their wedding. They'd probably be appalled if she said yes!'

On the right-hand corner of this wing is the Information Office, where Emma Goodey, the editor of the royal website, is updating a site which routinely attracts 300,000 visitors and several million hits every week. In the far corner, Jane Smith, the Palace's information officer and resident agony aunt is trying to prepare the day's Court Circular, the official list of royal activities which will be circulated to the newspapers. But she is busy fielding the sixth anguished call of the morning from the same lady caller in France who believes there is a Government conspiracy against her. 'Anyone can call the Palace and if they don't know who to talk to, they come through to me,' says Jane (it is not her real name – she avoids getting personal).

'Most people want help with something. When is the Queen next coming to Devon? How do I nominate someone for honours? Sometimes, they have a real problem and they want the Queen to help. It might be someone struggling with a pub quiz question – we don't help with those. And there are the hoaxers. I can usually spot them. I had someone last week asking if he could borrow the flag from the Palace. He sounded like a radio station. I just said that we were using it ourselves thank you very much.' Next door, in the press office, the Queen's Assistant Press Secretary, Stuart Neil, is dealing with a succession of American television networks who are busy making plans for the Queen's forthcoming state visit to the USA. No, she will not be doing any live interviews.

Left: Ladies-in-Waiting in the office.

The Main Players

THE LORD CHAMBERLAIN

Companies have a chairman. The Royal Household has the Lord Chamberlain, a conciliatory and erudite presence who is the chief link between the Monarch and her staff. This ancient position dates back a thousand years to the days when the Lord Chamberlain had the key to the Monarch's bedchamber and his jewels. To this day, the incumbent carries a special key of office, although no one has any idea what it unlocks. He chairs a monthly meeting of the five main heads of department and also liaises between all the other members of the Royal Family. 'You are there to listen to problems, to appoint good people and to give fearless advice,' says Lord Luce, the former Arts Minister, who recently retired as the seventh Lord Chamberlain of the present reign. 'You've got to lead the whole Household and make sure it's a happy place. If it's not happy, it's not doing its job for the Queen.'

Right: The Queen welcomes her new Lord Chamberlain, Earl Peel.

The Five Departments

Private Secretary's Office (PSO)

Run by the Private Secretary, with a Deputy Private Secretary and an Assistant Private Secretary, this is the official link between the Monarch and the world. The PSO runs her diary at home and overseas, administers her constitutional duties and deals with events as they arise. At any given time, one of the three private secretaries will be with the Queen, even during holidays and Christmas.

The Office's responsibilities also include overseeing the Press Office and the Co-Ordination and Research Unit, which helps plan the work of all the members of the Royal Family. The PSO handles between 50,000 and 100,000 pieces of correspondence in any given year and despatches thousands of cards for 100th birthdays and other anniversaries. The Queen's red boxes – which contain everything from state papers to internal memos – are prepared here.

Lord Chamberlain's Office (LCO)

This department runs all ceremonial events, large and small, and is responsible for a bewildering range of royal duties. Despite the historic title, it has very little to do with the Lord Chamberlain himself and is run by a senior courtier called the Comptroller, usually an ex-military man. Investitures, garden party invitations, royal weddings and funerals and most state occasions are arranged through here. The LCO has responsibility for the Central Chancery (decorations and regalia), the Ecclesiastical Household (the Queen's Chaplains), the Royal Medical Household, the Marshal of the Diplomatic Corps, the Royal Warrants, the Royal Mews (both horses and cars) and all ceremonial bodyguards, such as the Yeomen of the Guard and the Royal Company of Archers. If anyone has a fiendish question about some arcane aspect of royal life, this office and its surprisingly youthful team of experts will probably have the answer.

EⅡR

The Lord Chamberlain is commanded by Her Majesty to invite

....

....

to an Evening Reception at Buckingham Palace on Tuesday, 21st November 2006 at 8.30 p.m.

Evening Dress — White Tie
Full Ceremonial Evening Dress for Serving Officers
Decorations

Please reply in writing by 23rd October to:
State Invitations Secretary
Buckingham Palace, London SW1A 1.

LE MENU

Roulade Ballindall.

Salmis de .
Panchée .
Ch.

Pomme.

M.

LES VIN.
Riesling, Dom.
Château Batailley,
Royal Vintage 1963

MARDI LE 28 NOVEMBRE 2006

LE MENU

Cornets de Saumon Fumé et Crabe

Suprême de Faisan en Croute
Purée de Choux de Bruxelles
Carottes Glacées
Pommes Nouvelles Rissolées
Salade

Rhubarb Crumble and Ice Cream

LES VINS
Pouilly Fumé, Domaine Chibault,
André Dezat et Fils 2003
Château d' Angludet, Margaux 1990
Royal Vintage 1963

MARDI LE 5 DECEMBRE 2006

BUCKINGHAM PALACE

THE MASTER OF THE HOUSEHOLD'S DEPARTMENT

With around 250 staff, this is the largest department in the Palace and keeps the whole royal machine ticking over. The Master, usually a senior figure from the Services, is responsible for delivering all royal services, from cleaning and cooking to planning a state banquet or mending the roof. He is in charge of F Branch (food), G Branch (general staff such as footmen and builders), H branch (housekeeping) and C Branch (craftsmen). At any moment, this team might be planning a private luncheon for the Queen, a garden party for 8,000 or the installation of a new bathroom.

THE PRIVY PURSE AND TREASURER'S OFFICE

The Keeper of the Privy Purse, also known as the Treasurer, is the man in charge of the Monarchy's finances. As Treasurer, he manages the Queen's public funds from the Civil List, which cover her duties as Head of State, and also the Grants-in-Aid, Government funds to cover buildings maintenance and official travel. As Keeper of the Privy Purse, he supervises the Queen's private finances, most of them deriving from the Duchy of Lancaster. The Privy Purse funds other members of the Royal Family and the residences at Balmoral and Sandringham. The department also covers personnel matters, travel budgets and the finest stamp album in the world, the Royal Philatelic Collection.

THE ROYAL COLLECTION DEPARTMENT

This department restores and maintains all the royal paintings, furniture and other treasures. Although the collection belongs to the Queen as Sovereign, she cannot sell it and it receives no public funds. To maintain some of the world's finest art – it includes priceless works by Leonardo da Vinci, Van Dyck and Gainsborough – the Royal Collection needs the paying public. Around one million people visit Windsor Castle each year and nearly as many again visit Buckingham Palace, the Queen's Gallery next door and Edinburgh's Palace of Holyroodhouse. The Royal Collection also has shops and a range of merchandise which generate extra income worth nearly £10 million which is reinvested in the collection.

Other Royal Households

Aside from the Monarch, there are thirteen other members of the Royal Family who perform public duties. The Prince of Wales, the Duchess of Cornwall and Princes William and Harry have their own household, based at Clarence House and funded by the Duchy of Cornwall. The other members of the Royal Family have their own private offices – usually a private secretary and a couple of assistants – which are funded by the Queen from her Privy Purse income.

IN ATTENDANCE

The Queen likes to have dependable people around her to smooth any situation. If she embarks on a walkabout, she cannot shake every hand or grasp every bunch of flowers. And it is always useful to have extra eyes and ears. So, whenever you see the Queen at an engagement, two members of the supporting cast always stand out. One will be in a very elegant dress (though not so elegant that she upstages the Queen). The other will be in uniform.

Left: Commander Heber Ackland, Equerry to the Queen, accompanies the Queen and the Duke of Edinburgh.

LADIES-IN-WAITING

Unpaid and utterly trusted, ladies-in-waiting serve as assistants, letter-writers, bouquet-gatherers and general companions to the Queen in public and in private. At any engagement, at least one of them will be in attendance and, on a state visit overseas, there will usually be two. In public, they might help the Queen scoop up gifts or liaise with the local dignitaries. In private, they answer a lot of personal royal correspondence and are always on hand to meet and greet (and calm nerves) when visitors arrive to meet the Queen. Led by the Mistress of the Robes, they are often, though not exclusively, longstanding personal friends of the Royal Family.

EQUERRIES

Dating back to medieval times, the position of equerry once revolved around the Monarch's horses. Today's equerries are drawn from the Armed Forces and act as diary planners and quick-thinking Sir Walter Raleigh types who can be relied upon to drop a metaphorical cloak over any puddle in the royal path. The Queen has a Senior Equerry, an ex-Army officer who also doubles up as Deputy Master of the Household and is responsible for her more private social engagements. Below him is the Equerry, always a rising officer on secondment from the Armed Forces. The three Services take it in turns to fill this prized post but the Queen also has a temporary Equerry, traditionally an officer from the Coldstream Guards, who helps out at big occasions. When she is visiting one of her realms – Australia, Canada, New Zealand and so on – she will be assigned an equerry from that nation's armed forces. Other members of the Royal Family have their own equerries. An ability to ride a horse is no longer a prerequisite.

Above: Diana, Lady Farnham, a Lady-in-Waiting, assists the Queen in Romsey, Hampshire.

Above: The Palace lake. Above right: Buckingham Palace seen from the forty-acre grounds.

NORTH WING

We head down the North side of the Palace, the real nerve centre of the place. At one end, is the London residence of the Queen and Prince Philip. They live, quite literally, above the shop with their own side door, a 'Watch Out. Corgi About!' sign and a lot of white decor to counter the darkening effect of facing north. Today, in her Private Audience Room, the Queen is appointing a new Lord Chamberlain to oversee the Royal Household. Lord Luce has formally retired with a rousing send-off from the entire workforce and his successor, Earl Peel, arrives to be installed. 'This is your badge of office,' says the Queen, handing him a ceremonial key. 'I've heard all about it,' Lord Peel replies. 'You wear it in a very strange place,' the Queen explains. 'Dare I ask where?' the new Lord Chamberlain enquires delicately. The Queen points. 'Here, at the back – which always seems a silly place to put it because somebody might pinch it!' Below them is the Private Secretary's Office, led by the man in charge of the Queen's diary and her dealings with her various governments around the world. The retiring Private Secretary, Sir Robin Janvrin, a former Royal Navy officer and diplomat, has received the customary 11 a.m. call from his boss. He has gone upstairs to discuss the weightier matters of the moment.

When he has finished, the Queen rings down to her Deputy Private Secretary or her Assistant Private Secretary. A unique buzz lets them know that the Queen is on hold.

'Good morning, Ma'am,' they will say automatically. 'Are you free to come upstairs?' she always replies. Neither has ever answered 'No'. One of these two will go upstairs to run through more immediate affairs – Church and Services appointments or Royal Warrants which need approval, away-day programmes which need to be discussed. The Private Secretary's Office is the reception point for the 50,000 personal letters which the Queen receives in an average year (it can be double that in a big year like the Queen's 80th). Most royal intelligence-gathering is done here, too. What should the Monarchy be doing more of? What should it be steering well clear of? Some of this comes through the ancient network of Lord Lieutenants, the Monarch's representatives in the counties. Some of it evolves through a trusted reservoir of informal contacts – a canny retired Dean here, a perceptive business leader there. Some of it is hard marketing data.

We move out into the Private Secretary's Corridor, a long, dark stretch of red-carpeted gloom, interspersed with the odd bust or portrait. The other wings are full of light but this floor is for work. In one annexe, Warwick Hawkins is leafing through thick files of statistics and cross-checking with a computer screen. A senior civil servant on secondment from the Home Office, Warwick is in charge of the Co-Ordination and Research Unit (CRU) which serves as the royal database. With his team of three researchers, he will process the thousands of annual requests for a visit from a member of the Royal Family. He has a complex filtration process. A school in one county wants the Queen to celebrate its 200th birthday, but she visited that county last year. Is another member of the Royal Family due to be in the area? If so, when? As the Princess Royal puts it, 'We try to avoid each other.' If the Queen is visiting an area with several minority communities, the CRU will check these are all included at the appropriate locations. 'The Royal Family cannot go anywhere if they haven't got an invitation but some sections of society might not think of inviting them, so I might call a Lord Lieutenant and suggest a particular group,' Warwick explains.

He compiles a thick, closely guarded annual dossier called 'Analysis of Royal Engagements', which breaks down a year's royal work in the United Kingdom – usually around 2,500 engagements, not including foreign tours. These are then split up by sector – agriculture/elderly/faith/health and so on. The Queen visits the average county every four or five years, less in the case of smaller populations. 'If a visit is overdue, I might gently sound out the Lord Lieutenant. They usually bite your hand off.'

The London suburbs are, it transpires, an unlikely area of royal neglect. Since the Golden Jubilee, the Queen has been keen to put that right. 'A lot happens in London and a lot outside it, but the outer boroughs are huge, and yet there has been a tendency to overlook them.' Warwick's wall has a map of the capital covered in a multitude of little stickers. Where next? 'Bromley looks a pretty good candidate. It's big and it's got no dots.'

To one side, a narrow stairwell leads up to the Anniversaries Office, where Jo Wilson and a team of two are performing one of the Monarchy's happiest tasks – sending out congratulations. The tradition goes back to 1917, when George V decided to send a telegram to any royal subject reaching the age of 100. When the Queen came to the Throne, the annual tally of these telegrams was roughly 300 in Britain and another 100 in her other realms. Today, those figures are, respectively, 4,500 and 2,200 per year. Instead of a telegram, she sends a card with a photograph and a printed signature.

Centenarians are only part of the picture. Those who reach 105 get a card – and they continue receiving one for every subsequent year of their life. By far the biggest demand is for diamond (60th) wedding anniversary cards. In 2005, a bumper year because of the number of marriages at the end of the Second World War, the Queen sent out 24,000 diamond wedding cards around the world, 18,077 of them in Britain. Cards are also despatched for 65th and 70th (platinum) anniversaries and every year thereafter. 'We get some lovely thank-you letters and the Queen sees them,' says Jo, a former office administrator for a firm of accountants. 'They can be very touching,' she says, holding up a photograph of a diamond wedding couple with an inscription: 'You made their day'. Jo's fax machine hums ceaselessly with copies of birth and marriage certificates flooding in from relatives and care workers who want to notify the Palace that Granny's big day is looming. Every anniversary must be authenticated and every card will be despatched by special delivery two days in advance (if the anniversary falls on a Sunday, Jo must ensure the card lands on the Saturday). Each card is contained in a sealed package and woe betide the postman who fails to confirm delivery. 'Failure to do so by 09.30 will initiate an enquiry from The Palace,' reads the stern warning on the postal package.

Nearby, the Loyal Greetings Office is preparing one of the 1,500 loyal greetings sent out each year to organisations which request one. The members of the Royal Artillery Clerks Association have just sent a loyal greeting to their Captain General – the Queen – ahead of their 73rd anniversary reunion in Woolwich. The Queen has personally approved a reply: 'As your Captain General, I much appreciate your kind words and in return send my best wishes to you for a successful and memorable evening…' It always goes down well with the old soldiers.

Left: A corgi on sentry duty.

The Eleven O'Clock Meeting

When you have travelled the globe more times than you can remember, the prospect of a trip to Weston-Super-Mare might start to pall. But the Queen seems positively excited about her forthcoming trip to the Somerset coast. She has even been reading up on local issues. 'Last night's report from Parliament — I was rather intrigued by it,' she tells her Private Secretary, Sir Robin Janvrin. 'The Severn Estuary Barrage scheme. Do you know anything about it?'

Below: Sir Robin Janvrin and the Queen begin their eleven o'clock meeting.

Sir Robin promises to gather further details. 'It says it could generate five per cent of our electricity supply which sounds quite useful,' the Queen continues. 'It'll be relevant to the Weston-Super-Mare visit, Ma'am,' Sir Robin concurs. Furthermore, the Queen has a letter inviting her to tea when she is in the town. 'They'd be "more than happy to offer a refreshment", which I think is very kind of them,' she says with a smile.

And then the discussion switches to a new Transport Bill, the death of a soldier in Afghanistan and a Cabinet Minister in need of a travel permit. Des Browne is heading for a NATO summit but, as Defence Secretary, he can't leave British soil without his Sovereign's consent.

It is, in other words, a typical eleven o'clock meeting. The Private Secretary's Office is the Queen's official link with the wider world. And, every day, she likes to get up to speed on absolutely anything which might concern any of her sixteen realms.

Today, there is a letter from the Prime Minister of New Zealand about a new medal and another document from the Prime Ministers of both New Zealand and the Cook Islands concerning a new appointment. 'Two Prime Ministers on one page. It's not bad is it?' she remarks, signing her authority. Every day, she will sign a dozen documents with 'Approved, ER' or 'Elizabeth R'. Officially, it is not her signature but the 'Sign Manual'.

There are ordinary letters to be processed, too. The Queen sees a good cross-section of the thousands sent in each week. 'That's a "bluey" from somebody in Iraq,' she says, handing Sir Robin a Forces airmail. 'I have had quite a lot of letters about the Gurkha VC,' she adds. 'It's obviously worried people enormously, hasn't it?' The news that an 84-year-old war hero from Nepal has been denied medical treatment in Britain has indeed caused outrage. 'Shall I get more on that?' asks Sir Robin. 'I think it would be useful,' says the Queen. 'I've only read about it in the paper.' Days later, the decision is quietly reversed.

Sir Robin relays a request from the Chief of the Defence Staff. 'Jock Stirrup has asked if he can see you in the next two or three days.' 'Good Heavens,' snorts the Queen. 'He's optimistic!' The diary is, indeed, packed and there is a full investiture on the only suitable day. Sir Robin points out that there might be a short gap following the Queen's meeting with the outgoing Governor-General of Antigua and Barbuda. 'I think I could do that,' she says.

There is some more diary planning to be done. The Queen needs to juggle a lunch for the Order of Merit, the Hindu Festival of Diwali and the State Opening of Parliament. The solution is to let the Prince of Wales attend the Diwali celebrations. The Queen likes to follow the movements of all the family – 'Edward told me he's away for a week,' she says as she checks a message for the Earl of Wessex to take to the Falkland Islands – and she must approve all royal travel costs over £2,500. Today, there is a request from the Duke of Gloucester who has engagements all over Shropshire. 'Gosh, a school, a foundation stone, a district hospital...' the Queen murmurs as she reads the itinerary. 'Yes, of course he can have a helicopter. It's not a day we're using it.'

Finally, it is back to Weston-Super-Mare. This could be an eventful trip. For the first time, engineers are going to try to run the Royal Train on bio-diesel made from oilseed rape. 'It's quite expensive,' Sir Robin notes. 'Very,' says the Queen, looking at the figures. 'Well, it might get us to the West Country.'

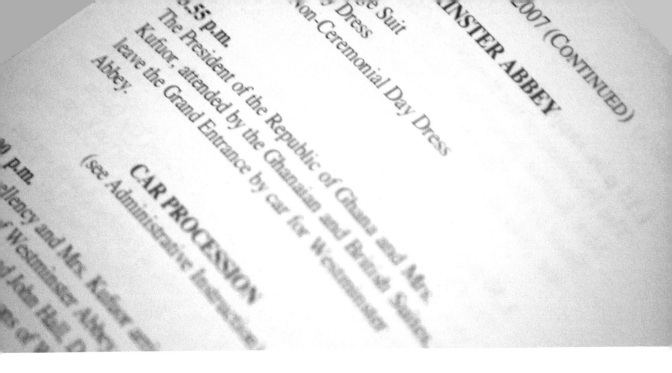

2007 (CONTINUED)

INSTER ABBEY

Non-Ceremonial Day Dress

Suit

Dress

.55 p.m.
The President of the Republic of Ghana and Mrs
Kufuor, attended by the Ghanian and British Suites,
leave the Grand Entrance by car for Westminster
Abbey.

CAR PROCESSION
(see Administrative Instruction)

.m.
ellency and Mrs Kufuor and
f Westminster
d John Hall D

Running down the other side of the grand but gloomy Private Secretary's Corridor, we find the Lord Chamberlain's Office (LCO), a team of ceremonial experts led by a man called the Comptroller. The present occupant of the post, Lieutenant-Colonel Andrew Ford, and Jonathan Spencer, his deputy, have overall responsibility for everything from cars to Crown Jewels to funerals and weddings. 'We don't have a rulebook full of protocol. We just try to do what makes sense,' says Jonathan, as he draws up the Ceremonial (the running order) for the Ghana state visit. In one office, Melissa Morris is picking her way through a list of names. She is the LCO official in charge of the Ecclesiastical Household – seventy clergy linked closely to the Queen. Some of these are domestic chaplains, parish priests for the various royal residences. Others are members of the College of Chaplains, a group of eminent clerics, limited to thirty-five, scattered around the country. They receive a free red cassock, a silver EIIR badge and the right to call themselves Chaplain to the Queen. 'It's like a knighthood for a priest,' says Melissa, a former teacher. A recent death means that there is a vacancy to fill. And Melissa has another list of names to examine. A retired admiral has just died, and someone must represent the Queen at the funeral. After the death of any senior public figure, it is Melissa's task to find a representative to pay condolences on the Queen's behalf. 'We read the death notices, and we need to move fast. The Queen must approve the choice. If it's, say, a former ambassador, we try to find someone who served at the same level at the same time.'

Next door, Alexander de Montfort is writing a letter to a company in London's East End which has just been awarded a Royal Warrant – the ultimate seal of approval – for making archive boxes for the Royal Household. David Waterman's family firm has been making boxes since 1897. When we finally see this letter arrive, David will be almost

Above: The 'Ceremonial' for the state visit of the President of Ghana.

speechless with emotion. Some of his staff will be in tears.

'It's wonderful to get one but horrible to lose one,' says Alexander, a former parliamentary researcher. The LCO is the link between the Palace and the Royal Warrant Holders' Association, the external body which polices the 800 companies who enjoy the right to use royal arms on their products. The chief criterion is that they must work for the Royal Household over a five-year period. 'They can be as unglamorous as you like – drains experts, whatever,' says Alexander. 'But we do have rules on where they can place the arms. If you are a loo hire company, we don't want the warrant on the loo.'

One of the LCO's more surreal tasks is organising regular state funerals and weddings, just in case one is actually required. Cometh the moment, State Invitations Secretary Alexander Scully will set up a well-rehearsed emergency operation using the Billiard Room and the Palace cinema, from where his team can despatch 2,000 invitations in a few hours. In his spacious red office, where two feather quills (purely decorative) sit before him, he is constantly redrafting lists of lists. 'I coordinate the guests. The basic job is to find people and get them there on the day.'

At the far end of the North Wing, the housekeepers are working hard on the grandest guest apartment in the building, the Belgian suite. This is where President Kufuor and his wife will be staying. On the walls, they will find a mix of framed Royal Family snaps going back for years (Princess Anne's first wedding is up there), along with some more traditional decoration. A huge portrait of Crown Prince Frederick of Prussia and a chandelier loom over the bed in the blue-decorated Orleans Room where the President and his wife will sleep. They will have a choice of two bathrooms – one green and one pink – and if they follow that vague whiff of chlorine, they will find themselves in the Palace swimming pool.

Above: The Queen meets author J.K. Rowling at a Palace reception.

WEST WING

The guests are already taking their seats in the Palace Ballroom, the largest room in the house. Ballroom it may be but no one has danced in here for years. This is the principal function room of the Palace, the place for investitures and the really big receptions. Today is a particularly unusual occasion because the Queen is presenting an award to a charity founded by her husband and supported by her youngest son. Prince Philip founded the Duke of Edinburgh's Awards in 1956 to promote self-discipline and confidence in young people. Now, fifty years later, it has helped millions in 120 countries and the Queen has decided to give it the ultimate seal of respectability, a Royal Charter, as well as a big party.

State trumpeters herald the arrival of the Queen in light blue. The Earl of Wessex, who has planned every aspect of this himself right down to the number of trumpeters, thanks his mother for the charter. She, in turn, thanks her husband for his work. 'You had the insight, courage and determination to establish the Award scheme fifty years ago,' she says. 'Since then, under your watchful eye, over five million young people have taken up the challenge.' There is much chuckling at the 'watchful eye' reference. Everyone, not least the Queen, knows that the Duke has been a demanding patron. She concludes on a strikingly personal note: 'For these remarkable achievements, you have my deep and enduring admiration, an admiration which words alone can never fully express.' It is an engaging blend of formal and family occasion.

Everyone retreats to the state rooms for lunchtime drinks and a party atmosphere soon develops. 'It's amazing. All you can do is gawp at all the nice decorations,' says Michelle Burns, a 25-year-old Gateshead youth worker. In fact, everyone has such a good time that some of them won't leave. 'We're just making a very small subtle hint,' whispers Ray Wheaton, the Page of the Chambers, as he implements his time-honoured guest-clearance strategy. He leads a line of footmen down the Picture Gallery, stop-starting in unison every few yards.

The West Wing is the part of the Palace where monarchs do their meeting and greeting. These treasure-packed halls and galleries were designed for entertaining and there is seldom a day when at least one of them is not in action. It might be an ambassadorial audience in the 1844 Room. Or it might be a relatively new innovation like the Christmas reception for 'achievers'. The latest includes comedian David Walliams, who has recently swum the English Channel. 'Were you covered in lard?' asks the Queen. 'She's more beautiful than I imagined,' says David afterwards. 'It's kind of weird when you meet someone that famous, there's almost a glow. Madonnas come and go but the Queen has been there from the moment I was born, so when you actually see her you want to have a good old look.'

THE LIVERY

From P.G. Wodehouse to countless films and period dramas, the butler has been an enduring – and often comic – mainstay of British fiction. At Buckingham Palace, however, the role is taken so seriously that the management is creating the world's first recognised qualification in it. The Queen does not have a butler as such. She has a Palace Steward, Nigel McEvoy, who arrived here twenty years ago and is now in charge of the forty Royal Household men and women dressed in the Palace uniform or livery. They start out as footmen, wearing dark tailcoats and red waistcoats, except on big occasions when they wear a 'state livery' of scarlet. The four most trusted footmen, who wear dark blue tailcoats, are called pages. For large events, extra waiters are hired from outside.

Above: The Yeoman of the Cellars, Robert Large, briefs his waiters before a state banquet.

On any given day, the footmen might be opening doors, greeting visitors, laying tables, polishing silver, serving drinks or waiting at table. 'We're perfectionists,' says Nigel. 'With the best will in the world, we won't always achieve perfection, so we're always very self-critical.' Nigel is working with Thames University to create a National Vocational Qualification for footmen. In addition to all their general duties, the footmen learn extra skills by circulating between Nigel's four heads of department, or yeomen, who also wear dark waistcoats. They are:
- The Yeoman of the Plate Pantry who is in charge of all silver and silver gilt plate
- The Yeoman of the Glass and China Pantry
- The Yeoman of the Cellars who, along with a Deputy Yeoman, looks after all the royal drink
- The Yeoman of Logistics who arranges all movements of baggage and office equipment.

Tonight's crowd includes the Queen's granddaughter, Zara Phillips, who is here because of her own achievements. The new world champion in the sport of eventing, she has just been voted BBC Sports Personality of the Year. Zara jokes with the Queen that the Royal Family and all the staff were behind the BBC's dial-in poll: 'They've all been voting on your phone bill!'

Another 'achiever' is television historian Dr David Starkey. 'I'm a huge believer in meritocracy. Everybody here is here because they have done something,' he says. 'That I think is very important.' He believes that innovations like this evening are long overdue because they show 'a Monarchy which is not, simply, aristocractic'.

Within hours, these rooms will have been cleared and set up for another event. And every summer, when the Queen and the Royal Family depart for Scotland, it is these apartments which are opened up to the paying public for a couple of months. In a good year, nearly 400,000 will come through the doors, raising around £6 million for the upkeep of the Royal Collection. They will marvel at the Throne Room (even if the Queen never sits on this throne) and they will take their time in the Picture Gallery, particularly when they learn that a Rembrandt, *The Shipbuilder and His Wife*, is the Queen's favourite painting.

But before any of the visitors arrive, the chatelaine performs one last inspection. 'No wonder the cupboards are bare,' the Queen jokes as she walks into the Ball Supper Room

Above: The Queen and her granddaughter, Zara Phillips, at a Palace reception for 'achievers'.

Above: The Queen inspects an exhibition of her own dresses in the Ball Supper Room.

to look at an exhibition of dresses she has worn over her reign. She spots a selection of heavily decorated numbers. 'What a lot of embroidery on them,' she sighs. 'They weigh a ton, too.' Turning round, she spots an old favourite: 'That's almost the first dress I ever had.' She proceeds into the Ballroom where a special exhibition of all her orders of chivalry has been laid out alongside all the overseas orders which she has received over the years. There is momentary pandemonium among the curators when no one can remember who designed a particular Australian medal. 'It drives me mad when I can't remember people's names,' she declares. She is not best pleased to discover that one of her decorations has been laid out with the ribbon of a male recipient. The curators smile weakly as she throws her hands up in mock despair and departs. Inspection done, the West Wing can open its doors.

SOUTH WING

Here lurk the number-crunchers. Every office has its finance director but few can boast a title to match that of Sir Alan Reid, the Keeper of the Privy Purse and Her Majesty's Treasurer. A straight-talking, football-mad Scot from the same Edinburgh school which produced Tony Blair, he is happy to stand his ground against all comers, be they critics of royal expenditure or a royal department in search of a bigger budget. 'We're audited by the big accounting firms and the National Audit Office. We have more transparent and efficient accounts than any other company or organisation,' says this former senior partner of a major international firm of accountants. 'Our Civil List accounts for last month came out on the second of this month. And, at 62p per person per year, we've got the best value Monarchy in Europe – even if we don't ride bicycles.' Sir Alan's office is decorated with an old Privy Purse, a huge silk pouch which must be replaced when a new Monarch takes the Throne. 'The present one came in very useful for storing Mars Bars at the Coronation,' he explains.

Next door are the royal travel department and the personnel department, which is responsible for the 1,100-strong royal payroll up and down the country. Of these, roughly 400 are staff paid for through state funding, 200 are private employees on the Queen's farms and estates and most of the rest work for the Royal Collection.

Further down the corridor, we find the Court Post Office – all brass, polish and pigeon holes with a special machine that stamps 'EIIR' on everything. Next door are the long-suffering Palace switchboard operators, who filter the outside world through this windowless annexe.

Upstairs, things are rather grander among the busts and portraits along the corridor that is home to the Master of the Household's Department. It is here that every aspect

Above: The Palace cellars. Above right: Unloading wine for the state banquet.

of royal entertaining, from tea for one to a state banquet will be arranged. The Master, by tradition, has no background in catering. Like his predecessors, Air Vice-Marshal David Walker has spent his professional career in the Forces – he was once seconded to the Palace as an Equerry to the Queen – but he is a firm believer in fresh ideas. Those who imagine that a hostess in her eighties always wants things done the same way are very wide of the mark.

'There is a changing approach to entertaining here,' he says. 'When I was Equerry, we did the same thing again and again. But there wasn't the focus on entertaining there is now.' His latest task is to accommodate 850 schoolchildren, 500 leading scientists and a dinosaur for a Palace tribute to the world of science. 'This will be the most ambitious reception we've yet done. I can't believe we're not more worried about it.'

Next door, one of two Deputy Masters, Edward Griffiths, is examining a sample of the carpet which is about to cover the wooden Ballroom floor forever. 'It's much more practical, and no one dances any more,' he says. An experienced hotelier and restaurateur, Edward runs a catering team of forty-nine, a general team (from footmen to roofers) of sixty-five and a housekeeping team of forty-four. Before any banquet, he will draw up menu options with the Queen's Chef, Mark Flanagan, and put them to

the Queen. Her only dislikes are raw food and messy dishes like spaghetti which can embarrass the eater. Most meals, though, are not for royalty. Hundreds of staff must be fed around the clock.

Edward is also drawing up bold plans for the guest accommodation. 'It may seem surprising given that we have 650 rooms, but we've only got six guest suites, which isn't many if you have a presidential delegation.' He is installing another three suites in what is known as the Hospital Wing, although the Master has just renamed it the 'Ambassadors' Floor' so as not to alarm future occupants.

A short distance away, the Master's Chief Clerk, Michael Jephson, is playing one of his games of three-dimensional chess. When not organising the big receptions, no one is better at the fine art of the seating plan, and there are 170 people to be placed at the upcoming state banquet for the President of Ghana. To Michael's immense relief, the old order of precedence was done away with a few years ago so that he can scatter members of the Royal Family around the table. 'People feel more comfortable if they see a member of the Royal Family at their end of the table.'

As well as inviting all the right people, he must have other people on standby to fill any last-minute gaps. A few people always have to cancel – even when it's dinner with the Queen. 'We organise an external banquet downstairs with Royal Household staff. They wear the same dress and have the same food, and we can slot them in upstairs at the last minute as required.'

A few rooms further on, we find the Queen's Senior Equerry, Lieutenant-Colonel Charles Richards, an urbane former Welsh Guards officer who also serves as the other Deputy Master of the Household. His duties cover all the Queen's private social arrangements, from holidays to 'dine and sleep' dinner parties. They also include selecting and inviting a cross-section of eight eminent people from all areas of British life to small private 'luncheons' with the Queen and Prince Philip. 'You can imagine the reaction I get when I pick up the phone to an actress or a charity executive and say, "Hello, this is Charles Richards from Buckingham Palace. I was wondering if you'd like to come to lunch with the Queen." They usually ask which one of their mates is winding them up.' A past master at finessing these occasions, he even has a special formula to make sure that those who are not sitting next to the Queen at lunch get equal time with her during drinks and coffee.

His team includes all the other Equerries and military staff on secondment from the Services, plus the Queen's Piper, the nearest thing to an official timekeeper in these parts. When you hear the pipes start up every morning beneath the Palace windows, you know it is 9.00 a.m. sharp. Right now, though, another of Charles's team is a few floors up on the roof, ready for action. When not working as an orderly, the Buckingham Palace Flag Sergeant is the man who must raise or lower the Royal Standard every time the Queen arrives or departs. And right now, it is coming down. Duty calls.

UNITING THE KINGDOM

The four jets from the Royal Air Force are so anxious to be on time that they arrive too soon. The diamond-shaped formation swoops low over Edinburgh Castle in a royal salute. The soldiers stand to attention and the crowd love it, but the intended target of the salute is still a full minute away. The Queen hides her disappointment as she emerges from the State Bentley to inspect the impressive new museum of the Royal Scots Dragoon Guards with its interactive reminders of heroics from Waterloo to Burma. She drops in on the souvenir shop, noticing various recordings by the regimental band. 'They're a very good band,' she tells the manager. As a proud Colonel-in-Chief, the Queen has heard them play on many occasions. 'I still enjoy listening to them after eleven years,' says the manager.

Outside, the crowds are ten-deep when the Queen emerges and walks across to see them. 'I'm from Australia,' one woman tells her. 'We're from Brazil!' 'Hungary!' 'Sweden!' The Queen nods and smiles in every direction. 'Sweden? I see.' An American lady is almost beside herself with excitement as she tells the Queen that she has just returned from the late Queen Mother's holiday home in northern Scotland. 'We've just been to the Castle of Mey. Your Mum had a lovely house. She collected shells like I did!' 'It was a very nice place for her,' the Queen replies. 'Oh, she was so beautiful,' the woman responds, while simultaneously pointing her video camera in the Queen's face.

Below: The Queen's bodyguard in Scotland – the Royal Company of Archers.

'She must have been a lovely woman!' The Queen climbs into her car as the American lady starts fanning herself. 'I'm shaking. I talked to the Queen!' But the Queen is not in Edinburgh today to boost tourism, nor simply to visit a favourite regiment. She is here undertaking what the Monarchy regards as one of its central roles: uniting the United Kingdom.

As a small nation comprising four small countries, the UK is not as united as it once was. Scotland has its own Parliament while Wales, Northern Ireland and London have Assemblies, and regional authorities take an increasingly elevated view of their own importance. Some of the tiniest town halls now boast a 'Cabinet Office'. Poll after poll shows that people increasingly regard themselves as something else first and British second. It does not suggest a rising tide of separatism so much as an increasing resentment towards central government. The Monarchy, though, is different. Like the Armed Forces, it is one of the few institutions to have a binding effect on this increasingly fractious country.

'I think people are at their best when you recognise the differences but you celebrate them in a unified way,' says the Prince of Wales. 'If you don't recognise these elements of diversity, then things can get more complicated. For instance, the military have regiments that reflect the tribal make-up of this country. People often work best if they are part of a recognisable unit that isn't too big and isn't too small but it's still part of the whole.'

Not everyone would agree, of course. There is plenty of shrieking and whistling as

Below: A royal visit to Cardiff to open the Senedd.

the Queen, Prince Philip, the Prince of Wales and the Duchess of Cornwall arrive in Cardiff to open the Senedd, the new £67 million Welsh Assembly building. Ranks of schoolchildren waving flags are upstaged by a small cluster of protest groups. A few placards are raised aloft with rather ponderous slogans like: 'An Oath of Allegiance to the People, Not The Crown'.

Neither the Queen nor the rest of her family appears to notice. Inside, she announces that this is a 'moment for the whole of Wales to celebrate'. There is big applause. The Royal Family did not insist on coming here. They were invited. Several of the protesters actually belong to the same political party as Lord Elis-Thomas, the Presiding Officer of the Assembly. He was the man who issued the royal invitations in the first place. And he is thrilled to have the Royal Family here to do the honours. 'It's just like a State Opening of Parliament,' he says proudly.

ON THE MOVE

It's a sweltering summer Saturday. Buckingham Palace is virtually deserted, but a removal truck has turned up. The Queen is off to Scotland for a week and the Royal Household does not travel light. The Palace's Yeoman of Logistics, Matthew King, is in charge of all royal luggage, whatever the trip. And, for this one, he has borrowed a detachment of soldiers from the Welsh Guards to help him.

Below: Loading and unloading for the trip to Holyroodhouse.
Below right: The bubble-wrapped 'knighting stool', ready for the journey.

The Queen will be spending her customary week at the Palace of Holyroodhouse, her Edinburgh residence. Since Scottish devolution, it has become an even more important part of her calendar. Normally, the place is inhabited by a skeleton staff, so all the supplies for a Monarch and her Court are taken up from London. There will be no time for shopping in Edinburgh. Matthew supervises crates of biscuits, chocolates, crisps, napkins, coffee and kitchen towels. It is a bizarre cargo. No sooner has a mountain of loo roll been packed into the lorry than a huge crate of silver appears from the vaults followed by piles of red boxes, several old leather suitcases and a curious wooden creation covered in bubble wrap. This turns out to be the 'knighting stool', the contraption on which a would-be knight must kneel while the Queen dubs him with her sword. Her staff have thought of everything.

The following morning, it all arrives at Holyroodhouse. Resident Superintendent Geoff Mackrell is doing his rounds starting at the front door where the carpet is an interesting shade. 'We don't have red carpets,' he explains. 'Blue is our house colour.' Very Scottish. Some of this Palace dates back to 1128 and it can be tricky adapting it to the needs of a modern head of state with eighty staff in tow. For most of the year, these rooms are open to the general public but, like all the staff, he is delighted to see them inhabited from time to time, even if there can be occasional problems with a ceiling held together by seventeenth-century horsehair and egg white. To make things more

interesting, a family of swallows has taken up residence just above the door through which the Queen will need to pass several times each day.

At the front door, the Holyroodhouse gardeners are starting to lay out displays to welcome the Queen. There are lilies, petunias, cornflowers, poppies, delphiniums, zinnias and sweet peas, all of them reared just round the corner in the royal greenhouses where the head gardener plays them a steady diet of Classic FM. Alison Robertson, whose husband used to run the local church, arrives with the seven-pound pot of marmalade which she makes for the Monarch whenever she is in Scotland. 'I call it the Queen's Marmalade. I know she enjoys it because I visited her once at Balmoral and she said, "I've finished your marmalade today"!'

Upstairs, royal upholsterer Allan Coggin is steaming every single curtain by hand. Robert Ball, the Queen's clockmaker for twenty-three years, is winding up all thirty-eight clocks, a relatively simple task compared to the 630 he has to look after at Buckingham Palace. A Guard of Honour stands rigidly to attention as the Queen arrives. The Lord Provost of Edinburgh goes through the ritual of presenting the Queen with the keys to the city. By a tradition she knows better than anyone, she hands them back, declaring: 'I return these keys, being perfectly convinced that they cannot be placed in better hands than those of the Lord Provost and Councillors of my good City of Edinburgh.' And with that, it's time to get cracking. Much as she may enjoy all this, the Monarch is not on holiday.

Among the first people the Queen meets are the main players from the new Scottish Parliament just up the road. The (then) First Minister, Jack McConnell, has arrived for an audience of the Queen in the Evening Drawing Room. He is announced by the Equerry and, despite the absence of a bow or a 'Your Majesty', he is all smiles. 'Good morning. How are you?' he asks the Queen. 'Fine, thank you. It's a lot cooler here than it is in the South.' 'It's been very thundery,' says Mr McConnell. 'I believe it was very, very wet on Monday,' the Queen replies. With the meteorological preamble out of the way, the talk turns to more serious matters and all officials leave the room. Mr McConnell's chat will be treated just like the Queen's conversations with the Prime Minister – confidentially.

The Duke of Edinburgh, meanwhile, is at the Royal College of Surgeons of Edinburgh (of which he is patron). He has come to open the college's new Quincentenary Hall, except that the builders have not finished it. There is a plaque for him to unveil in another room but the string doesn't work. Once the laughter subsides, he presents them with a parchment. 'I've been asked to present this scroll from the Queen to mark the occasion. You want to frame it before it gets too crumpled.' He is finally invited to use the latest keyhole technology to conduct a spot of imitation knee surgery on a length of pig intestine. After fiddling around unsuccessfully for a few moments, he realises he is about

Below: A gardener prepares for the largest garden party of the year at Holyroodhouse.

to cripple his putative patient. 'I think I'll leave it,' he says, grimacing.

The main event of the entire week, as always, will take place out on the Holyroodhouse lawns. It is in Edinburgh that the Queen holds her largest garden party of the year – and it often turns out to be the wettest. The guests are certainly the hungriest. At a Buckingham Palace party, 8,000 guests each consume an average of eight items of food. At Holyroodhouse, up to 10,000 guests scoff their way through an average of fourteen items. The Deputy Master of the Household, Edward Griffiths, has added some Scottish touches to the menu – shortbread and Dundee cake. Some things are the same in London or Edinburgh. 'How could we possibly serve tea without having classic cucumber sandwiches and strawberry tart?' asks Edward. How indeed? Every cucumber sandwich has been made with rock salt and dill, every crust removed by a team of thirty-two chefs who have been working since dawn.

'We British people love to queue,' he says, 'and generally, as soon as a queue starts, it will get longer.' Each serving station will serve several hundred people with exactly the same selection. With just minutes to go, the caterers watch nervously as Edward ticks everything off:

'We start with the Dundee cake, mini lemon tarts, Opera Gateau which is coffee and chocolate, mini scones filled with strawberry and Chantilly cream, little choux buns filled with coffee cream, classic strawberry tart, mini chocolate brownies, cherry tart, iced ginger and sponge, shortbread, strawberry tartlets…' Next come sandwiches and rolls: 'The blini with smoked salmon, the smoked trout with apple, the cheese and the chutney, the classic cucumber with dill and rock salt, egg and cucumber and then ham with mayonnaise. Plus soft drinks: pressed apple juice, iced coffee, still lemonade and then tea which is the Garden Party blend.'

Everything is waiting in pristine condition beneath chilled J-cloths as the gates open. The Army and the police are not the only guards on duty here. Whenever the Monarch is in Scotland, she is protected by her Scottish Bodyguard, the Royal Company of Archers. They are not trained bodyguards and their archery skills are mixed, to say the least. They consist of around 500 well-connected Scottish men who elect their own members, buy their own uniforms and provide an unpaid escort to the Monarch and other members of the Royal Family on formal occasions. Today, in their dark green uniforms and their Balmoral bonnets, they will mark the lanes through the crowds. Also on parade are the High Constables of Holyroodhouse, a self-selecting corps of thirty Edinburgh gentlemen, whose ancient duty is to guard this palace when the Monarch is in residence. Dressed in blue tailcoats, a silk top hat turned up at the side and white gloves, they carry silver or wooden batons, depending on their seniority. There is a friendly rivalry between the two organisations. Mingling together before the party, it is as if a Robin Hood convention has double-booked with a conference of circus ringmasters.

The guests represent a broad cross-section of Scottish life. For one couple, today is long overdue – by some sixty years in fact. John Love was a Royal Air Force pilot during the

Above left and right: Edward Griffiths, Deputy Master of the Household, inspects preparations for the Holyroodhouse garden party.

Second World War. In 1945, he volunteered to fly a glider full of troops into Germany. Badly injured by enemy anti-aircraft guns, he pressed on and managed to land his plane and his men in the thick of the action. For his bravery, he was awarded the Distinguished Flying Cross, one of the highest decorations for gallantry.

He was due to receive his award at Buckingham Palace but the King cancelled at the last minute and Mr Love received a letter of apology and his DFC through the post in 1946. At the time, he was sad but stoical. At least he was alive. Six decades later, the story of Mr Love's cancelled appointment reached the ears of a Lord Lieutenant, one of the Monarch's county representatives. As a result, the Loves have been invited here today so that the King's daughter can meet them in person and make amends. The couple believe it has been well worth the wait. 'We're thrilled,' says Mrs Love.

At 4 p.m., Ray Wheaton, the Page of the Chambers, opens a garden door and the Queen and Prince Philip emerge on to the lawn. The National Anthem strikes up and seems to send some offensive signal to the elements because, within moments, there is a darkening up above. There is the ominous sound of thunder and it is not far away. The Queen and the Duke of Edinburgh ignore it, as do most of the guests. Among the first to get a royal introduction in the Duke's lane are William and Nancy Allan from Irvine, Ayrshire. They were invited in recognition of Mrs Allan's thirty-five years of voluntary work for the Girl Guide movement. 'It's made my day,' says Mr Allan afterwards. 'It can rain if it likes.' And it does.

The Queen and the Duke raise their umbrellas, but there is no question of rushing for cover – or even of speeding up the royal progress across the lawn. If people are prepared to get soaked waiting to see the Royal Family, then it would be pretty rude to let them down. In any case, the rain makes a rather entertaining talking point. At one point, the Duke meets a couple who are cowering beneath a big yellow golfing umbrella with a Renault corporate logo on it. So talk turns to cars. The Duke has been enjoying a commercial in which people do a bottom-wiggling dance to simulate the outsized rear end of the Renault Megane. To the delight of the crowd and the astonishment of the umbrella-holder, the Duke gamely performs his own version. 'Do you do this?' he asks the couple, attempting the dance himself. They do not.

The rain is bucketing down. 'I think everyone's running away, Sir,' says one of the escorting Archers. The Duke is having a whale of a time, though. He has no intention of giving up. Next up is James Malone from Lanarkshire, an alumnus of the School of Infantry in Hythe. 'Were you there in the war?' asks the Duke. 'I'm not that old,' says Mr Malone with a laugh. 'Well I am!' says the Duke. Jackie Hampton and Jackie Sim, both from Brechin and both invited for services to the community, are ushered into the Duke's lane with their respective daughters, Nicola and Felicity. He praises their resilience during

Below: The Duke of Edinburgh, undaunted by the rain.

the storm. 'Stand by for rising damp!' he says, noting Felicity's open-toed shoes.

The royal couple battle on beneath umbrellas for a full hour until they reach the Royal Tea Tent. Mr Love is glowing after finally meeting his Monarch, sixty years on. For Timothy Wright, it has been a great day, too. The new boy among the High Constables, he has been on duty in his blue tails and turned-up hat for the first time. Just as he is about to receive the instruction to stand down, however, he has a new challenge. Two lady guests from Glasgow have had a wonderful day and round it off by chatting up this young man in a uniform. 'You're handsome,' says one as they each grab an arm. They sing the praises of the day, of the Queen, of the cherry slices and the chocolate cake. And the highlight? 'Standing with you, darling,' they say, squeezing Timothy's arms and inviting him on a winter cruise. It is just as well that the royal caterers do not serve anything stronger than iced coffee.

Below: New High Constable Timothy Wright and admirers at the Holyroodhouse garden party.

Right: Former
Conservative Party
leader Michael Howard
was among the guests
at St James's Palace
marking the anniversary
of the resettlement of
Jews in England.

UNITING THE COMMUNITIES

Buckingham Palace's Regency Room is different today. Normally, this comfortable green-coloured ground-floor sitting room, dominated by Stroehling's portrait of Princess Sophia, is a place for royal drinks. Today, it is full of wires and sound equipment. The Queen is recording her Christmas Broadcast to the nation. She reads it through twice, conscious that it must be delivered inside a narrow time band. 'Can you fit it all in?' she asks the producer. He can.

This is a message to a multicultural Britain of all religions and none and a Commonwealth of Nations of every race and creed. The Queen will take a Christian theme but her message will be entirely ecumenical. She made a Coronation oath to maintain the Church of England and a subsequent oath to preserve the Church of Scotland. According to the preface to the 39 Articles of the Church of England, she is 'Defender of the Faith'. She is not, contrary to popular misconception, the 'Head' of the Church of England as that position is occupied by God. But she is its Supreme Governor. And however much some public bodies may shy away from all overt religious imagery, the Queen does not. She takes the simple view that she is the Christian head of a multi-faith country. So, in one section of her broadcast, she quotes 'Christ' and 'Saint Paul'. But then she draws a more general conclusion: 'People of different faiths are bound together by the need to help the younger generation to become considerate and active citizens.'

Just as the Monarchy is concerned with 'uniting the kingdom' geographically, so it is determined to do the same in terms of different faiths and ethnic groups. 'We do not want to do box-ticking,' says Warwick Hawkins, the head of the Palace's Co-Ordination and Research Unit. 'But we want to make sure that we are always thinking of ways of including every section of society in whatever we do.' At most state occasions, all the major – and minor – faiths will be represented. Hidden away at the lower end of Windsor Castle is St George's House, a conference centre for all faiths, founded by Prince Philip. The Prince of Wales has been patron of Oxford's Centre for Islamic Studies since 1993.

On regional tours, minority demographics will be reflected in the programme. An away-day to West Yorkshire, for example, takes the Queen to an area with several large British-Asian communities. So, as well as an opera recital and a tour of the new police headquarters, the itinerary includes Bradford's Hindu Temple and a Kashmiri curry lunch in Huddersfield.

It is a cold, wet evening but they are queuing round the block to get into St James's Palace, the other big royal entertainment venue just up the Mall from Buckingham Palace.

Up and down the country, Britain's Jewish communities have been organising events to mark the 350th anniversary of the resettlement of Jews in England following their expulsion in 1290. And tonight's event is the climax of the celebrations. The anniversary organisers contacted the Queen's staff to discuss ways of including the Monarch in the event. The answer seemed pretty straightforward: a party at the Palace.

No matter that it was a Monarch – Edward I – who expelled the Jews and that it was a regicidal republican – Oliver Cromwell – who invited them back. These guests are all absolutely thrilled that they have been invited to St James's to meet the Queen and Prince Philip. 'I think the Monarchy carries a tremendous amount of stability and we Jewish people love stability,' says Rabbi Norman Zalud, who has travelled down from Liverpool for the party. The guests have been split into groups – the Queen does not want one long greeting line – and the ladies are frantically practising their curtsying. Outside caterers have been brought in to ensure that the food is kosher and the Palace is buzzing as the Queen appears through the Throne Room door with Prince Philip. Even the hired waiters are trying to take pictures on their mobile phones, until someone warns them that they are being paid to serve the drinks. The conversation flows, even when the room is suddenly cast into darkness.

The Queen has just reached Robert Rossano and Matthew Granger, both 22-year-old representatives of Jewish youth groups, when a power cut occurs. Quick as a flash, the young men make light of the situation. 'Maybe someone forgot to pay the bill?' says Robert. 'Are we expecting a cake?' asks Matthew. The Queen laughs and carries on. It is a surreal conversation, and it is a full half-minute before someone restores power, whereupon the Queen reappears in mid-conversation talking to Paula Scott from Nottingham. 'It is quite difficult, with no eye contact, to carry on a discussion in any meaningful way,' says Paula afterwards. 'But it didn't seem to knock her off her stride at all.' Robert cannot wait to tell his mother what has happened. 'Before I even came

Left: The Royal Maundy service.

here tonight, she told me to give her a call straight away. It's almost more of an event for her.'

Among the other guests is the former Conservative Party leader, Michael Howard. Isn't it ironic to find a Monarch and 500 subjects throwing a party, effectively, in honour of Oliver Cromwell? 'Not everything Cromwell did was bad,' says Mr Howard with a laugh. 'Most of them were – but not everything.' At the end, the Queen receives a *Hannuka* candlestick from the Chief Rabbi and the Duke receives a *Kiddish* cup. Everyone goes home happy. Except, presumably, a certain electrician, who must fear for his job.

ROYAL MAUNDY

Wherever she is in the world, the Queen will attend Church on Sunday morning. It might be a Church of Scotland service on a Highland hillside. It might be a tiny Anglican chapel in a Guyanese rainforest, where she once found herself in 1994. But it is religion which governs much of the Monarch's calendar. Christmas is the time to depart for Sandringham. At Easter, she moves her entire Court to Windsor Castle for a month. But, just before that, she performs one of the oldest royal rituals in existence. And it is one which she has embraced more enthusiastically than any other Monarch for centuries.

From the earliest days of royalty, Maundy Thursday – the day before Good Friday – was an occasion on which monarchs would feed and clothe a selection of poor people, wash their feet and give them some alms money. The tradition follows Christ's Last Supper, when he washed the feet of his disciples and ordered them to love one another.

Below: The Yeomen of the Guard rehearse their Maundy duties.

Some monarchs have proved more penitent than others. Elizabeth I only washed the feet of the poor after the same feet had been washed already. Charles I and Charles II avoided all foot-washing because of plague fears. James II washed a creditable fifty-two pairs of feet in 1685 but, thereafter, most monarchs ceased to take much interest in the ritual. The foot-washing was dropped in favour of a cash gift, known as Maundy Money, and Sovereigns were happy to leave the distribution to a senior bishop with the title of Lord High Almoner. It was not until Maundy Thursday in 1932 that George V revived the tradition of royal attendance with a one-off appearance at Westminster Abbey. The Queen's father, George VI, attended a few times. But it is the Queen who has completely revived the ceremony in its present form. She attends every year and, for more than forty years, she has taken the ceremony out of London to a different cathedral each year (another nod to regional sentiments).

So, the people of Guildford are particularly excited as they await the royal convoy outside their modern, red-brick cathedral – a building hitherto best known, perhaps, for its appearance in a horror film, *The Omen*. Inside, the Lord High Almoner is making a final check of all the Maundy Money which the Queen will be handing out. It is a complicated process. The recipients will be eighty women and eighty men – one for each year of the Monarch's life – and they will all be elderly. These days, they are chosen for their contribution to local life and not on grounds of poverty. Each of them will receive a red purse containing the traditional sum of £5.50 and a white purse containing 80p (a penny for each year of the Queen's life). But these coins are worth far more than their face value. 'What we see today is, quite genuinely, an act of humility on the part of the Queen,' says the Lord High Almoner, Nigel McCulloch, whose day job is Bishop of Manchester. It is a challenge for the Yeomen of the Guard who, by tradition, must process the Maundy Money into the service on ancient gold dishes. The dishes are so large that the Yeomen must carry them on their heads. It is a moment of pure comedy, as this bunch of retired soldiers in Tudor fancy dress rehearse their routines. In fact, there is plenty of fancy dress today. The Queen's attendants are all carrying towels as a reminder of the old foot-washing routine. Other people carry bags of herbs, an aromatic throwback to the days when herbs were thought to ward off infection. After a short service and a lesson read by the Duke of Edinburgh, the Queen moves through the cathedral dispensing medieval largesse to the soaring sounds of the cathedral choir. It all culminates in the sublime explosion of Handel's mighty 'Zadok the Priest', as the Queen reaches the end of the line. 'Many happy returns,' she tells a stunned Ruth Gillard, who has no idea how the Monarch knows that it is her birthday. It is a timeless scene, neither contrived nor comically out of date. Afterwards, the Queen proceeds outside to a series of walkabouts while the 'poor' of Guildford are left feeling thoroughly honoured.

THE ROYAL CAR FLEET

Built in 1825, the Royal Mews behind Buckingham Palace contains some of the finest horse accommodation anywhere in the world. Behind the grand façade, though, is a row of garages where seven chauffeurs look after the Queen's twenty-four vehicles. At the top of the royal fleet are the five State Cars which are used for the big public occasions. Two are claret-coloured, LPG-powered State Bentleys, built for the 2002 Golden Jubilee. Each has a huge goldfish bowl rear for optimum royal visibility at low speeds. On being informed that each has a top speed of 160 mph, the Queen replied: 'But what's it like at two miles an hour?' The boot space is tiny, with room for a fire extinguisher, a cleaning kit, an umbrella and a few red boxes. Also in the main garage are three petrol Rolls-Royces, a 1949 Phantom 6, a 1977 Phantom 6 and a 1985 Phantom 4. None of the cars has satellite navigation. The Duke of Edinburgh is a firm believer in the road atlas. Next in line are two Daimler limousines, often used by other members of the Royal Family. For more functional travel – and, more often, for staff movements – there are four Jaguar estates, a Jaguar saloon, a Vauxhall estate, two Land-Rovers, a Freelander and a Range Rover which the Queen uses to transport her corgis en masse. For royal retinues, there are three Caravel people carriers and an Iveco eight-seat minivan. The two most unusual vehicles belong to the Duke of Edinburgh. One is a London cab which he uses in the capital (unusually, it is dark green and has a passenger seat for a policeman but no For Hire sign). The other is the 'Jumbo', a fifteen-seat, all-terrain minibus for shooting parties. Built from a Land-Rover chassis, it has a trailer for guns and dogs. How are they are kept so spotless? Royal chauffeur Danny Martell has a simple formula: 'Clean sponge, clean chamois-leather, clean water.'

Left: One of the State Bentleys.

'I just wanted to give her a big hug,' says a lady called Rosemary, who was chosen as one of the 160 as a reward for her Mothers' Union work. She is adamant that she will not be spending her Maundy Money. 'I might have a little case made for it so that I can see it in my living room. You're meant to enjoy them aren't you?' The Supreme Governor would certainly agree.

THE ROYAL NETWORK

The views are spectacular through the drawing room windows – a vast stretch of the South Downs with a vineyard creeping up the side of an adjacent hill. The house is pretty but not grand, being a large cottage which once served the big house at the end of this drive. Round here, though, it is, effectively, Buckingham Palace. This is both home and headquarters to the woman who is, de facto, the Queen in this county.

Since Tudor times, the Monarch has had a representative in every county – the Lord Lieutenant. Originally, these were powerful local men who were expected to raise armies. Today, they are ninety-eight men or women who stand in for the Queen at official occasions, who serve as her eyes and ears around their particular county, who orchestrate all royal visits, sit on umpteen local bodies and serve as a quasi-royal figurehead. It verges on a full-time job but their only reward is a military-style uniform for men and a brooch for women. There is no pay. Selected by the Prime Minister, they are not necessarily (though often) members of the county set. But they are all active, public-spirited people of independent means at the latter end of their working lives (retirement is compulsory at 75). And when the Monarch comes to visit, they drop everything.

'There really is no greater honour than welcoming the Queen to your county. It's the best bit of the job,' says Phyllida Stewart-Roberts, the Lord Lieutenant (it's 'Lord' regardless of gender) of East Sussex. She has a few weeks to go before the Queen arrives in the county for what the Palace calls an away-day, and it is down to her to ensure that every second of the day is well used. So she has summoned a small team to go through the whole thing in microscopic detail at her home – right down to the length of time the lunch guests will have for each course.

Phyllida has been in this position since 2000. A banker's wife, a mother and a grandmother, she had devoted much of her adult life to public causes like the St John's Ambulance and had already served as a Vice Lord Lieutenant when Downing Street invited her to take the job. Within a year, the Queen came down to Brighton to grant the place city status and Phyllida was in charge. She has vivid memories of the excitement when the Queen met a *Big Issue* seller and bought a copy (as the Queen genuinely doesn't carry cash, Phyllida provided the pound coin). Since then, there have been occasional royal visits by other members of the Royal Family but not many. The last visit, several

months back, would have been by the Duke of Gloucester but he was diverted at the last minute to attend the funeral of the King of Tonga.

'We are not a rich county. We are very rural and we have our fair share of problems. There are only twelve miles of dual carriageway in the whole county so it's hard to attract big business,' says Phyllida. Assisted by a network of thirty-five honorary Deputy Lieutenants, she tries to keep tabs on local issues and makes a point of recognising people who have done their bit. Among her happier tasks is nominating forty-five couples to be invited to a Buckingham Palace garden party each year. Most of her time is spent on panels of magistrates or worthy local causes, visiting local organisations on behalf of the Queen – Scouts, charities, reserve forces and so on. Her manner is gently workmanlike rather than regal. Does she feel like a mini-Monarch? 'Oh no,' she says firmly. 'My role is representing the Queen, not being her.'

Like all Lord Lieutenants, she routinely informs the Palace when a local organisation wants a royal visit. But, six months ago, she received a call out of the blue from the Palace. It was Edward Young, the Queen's Assistant Private Secretary, suggesting that Phyllida might like to conjure up a theoretical visit to Brighton, with the emphasis on fun, youth and voluntary work. The fresher the better. It should be entirely confidential and no one should get their hopes up. Brighton was simply one of many ideas under consideration. Once again, the Palace's Co-Ordination and Research Unit had been nosing through its database and had suggested that Brighton, as a major city of 250,000 people, seemed overdue for a spot of regal attention. Phyllida jumped into action, teamed up with the city council's chief executive, and produced a long list of suggestions. She went up to the Palace with her list. Edward Young came down to Brighton twice to check it all out. Once the police were happy, Phyllida was thrilled to receive a quiet thumbs-up. Like a

good drink, this visit has been refined and refined again. Edward has been keen to weed out superfluous dignitaries. Phyllida has had to field many angry calls from many self-important local people wanting to know why they have not been invited to anything.

And now Her Majesty's Lord Lieutenant for East Sussex is nervously pacing Platform One of the railway station, waiting for the Royal Train. 'I haven't had much breakfast,' she admits. The platform is sealed off from commuters. In days gone by, there would have been a 'chain gang' of mayoral worthies in full regalia lined up with their spouses. But the Queen has had enough of all that over the years. Today, the greeting line consists of just Phyllida and the station manager. The Queen's chauffeur, Danny Martell, an ex-Army driver, is waiting with 'Bent 2', the second of the Queen's two State Bentleys. He drove it down the day before and has now opened up the glass panel at the back to improve visibility (within and without) and has inserted a shield with the Queen's arms on the roof. Above the radiator grill he has screwed in the Queen's mascot, a silver model of St George slaying the dragon (in Scotland, the mascot is a lion).

The Royal Train glides in at jogging pace to hit its 10.10 arrival slot on the dot and Phyllida performs a model curtsy as she welcomes the Queen and Prince Philip. The crowds are several deep outside the Theatre Royal, the Queen's first destination. It is celebrating its 200th birthday with a concert by local children. After the recitals are over, the royal couple meet some of the staff. Prince Philip quizzes the theatre fundraisers. 'Got any friends left?' he asks mischievously. There are whoops of excitement as the royal couple step out onto the balcony to watch a few minutes of a bizarre 'bicycle ballet' display below, even bigger whoops when they emerge for a walkabout. Phyllida has arranged for a team of local cadets to gather up all the flowers given to the Queen and there are hundreds of bouquets. One day, perhaps, the British public will learn that

Left: Bicycle ballet
in Brighton.

flowers should be presented without their plastic wrapping. Today, as usual, nearly all are in cellophane. The Queen does not seem bothered. She spends a long time on one side of the road chatting to mothers and children from a Montessori school. On the other, local estate agent Martina Packham is terrified she is going to be ignored. 'Welcome, Your Majesty!' she keeps shouting. The Queen spots her and walks over, whereupon Martina is dumbstruck. 'My legs went all funny,' she says afterwards. 'I'm actually quite emotional.' And with that, tears well in her eyes.

The plan is for the Queen to proceed by car to the city library at the far end of the road. But it is a nice day and she decides to ignore the schedule and her eighty years. She walks the whole 300-yard route. Phyllida is thrilled. The Queen is obviously enjoying herself. A percussion orchestra of pensioners called Silver Sounds are playing tins and dustbins outside the library. Inside, amid a group of young mothers, the Queen watches a display of 'baby boogie'. So much for the old days of library signs saying 'Silence, Please'.

At a reception for local groups – from the Chinese community to the 'Gay Elderly Men's Society' – the Queen works the entire room one way, with Prince Philip going the other. 'It's good to get them away from the television,' the Queen tells Ann Martin, who organises youth gymnastics. She has a long chat with Andy Dalby-Welsh, 28, a member of England's blind cricket team. Her Assistant Private Secretary, Edward Young, is not happy, though. He wants music at these events because it softens the atmosphere and encourages people to talk rather than eavesdrop on the Queen. As usual, though, some local official has second-guessed the Queen's wishes and told the musicians to shut up. To their delight, Edward marches up to their balcony and begs them to continue. On the way out, the Queen even stops for a chat. It makes their day.

After a lunch of ham and chicken terrine, Sussex lamb and Sussex cheese up on the hill at the local racecourse (sadly, there's no racing), the royal convoy takes the less attractive road back down to the 'challenged' social backwater of Whitehawk for the afternoon. The Queen visits the nursery school. Shane Huggins presents his flowers. The Duke meets young people at a youth club built in memory of a murdered teenager. Back at the station, the Queen thanks Phyllida for her efforts and mulls over the day. She has been particularly struck by her visit to Whitehawk and its stories of deprivation as well as the sight of a small child preferring a computer screen to the company of other children. When it is all over, Phyllida is bursting with pride and relief. Her corner of Britain has been saluted by the Head of State. Some people will never forget it. Some will shrug and move on. There will soon be similar scenes in another county – Hampshire, for example, where the Queen will shortly be celebrating 400 years of the Borough of Romsey. This is the bread-and-butter work of the Monarchy. Brighton has been a textbook display. The Head of Nation has done what she has always done. Differently.

CHAPTER TWO

FAMILY BUSINESS

As any psychiatrist will testify, it is one of the most common dreams among the British. There you are, sitting at home, and a member of the Royal Family drops in for a cup of tea. But for Duncan Whittington, it is no dream. He is sitting in his house in Jarrow, outside Newcastle-upon-Tyne, and the police are in the garden conducting security checks. In the kitchen, his mother and her friends are boiling kettles and slicing cakes. The doorbell goes, and another neighbour turns up with yet more cakes and a smart silver cake stand. She wants her cakes looking immaculate. This is going to be some tea party. The Prince of Wales and the Duchess of Cornwall, no less, are on their way to Duncan's house.

Duncan is a volunteer for a charity called Toc H. Named after a classless refuge for troops during the First World War, it is promoting cross-community friendship through friendly chats over tea and cake. Today, all its efforts are about to receive royal recognition. 'At the end of the day, it's just folk coming together,' says Duncan. 'But I think my mum's in shock.'

There is a similar excitement at a refuge for the homeless as the residents find that Prince William is making breakfast. The exhibitors at a trade fair are buzzing, too, as they await the Duke of York. There is nothing sentimental about it. The Duke's hosts are hard-edged business people. 'This is "New Royal Family",' says Sir Digby (now Lord) Jones, former Director-General of the Confederation of British Industry. 'We do lots of things wrong in Britain, but we do some things incredibly well, and the Royal Family is one of them.'

For all the Monarchy's prominence, most of its work does not surface on the radar of the national media. It will, though, be faithfully recorded in the Court Circular, the official register of royal duties which is printed in certain newspapers. In Berkshire, royal memorabilia collector and retired insurance broker Tim O'Donovan has faithfully logged every engagement since 1979 (he noted 3,956 in 2006). But the family are not doing it for headlines.

'We're trying to recognise excellence, good work. So much of what we read is negative,' explains the Earl of Wessex. 'There are a lot of people doing very good work, and every now and then it's nice to be able to give them a pat on the back.'

The Royal Family do not tour the country and the globe, saluting the worthy and opening things, just because they enjoy it. Very often they do it in support of patronages – the thousands of charities and organisations which have a royal patron or president. 'They don't often get the credit that they deserve for a lot of the work they do,' says former Prime Minister Tony Blair. 'I think they'd be the first to say it's a privilege for them to be in that position. But I think that it's also the case that they give a lot back to the country. I genuinely believe that.'

The chief reason why the Prince of Wales is heading for Duncan Whittington's house, why the Duke of York is on his way to the trade fair, is that this is the basic duty of royalty. The family call this 'supporting the Queen'. And, with the exception of the Prince of Wales, the Queen funds their activities in return. As the Queen herself is fond of remarking: 'I can't go everywhere and I can't do everything!' Indeed she can't. That is why the modern Monarchy has to be a family business.

Left: The Prince of Wales and the Duchess of Cornwall arrive for tea in Jarrow.

The Royal Accounts

The latest figures show that the annual cost of the Monarchy to the British public is roughly £37 million. The largest portion of that – some £16 million – is spent maintaining buildings, like Buckingham Palace, which belong to the State rather than to the Queen as an individual.

The second major public expense is the Civil List payment of £7.9 million per year, which pays for the Queen's duties as Head of State. Largely spent on staff salaries, this figure has stayed the same since it was fixed in 1990, and it will not be altered until the next review in 2010. Today these costs are actually more than £11 million but, because of economies in past years, there is a surplus to play with. A further substantial public cost – some £5.5 million – is that of official travel for members of the Royal Family.

Many of the Monarchy's costs, though, are met not by the public but by the Privy Purse, the Sovereign's private income. Much of this comes from the Duchy of Lancaster, a portfolio of farms and commercial property. By a tradition dating back to 1399, the Monarch receives the annual revenues of the Duchy, currently around £10 million (on which the Queen pays tax). It is these funds, rather than the taxpayer, which support the other members of the Royal Family. The Privy Purse also funds everything from the private residences at Balmoral and Sandringham to racing stables, royal choristers, scholarships, endowments and prizes for everything from exploration to essays on the Bible to the trophy for the 'Best Bull in Jersey'.

Neither the Queen nor the State pays anything to the Prince of Wales, who receives his own independent income from the revenues of the Duchy of Cornwall. An ancient mixture of rural and urban holdings, this estate generates around £14 million a year before tax and funds the Prince's entire operation, from staff and offices to the Duchess of Cornwall and his sons. The Prince cannot sell the Duchy of Cornwall any more than the Queen can sell the Duchy of Lancaster. And everything must be fully audited.

Royal finances are usually the main source of criticism levelled at the Monarchy. Even when a debate on a particular royal issue has no financial implications, the cost of the institution is eventually thrown into the mix. Misconceptions are rife. It is often assumed that the Queen owns the Crown Estate, vast tracts of countryside and seashore which generate hundreds of millions of pounds each year. In fact, since the days of George III, the State has received the surplus from the Crown Estate (just under £200 million per year) in exchange for the Civil List allowance (£7.9 million).

Left: The Prince of Wales joins his family for Trooping the Colour.

THE PRINCE OF WALES

No heir to the Throne has been better prepared than the present Prince of Wales. Edward VII was 59 when he took the Throne and William IV was 64, but neither had come to know the country nearly as well as today's first-in-line. William was a sailor who had not been expected to reign, and Edward was more interested in shooting and cards than inner-city regeneration. Prince Charles, born in 1948, is of a similar age. But he has rewritten the rules to become an active champion of everything from Forces welfare to derelict buildings.

'The maddening thing,' he says, 'is you go trying to put people at their ease and then you have to disappear just as they are realising that you're vaguely human.'

It is, though, a serious mistake to see Prince Charles as some sort of coiled spring eagerly waiting for the Big Job. Neither he nor his staff will dwell on the next reign for the simple reason that it is regarded as extremely bad form to contemplate the end of the present one. When the time comes, so the feeling goes, it comes. The future King Charles may actually regard a Sovereign's existence as less fulfilling than his present position. For now, he is happy to deputise for the Queen at events such as investitures. He is also being eased into more sensitive territory such as Commonwealth summits, previously regarded as Monarch-only affairs. But it's not about a subtle handover. It is simply that same old royal business of 'supporting the Queen'.

'I'm taking an interest and trying to see if there are ways of improving some of the ways things are done, to remind people of things that are missed out or groups of people who are having difficulty,' the Prince explains during a quiet moment. 'I'm just doing what I consider is my duty, really. Sometimes rather an old-fashioned concept, it seems. But none the less it's quite important.'

It is a view which has been absorbed both by his sons and by his wife, the Duchess of Cornwall. Since their marriage in 2005, the former Camilla Parker Bowles has accompanied the Prince on hundreds of trips, and she has also started carrying out some of her own engagements, many of them in connection with the National Osteoporosis Society. This is a charity devoted to fighting the debilitating disease which afflicted the Duchess's late mother, and her involvement – be it a conference or a storm-battered sponsored walk through the Scottish Highlands – has raised its profile substantially. The Duchess is also patron or president of forty other organisations. At a time when most of her contemporaries are reaching retirement, she is embarking on a new career.

The Prince's royal role began in earnest in 1976 after he left the Royal Navy and used his Forces pension to start up the Prince's Trust for disadvantaged young people. Today, the Trust is part of a charitable network raising more than £100 million each year. In addition to performing the more traditional royal duties – more than 600 a year – he is well known for his contributions to public debates on the environment, architecture and education. These have prompted some critics to suggest that he is straying into dangerous constitutional territory because his views are not always in line with Government policy. Some call him a 'meddler'. But he has been at this game far longer than most politicians and he knows his constitutional limits. As for 'meddling', he only partially disputes the charge. 'Some may call it meddling,' he says, 'but if you actually go round the country over and over again, I think you'd be criminally negligent not to try and do something [about] the problems and complications people are facing. If one can at least bring people together to look at the situation as a whole, then I will go on trying to do that.' In any case, ministers see him as an asset rather than an irritant, according to one former Prime Minister.

'When you look at what he's done on the environment, on agriculture, on housing, on the Prince's Trust, he's done some amazing stuff,' says Tony Blair. 'All this stuff written about Charles interfering with Government or getting political – I never found him the slightest bit like that at all. It's sensible if he's out and he's talking to people. He did this a lot in my time, for example, when the farming industry was going through a very difficult time. He would represent their views or ask about certain issues, but I never found it a problem, honestly never.'

As we follow the Prince around Merseyside for a day, there is plenty for both his critics and fans to dwell on. Receiving an honorary degree from Liverpool John Moores University, he delivers a sustained assault on the argument that science alone holds the answers to the world's problems. In the suburb of Toxteth, the scene of terrible riots in

Right: 'I'll be mother.' The Prince makes the tea at Duncan Whittington's house.

1981, he is appalled to discover that the local council is preparing to tear down a terrace of Victorian houses. An assembly of faith leaders tell him that the street is a model of happy multicultural coexistence. The Prince voices his dismay, makes a note of the street name and slides it into his pocket. Is a bit more discreet 'meddling' in the offing? 'I couldn't possibly comment,' he says with a sly grin.

He does not see his interventions as a case of wielding influence but as using the wisdom of experience. 'To have that cumulative awareness enables you to have some sort of perspective. You see things coming round again once you get to a certain age,' he explains. Certainly, of all the national figures who visited Toxteth after the riots, the Prince is the only one still active in public life. And no one in Toxteth disagrees with a word he has said. They are just pleased that he has made the effort to come.

So, too, are the cake-makers of Jarrow. It is another day, the Royal Train has arrived overnight in another region, and the Prince and the Duchess arrive at Duncan Whittington's house. 'I hope this isn't too much of an invasion,' says the Prince as Duncan introduces the guests, a dozen people from different communities across the North.

'It's very nice to have a cup of tea,' says the Duchess, sitting down next to Duncan. 'It's just what you need at the end of the day.' The Prince dutifully pours some milk into her cup as she asks Duncan about his 'Tea and Cake' campaign. 'So it's every age? Every religion? … You discuss everything?' The Duchess has proved a fast learner in the fine art of asking questions. As a means of propelling a conversation along, it has no equal. She is presented with a huge piece of carrot cake and an introduction to a guest called Heather, all at the same time. 'I'm going to drop everything down me,' she says cheerfully, but doesn't.

For the best part of an hour, the conversation ranges from cake to housing issues to Parkinson's disease and back to cake before it is time to go. On the way out, Duncan lures his mother out of the kitchen to meet the royal couple. 'You've done a fantastic job,' the Prince assures her. 'There's a lot of cake in there.' The convoy departs. Half of Jarrow charges through Duncan's door in search of surplus cake and a gossip. Duncan is rather lost for words. Was it all just a dream?

COUNTRY PRINCE

If the Prince of Wales was not royal, it is a safe bet that he would be a farmer. For all his interest in the built environment and the problems of urban life, he

The Royal Train

Though one of the slower creatures on Britain's rail network, the Royal Train is never more than fifteen seconds early or late. Rocket-proof and discreet, it is designed to deliver members of the Royal Family and their entourage to early starts anywhere in the country, so it usually leaves the night before and has plenty of time to meander along the back routes to any destination in mainland Britain. Those expecting a 'Palace on wheels' will be disappointed, though.

Instead of Orient Express-style opulence, it resembles a dated motel with green and pink plastic bathroom suites, strip lights (not chandeliers) and plastic walls (these carriages were converted from old commuter trains in the Seventies). Wooden loo seats and Victorian prints are the only concessions to history, along with the terminology. Edward VII wanted his train to be as near as possible to a ship and all the bedrooms are still called 'berths', just as all dining areas are 'messes'. The Queen, Prince Philip and the Prince of Wales each have their own carriage, or 'saloon', with a single bed, a bathroom, a sitting area, a desk and a small dining area. Staff have their own cabins in other carriages, size depending on seniority. A Lady-in-Waiting will have a cabin ten feet by six feet with a chunky old Roberts radio by the bed and an ancient air-conditioning switch. The bathrooms have proper baths with shower attachments. There are no duvets on the Royal Train. Everyone has traditional bed linen (sheets must come nine inches over the edge of the eiderdown). To the rear is the Household Saloon where the staff eat, socialise and watch television. Today's passengers are much less demanding than their predecessors. Queen Victoria refused to eat or heed the call of nature while in motion and the train had to stop at the nearest station. Queen Mary would always order the train to slow to a pedestrian crawl at 7.30 every morning. She complained that if it went any faster, water would slosh out of her bath.

Below: The Royal Train being pulled by a steam locomotive during the Golden Jubilee.

By Appointment to
Her Majesty The Queen
Royal Train Operator
English Welsh & Scottish Railway Ltd
London

seems at his happiest in a pair of boots stomping through a field to inspect a rare breed of sheep or a new tree plantation. As Duke of Cornwall, he is not merely the titular head of a big rural estate spanning 140,000 acres of England and Wales, but also a hands-on landlord.

The Prince enjoys his ducal responsibilities, paying regular visits to the bottom left-hand corner of the kingdom. 'It is a very special part of the world,' he says as he visits the twin seaside villages of Kingsand and Cawsand on this less fashionable stretch of Cornish coast. 'A lot of it is to do with the climate and that, in itself, makes the landscape different.' These villages haven't had a royal visit since the fifteenth century. Today, everyone turns out to greet the Prince and the Duchess.

It pours with rain, but the Prince is happy. 'Sometimes shared discomfort can be quite a good thing,' he says. 'It's a blessing – rain, we should always remember that.' He meets the parish council in the Rising Sun pub. Afterwards, landlord John Moore is surprised by his own emotions. 'What a gentleman. He met all the family,' says John, his words tailing off. 'Sorry, I'm welling up…' The Prince is keen to salute all the little local organisations which, he believes, are crucial to places like this. He drops in on the Post Office, both churches, the sports clubs, the self-help groups and the seafront village hall (he donated the money for its new floor). He ends up meeting some people three times over. 'The whole aim is to encourage and thank and generally see what people are doing to contribute to keeping communities going,' he explains.

He meets Doll Jago, 94, the oldest woman in the area. Edie Acton, now in a wheelchair, shows him a picture of the one-ton basking shark she caught with a dinghy and a net

Right: The Prince of Wales and the Duchess of Cornwall bid farewell to the Andersons.

Left: The Prince of Wales and the Duchess of
Cornwall during a visit to the Wiltshire Wildlife
Trust.

in the 1940s. Local resident Ben Satterthwaite has organised a party and erected a model of the Queen holding a bunch of fresh flowers. A tug of a cord makes her arm wave and a corgi jump. To the delight of the party and the press, the Prince pulls the rope. 'We'll be talking about the visit for the next 523 years until our next royal visit,' says Tony Carne, chairman of the parish council.

As British farming has endured a succession of economic setbacks in recent years, the Prince has, increasingly, been one of the countryside's most high-profile supporters. Given the political sensitivities over issues such as crop subsidies and fox hunting and his position within the constitutional framework, he has to tread carefully.

At Dunterley Farm, up near the English border with Scotland, he is already something of a hero. Colin and Michelle Anderson have turned their 1,600-acre hill farm into a model of princely organic ideals. Not long ago, the couple were astonished to receive a call from a lady at the local Lord Lieutenant's office asking if they would mind showing their farm to the Prince. 'I told her to put it in writing because I didn't believe it,' says Colin. There is still disbelief as the royal helicopter looms into view. 'That's Charles and Camilla in our field!' gasps elder daughter Tracy as the visitors appear.

'You're awfully brave,' the Prince tells Colin, who has turned out in shirt and tie but no coat. It is sunny but freezing. 'Lovely to see you,' says the Duchess. 'It's a joy to be here.'

The visitors are introduced to two pedigree Aberdeen Angus cattle called Charles and Camilla. They were named at the time of the Prince's wedding in 2005, but Colin has been very worried that it might seem a little disrespectful. 'Spot the likeness!' says the Duchess. 'You're not meant to say things like that,' laughs Michelle. Phew. No offence, then. The Prince says he is delighted that Colin is embracing the famous Scottish breed, even if many Scottish farmers prefer cheaper European breeds. 'Why can't we persuade Scotsmen to do the same rather than have these ghastly continentals,' he sighs. The Duchess has heard it all before. 'He minds so much about the farmers,' she tells Michelle proudly. 'We know that,' she replies.

They move on to look at the Andersons' sheep, all traditional breeds. 'Do you have sheep?' asks Michelle. 'We mow the lawn with little tiny black ones,' the Duchess replies fondly. 'They make everything neat and tidy.'

The Prince is thrilled when a 93-year-old local walking-stick-maker presents him with a horn-tipped walking stick. 'It's a third leg to me,' the Prince replies, striding off with his new present. As he leaves, Colin grabs him warmly by the hand and plucks up the courage to say a few informal words. 'You keep chipping away at the Government because you've been doing a fantastic job over the years,' he says. 'You don't know what I get up to, even if it kills me,' the Prince replies with a wry smile. 'You're so important to this country. You're the backbone.' He parts with an invitation for the Andersons to visit his own operation at Highgrove. Michelle is still trying to take it all in. 'I want them back. Wonderful people. It's just blown me away – this day. Why can't it happen tomorrow?'

TOWN PRINCE

Most of the passengers in the third carriage of the 10.20 from Waterloo to Exeter do not look up from their newspapers. The few that do are astonished. But, with the classic studied indifference of the British travelling public, they refuse to become excited. The Heir to the Throne has just sat down. Better to carry on as if nothing has happened. The Prince is on his way to Woking – a Surrey commuter town thirty miles from London – for two reasons. First, Woking has established itself as a beacon of environmental good practice and the Prince wants to show his support. Second, the town hasn't had a royal visit for a while and the Prince is, once again, 'supporting the Queen'.

There is the usual media scrum as the Prince alights at Woking, squeezing past open-mouthed passengers on the platform. His itinerary has been in the local paper, however, and substantial crowds line every step of his route from the solar-powered railway station canopy to the recycling exhibition in the shopping centre to the waste management seminar at a local restaurant. The crowds are not lining the roads to talk about the environment, though. They are just here to see the future King. The Prince knows it and plunges straight in. 'How did you know I was coming?' he asks one woman who has been waiting for hours. 'It's in the paper,' she replies. 'It must be true, then!' he says. A disconcerting new trend in royal walkabouts is the way that people want to film the royal subject with their mobile telephones while simultaneously attempting a conversation. 'You'll ruin your machines if you point them at me!' the Prince tells one group of phone-thrusters. As he says later: 'You never quite know which bits of you they are recording.'

The staff of an Italian restaurant have decamped onto the street and a lively discussion ensues about pasta. Another Italian man offers the prince a haircut. 'I've

Below: St George's Day in Toxteth – the Prince visits a community centre.

just had one, thank you very much,' he says. Across the street, the workers at a Marie Curie charity shop start dancing for joy when their patron drops in. As the Prince says later: 'I enjoy people and meeting them, and the awful thing is I suspect I was merely interrupting their shopping activities so the poor things had no alternative but to stand until I'd gone past.' It is typical Prince of Wales self-deprecation. In the course of more than half an hour he does not encounter a single unfriendly voice. Before his arrival, two women in separate sections of the crowd had been criticising him (one in relation to his late ex-wife, another taking issue with his environmental messages). Afterwards, having shaken his hand and had a chat, they both admit to being charmed, faintly embarrassed by their earlier remarks and really rather excited by it all.

It is a long walkabout. But it was the Prince who wanted to come here after learning of Woking Borough Council's record in waste recycling. He asked one of his favourite charities, Business in the Community, to gather together a selection of like-minded councils and business people for a brainstorming session in Woking. So, around a hundred of them are seated in a restaurant. It is an eminent assembly. The guests include Stuart Rose, the chief executive of Marks and Spencer. The speakers outline their victories and defeats in the war on waste. It is music to the Prince's ears. He regularly intervenes with observations and questions. 'I've reached the stage where some of my godchildren are in their thirties and lecturing me about corporate responsibility,' he tells them before moving on to visit almshouses in another part of Surrey. It is a normal day – a celebration of favourite princely themes while saluting another slice of British life. And, bizarrely, he does the whole lot on nothing more than a glass of water. 'I can't function if I have lunch,' he admits. 'I've got to the age where I don't need it. Like a camel, I can keep going on what I had the night before.'

THE YOUNG PRINCES

The Prince has always made it clear that his sons will not be shoved into royal duties against their will. Having had his own education and early career mapped out by a committee involving everyone from the Archbishop of Canterbury to the Prime Minister, he remains determined that Princes William and Harry should follow their instincts and their own sense of duty rather than some dusty blueprint.

For the moment, their duty lies in the secondary family business – the Services. The Windsors are very much a Forces family. Generation after generation has served in uniform. 'The connection between the Crown and the Armed Forces has always been incredibly close,' says the Prince of Wales, himself a former Royal Navy officer and pilot, during an afternoon with the men and women of the Army Air Corps who are on guard duty outside the royal palaces for the first time. The Prince is proud to be their Colonel-in-Chief.

'When the British Armed Forces are so heavily stretched in different parts of the world – many of them being shot at, mortared, rocketed on a regular basis – there's even more reason to remind people what an incredibly difficult job they're doing. We're very lucky to have them.' Some of his earliest memories are of watching the Palace sentries as a boy, and he is a firm believer that the Forces are, in essence, one large family of which he is a part. 'It's very important to have that experience with other people, and to be responsible for other people and to help look after them.'

It is a proud day for the Windsor clan as they gather at Sandhurst to watch the latest royal recruit passing out. Prince William has just followed his younger brother through the rigours of Army officer training and, like him, is about to become a second lieutenant – or 'cornet' – in the Blues and Royals. 'Mr Wales', as he is known, has endured the same treatment as every other cadet here but his presence at the passing-out parade has brought a media circus to the Royal Military Academy, not least because royal girlfriend of the moment Kate Middleton is in the crowd.

The marching, needless to say, is faultless, and the Queen is invited to inspect her latest intake of officers. She pauses briefly as she passes her grandson and is unable to restrain a smile which manages to crack the stern features on the supposedly inscrutable face of Mr Wales. 'This is a milestone,' she declares in her speech to the parade, 'a day when you prepare to start on this demanding but most rewarding of careers. I'm speaking to every individual one of you when I say you are all very special people.'

Afterwards, the cadets are reunited with their families. 'Didn't you think my speech

Right: The Queen inspects her grandson and his fellow Sandhurst cadets.
Overleaf: Princes William and Harry in bowler hats, traditional officer headgear at Household Cavalry events.

was commendably short?' the Queen asks Prince William ('commendably short' is a
family phrase for any speech that does not leave the audience yawning). They all admire
a portrait of the royal gathering at Prince Harry's passing-out parade. 'It's come out very
well,' notes the Queen. When it is time for the royal party to leave, the Prince dutifully
follows them out to the waiting cars. He kisses them all goodbye. And then he stands
rigidly to attention and salutes his family. After all, he is now in the service of the Crown
that will one day be his.

For both the young Princes, though, there are still royal responsibilities beyond the
Army. Nobody has forced these on them. A small team on their father's Clarence House
staff ensure that the royal side of their lives continues in tandem with their military
careers.

And so it is that Prince Harry finds himself in a cramped St James's Palace meeting
room with the board of Sentebale, a charity he created to help deprived children in
Lesotho, where he spent some months after leaving school. He explains that he plans to
give them a share of the proceeds from the big concert which the brothers are planning
for the tenth anniversary of the death of their mother, Diana, Princess of Wales. The
charity is duly grateful. 'It would have been slightly wrong not to, wouldn't it?' the Prince
replies with a grin.

Prince William has his own expanding range of patronages. Some reflect his own
interests – like TUSK, a small UK charity devoted to African wildlife. Others were held
by his mother. These include Centrepoint, a charity for homeless young people and the
first to claim the Prince as its patron. During a break from Army training, he makes a
dawn start to visit a London hostel and help with the breakfast arrangements. There is
no protocol as he arrives. This is a 'jeans and T-shirt' engagement. The chief executive,
Anthony Lawton, gives him a progress report on the charity's work. One company has
just said that its staff are going to raise a million pounds. 'Are they really? Awesome,' says
the Prince. People are starting to surface and are, to say the least, startled when they find
the future King making them coffee and toast.

The Prince drops in to the office to meet Stuart Cox, one of the workers, who is the
same age as him. Having been homeless and jobless, Stuart is now determined to put
his life back together. 'You're one of the most valuable people Centrepoint has at the
moment because you've been through the system and come out the way you have,' the
Prince tells him. The conversation is easy. Despite his young years, the Prince is already
one of the best conversationalists in the Windsor line-up. 'He listens and connects,' says
Stuart afterwards.

Much of the visit involves simply listening to people's stories. Anthony Lawton is very
grateful. Christmas, always a tough time here, is fast approaching but this has been a

big boost to morale. 'He matters, he's here with us and maybe, in some way, that makes people think, "I matter",' says Anthony. That, in essence, is the Prince's job for life.

THE DUKE OF EDINBURGH

No Monarch in history has travelled as far or met as many people as the present occupant of the Throne. Nor, for that matter, has any consort. Despite his complaint in the early years that he felt like an 'amoeba' because of his subordinate position to the Queen, Prince Philip has been performing duties on her behalf for longer than anyone else. Created Duke of Edinburgh in 1947, he has carved out his own distinct range of interests, notably in the fields of youth welfare, science and conservation. His Duke of Edinburgh Awards are now a global institution embraced by millions. He has been *paterfamilias* to the most scrutinised family on the planet. But his primary role, as far as the Monarchy is concerned, is to be a pillar of strength a couple of paces back from the head of the procession. As the Queen put it on their golden wedding anniversary: 'He has, quite simply, been my strength and stay all these years.' Sometimes, he has to be a substitute, too.

It is the biggest non-footballing day in the modern history of Arsenal Football Club. The London club, one of the biggest in the world, has recently moved into a superb new stadium and the Queen has agreed to open it. Arsenal director Ken Friar has been put in charge of organising the visit. 'We've had some historic days but none more so than today,' says Ken, who has been here for more than fifty years. The club visitors' book contains the signature of the present Prince of Wales and of the previous one. But Arsenal have never entertained the Monarch.

Ken has planned every inch of the royal route and runs through every contingency with his staff. Yes, an executive lift will be on the same floor as the Queen at all times. Yes, a lift engineer is on site. Yes, the pen next to the visitors' book contains ink. 'Unless something else has slipped both of us or the staff, I think we're there, aren't we?' he asks his team. They agree. 'I think the only thing we've perhaps not covered is the Queen changing her mind and not turning up,' he jokes. What a preposterous idea.

Moments later, Ken receives a message that he should call the Palace. He continues his tour before diverting into a quiet room to call the Palace. 'Maybe she's not coming,' he jokes. And, suddenly, Ken Friar looks like Arsenal have lost the biggest game in their history. 'Right, right,' he murmurs. 'Well, I'm extremely sorry to hear that, but obviously we have to understand.' He puts down his phone in disbelief. 'The Queen is not coming,' he murmurs. 'The Queen's injured her back. The one thing we haven't forecast…'

Moments later, the Queen's Private Secretary, Sir Robin Janvrin, calls to pass on the Queen's regrets. 'I can only apologise,' he says. 'It wasn't too bad until the day before yesterday.' Ken passes on his best wishes. Deep down, he is distraught. 'The planning for this has gone back for two years,' he sighs. 'It's like losing a Cup Final.'

But all is not lost. The Duke of Edinburgh is coming. There will be a royal opening after all. It will be too late to alter the plaque but this is a football club. People get substituted. 'We know about injuries,' says the manager, Arsène Wenger, who has met the Queen before. 'We wish her to be fit again very quickly because she has a busy schedule like we have.'

Word spreads through the surrounding streets. 'We're gutted, absolutely gutted,' says a woman outside the ground. But there is still an enthusiastic welcome for the Duke as he arrives at the site of the club's ICT computer centre and museum. Today is not all about football. The club's Old Etonian chairman, Peter Hill-Wood, explains that the new £390 million complex also includes 'affordable housing' for local people. 'Nothing's affordable if you can't afford it,' the Duke observes. Out on the pitch, his football banter needs a little polishing. 'When are you on next?' he asks team captain, Thierry Henry, as if this were a theatrical act. Thierry introduces him to the players and the Duke is intrigued by the range of nationalities and the problems of injury. 'How many walking wounded have you got?' he asks. 'They're supposed to be fit,' Thierry replies with a laugh.

The Duke is ushered up to the Diamond Club, Arsenal's most palatial hospitality area, where the directors and club staff have gathered to watch him unveil the wrongly worded plaque. 'The Queen has asked me to tell you how very disappointed she is,' he

Right: The Duke of Edinburgh meets Arsenal football club manager Arsène Wenger.

says. 'I'm delighted to be able to stand in for her. You will have, second to her, the world's most experenced plaque-unveiler!'

For all the disappointment, it has still been a big day. Thierry Henry says he has been 'thrilled' to meet the Duke, although, being French, he had to ask his British wife how to bow. 'For me it's pretty strange because, obviously, we have a president. We don't have a queen or a king. We used to have one but I won't tell the story – I think we all know it.'

As in football, so with royalty. A swift substitution and a bit of teamwork have saved the day. A few months later, Arsenal have a happier surprise. To make up for her no-show, the Queen invites them all round for tea and a tour of the Palace.

Despite his years – he was born in 1921 – the Duke of Edinburgh does not show the slightest inclination to slow down. He performs hundreds of engagements every year and remains firmly attached to all his organisations, wherever they happen to be. So, the morning after returning from a foreign tour with the Queen, he is packing his bags again. It is not the obvious destination for a weekend break, particularly if you happen to be 85. But the Duke of Edinburgh is positively exuberant at the prospect of a couple of days of winter sun – in Iraq.

The Queen and the Duke are unique among the world's 'first couples', in that they both served in uniform during the Second World War. The Queen was a second subaltern on vehicle maintenance duties in the Auxiliary Territorial Service. The

Below: Prince Philip at the Diplomatic Reception.

Duke served all over the world in the Royal Navy and was mentioned in despatches. Since leaving the Royal Navy, he has spread his patronages widely across all three Services and he takes them very seriously. So, when he received an open-ended invitation from one of his regiments to visit Iraq, he kept it in mind. That is why, many months later, he is en route to the Shaibah airfield outside Basra in southern Iraq.

The Queen's Royal Hussars (QRH) have seen a few things in their time. Their regimental ancestors were at Waterloo, the Charge of the Light Brigade and the Normandy landings. With eight Victoria Crosses to their credit and Winston Churchill among their old boys (the regiment stood guard over his coffin), they are not easily impressed. Even so, they have never welcomed a royal Colonel-in-Chief to a combat situation. 'He'll be pretty secure. There's no doubt there are dangers, but if we didn't think we could protect him properly, we wouldn't have invited him,' says Lieutenant Colonel David Labouchere, commanding officer of the QRH, as he gathers his men in from the desert for the royal visit.

The Duke's connection with the regiment goes back to the Coronation year of 1953 and the Hussars know that they will need to be on the ball. 'He'll be very sharp, he always is,' says David. 'And he will know an awful lot more than people give him credit for.'

Right now, the Duke is coming in to land in a four-engined BAe146 aircraft of 32 (The Royal) Squadron. Flight Lieutenant Dave Coombs is entering one of the most dangerous flying zones on Earth but he is fairly relaxed. 'We'll do a tactical approach into Basra. It's a fairly dirty dive from high altitude close into the airfield. It's not that scary.' Really?

The soldiers are reaching the end of a six-month tour of duty, and this visit will be a bonus. As the Duke's plane starts its 'dirty dive', they are preparing various displays. An anti-explosives sniffer dog called Simba has been brushed for the occasion. Soldiers, fresh in from overnight desert patrols, are stripping weapons and repairing vehicles. The bagpipes are playing as the royal guest steps onto the sand-blown tarmac. The Duke is being accompanied on the trip by the QRH's honorary Colonel, Major General Arthur Denaro, who commanded the regiment here during the first Gulf War. 'It is a remarkable thing that someone of his years is flying out to an extremely hot and quite dangerous country to visit soldiers. People talk about the risk of this trip, but he's not a man who is afraid of risk, given his own wartime experience,' says the General. The formalities are kept to a minimum as the Duke arrives in military desert kit, albeit with the best-pressed trousers in Iraq. Some of the regiment are out on patrol, and one squadron of tanks has just been summoned

north to deal with an outbreak of violence. But everyone else has regrouped here on the outskirts of Basra for the big day. The Duke is full of questions as he meets the men of Headquarters Squadron, grilling them on the logistics of airborne supply drops by night.

'He's a down-to-earth kind of guy. What did he say he was? An octavian? He must be 80-ish. I can't imagine my grandad saying, "I'll just pop out to Iraq to see some of my mates",' says Warrant Officer Cas Potter.

The men of A Squadron show the Duke their 'Snatch' wagons, light Land-Rovers which they use to escort supply convoys and launch counter-insurgency strikes. Most of them are out on patrol at the moment. 'Been shot at?' asks the Duke. 'We were engaged last week in an urban area,' says Major Jamie Howard. 'Thankfully, one of the sentries returned fire and killed the insurgent.' 'Oh good,' says the Duke.

He views a perplexing array of defused roadside bombs and a display of hand grenades. 'An Afghan cricket ball!' he jokes. After more inspections and meetings, the day concludes with a gathering of around a thousand men and women in front of a Challenger tank.

Left and far left: The Duke
meets the Queen's Royal
Hussars in Iraq.

There is no bunting, no brass band. The only overt indicator that a royal visit is in progress is the sign on a solitary plastic lavatory cubicle next to the track. It reads: 'VIP ONLY DO NOT USE'.

Speaking without notes, the VIP tells them: 'Everyone at home has been following what's been going on with a great deal of sympathy for those of you at the sharp end.' He is keen to reassure these soldiers that their efforts do have a purpose, whatever the media says. 'It's a role which the British Services have been doing for a great many years and very often getting killed in the process. If you just imagine, with a bit of luck, you could do with this place what previous British people have done for the Gulf states. Look at them now. It happened because of people like you – mind you, that and a bit of oil!' He concludes by wishing them a decent spell of leave – 'but don't overdo it.'

The regiment responds with three cheers above the hum of ground and air traffic. The soldiers get back to work. Many will be on patrol within the hour. In a few weeks' time, his Hussars are having a homecoming dinner in London. It is already in the Duke's diary.

THE PRINCESS ROYAL

Right: The Princess Royal at St George's Chapel, Windsor on Easter Day.

She doesn't like being photographed. She doesn't like small talk and regards publicity stunts as something to be scraped off the sole of a shoe. Perhaps that is why the Princess Royal remains one of the most admired members of the Royal Family in modern times.

Born Princess Anne (she was made Princess Royal in 1987), the only daughter of the Queen and Prince Philip has now been doing royal engagements for forty years – longer than any of her siblings. Unlike her brothers, she neither went to university nor joined the Armed Forces. 'Occasionally, you remember with a cold sweat how awful you were when you started, how crass everything you said seemed to be,' she says. 'I rather hope I may have improved. It is about being around for a long time.'

On leaving her Kent boarding school, Benenden, in 1968, she immediately started public duties, while simultaneously becoming one of the most successful three-day-event riders of her generation. Since then, she has become an active patron or supporter of more than 200 organisations and twenty-three different service units around the world – from the 8th Canadian Hussars to the Royal New Zealand Corps of Signals.

Every year, she carries out at least three major overseas tours on behalf of the Queen, preferring to travel with a tiny team and even doing her own washing rather than run the risk of souvenir hunters in the hotel laundry. It is often the Princess who is sent to represent the Sovereign in the less accessible remnants of Empire. Her 2007 schedule began amid glaciers and penguins with a visit to the British Antarctic Territory with her husband, Rear Admiral Timothy Laurence.

These days, her workmanlike manner is no longer seen as a shortcoming. She has made it a virtue. It has become accepted media shorthand to describe the Princess as 'the hardest-working royal'. She undertakes more engagements than anyone else – over 600 a year. After an adult life spent going round the country – and the world – time after time, the Princess has personally encountered well over a million people. She is rather like Big Ben. The British public may not have much idea of what makes her tick. Nor do they need to see or hear her to know that the Princess is there. It is taken for granted. They simply like the fact that she does what she does and they would be rather sad and cross if she stopped. There is, though, little chance of that.

On a breezy Hampshire runway, Mary Fagan, the Lord Lieutenant of the county, has done this more times than she can remember. 'I see a lot of the Princess Royal,' she says. 'She does up to five engagements in a day and she speaks beautifully without notes.' Today, in fact, the Princess does not have five engagements. She has seven.

The Princess hits the ground running. First stop: a Save the Children charity shop in Eastleigh. Save the Children became her first major patronage when she was appointed its patron in 1970 and she likes to witness its work, from refugee camps to the high street. Ten volunteers and the local mayor are all chatting noisily as the royal car pulls up outside. The volume drops. Over the years, the Princess has become more knowledgeable about charity shops than many people who work in them. 'It's extraordinary what people think is acceptable to dump,' she tells one group of staff who are nodding in agreement. 'The sorting is critical.' The Princess meets Daphne who has been helping here for nineteen years. 'That's nearly as long as the shop,' says the Princess. Daphne blushes.

There is a rather different atmosphere at the next stop, a conference for Victim Support, a voluntary organisation which helps crime victims. As president, the Princess is clearly up to speed on developments and delivers a long speech on the need to improve support systems for intimidated witnesses. 'Is there equal access to justice for all members of society?' she asks in conclusion. 'If we consider the answer is "no", then consider what each of us can do to change that answer to "yes".'

The voluntary sector is a major facet of the Princess's work. The theme continues a few miles away, as she opens a new Citizens' Advice Bureau in Gosport. And she has strong views about vetting volunteers. 'The Criminal Records Bureau has made a fundamental change in terms of the relationship,' she tells us later. 'It does imply a startling lack of trust in the Great British public to feel they're all potentially guilty. And everyone else has to have qualifications!' But her strategy is to get on with it rather than grumble. Her helicopter whisks her back to London. The Princess's day is not over. It has only just started.

Waiting for her outside her Buckingham Palace study is Salva Kiir, the Vice President of Sudan, who is passing through London. The Princess talks to him privately, not as a politician but as an experienced figure from the charity sector. No sooner is he out of the door than three men in suits arrive for a lengthy chat about food. For the last seventeen years, the Princess has been patron of the British Nutrition Foundation, which wants to use the 2012 London Olympics to promote healthier eating. The Princess, who also sits on the International Olympic Committee, is not short of ideas.

Left: The Princess Royal visits a Citizens' Advice Bureau in Gosport.
Right: The Princess Royal meets the Christmas Day crowds at Sandringham.

Left: The Duke of York,
with his daughters,
Princess Beatrice (left)
and Princess Eugenie.

'She's been our patron for seventeen years and that's longer than a lot of our employees,' says Director-General Robert Pickard. The secretary, Peter Leigh, politely interjects: '*All* our employees.'

The Princess herself has not had much time for food today. She has invited several hundred 'young achievers' from the St John Ambulance organisation to a reception at Buckingham Palace. They are cadets from all over the country and have come in uniform so the Princess switches into her own – that of Commandant-in-Chief – for the gathering in the Bow Room. 'Did you volunteer or were you volunteered? What were you after?' she asks one girl. 'A social life,' comes the reply. She applauds them all for volunteering at an early age. 'The sooner you start, the easier it is,' she remarks, and they all nod. It is a rather uplifting occasion, full of stories of young people making a difference to other people's lives – and even saving them. 'Sometimes people see First Aid as not relevant when it's wholly relevant,' she assures one group, 'and it can make a real difference. You're the practitioners.'

The Princess's official day is still not over. She changes again into an evening dress and heads to the City of London. She is the guest of honour at a dinner for the Whitley Fund for Nature, a charity which gives grants for outstanding conservation work around the world. The Princess's host is brewing heir Edward Whitley, the charity's founder. 'We look for pragmatic and successful conservationists,' he says. 'When they meet the Princess Royal, they get a very thorough grilling and they need to justify their existence. Since she became patron, our charity's grown tenfold.'

Tonight's dinner is in honour of recent beneficiaries, including Claudio Padua, a Brazilian conservationist who has met the Princess during her travels. 'I want to tell you how important your international work is,' he tells her. But she has not come here to be thanked. 'Networks are quite handy, aren't they?' she says. 'None of you has had any easy start.' She starts grilling Claudio on his research and his generation of local support. 'It has to make sense to the local populations, doesn't it? It has to have something to offer them. You've set real standards for others to follow.' 'Thank you,' he replies. 'It's nothing to do with me!' says the Princess, deflecting another compliment. It is approaching midnight by the time she gets back to her apartment at St James's Palace.

THE DUKE OF YORK

It's a nightmare for any public speaker. For a member of the Royal Family, it's virtually a daily occurrence. You are in the middle of making a carefully prepared speech when someone's mobile telephone shrieks into life. And it happens all the time to the Duke of York. He has just started his address to a room full of important businessmen when, sure enough, an irksome trill suddenly fills the air. But since he is at a major international trade fair for the mobile telephone industry, he can only make a joke of it: 'This is a mobile phone event – so please turn your mobile phones off.'

Born in 1960, Prince Andrew was created Duke of York in 1986. Since leaving the Royal Navy in 2001, after a 22-year career, the Queen's second son has spent an increasing amount of his time promoting British companies at home and abroad as the United Kingdom's Special Representative for Trade and Investment. He cannot be a salesman but he can certainly do his bit on the marketing side for what he likes to call 'Team UK'. In 2006, 293 of his 446 official engagements were trade related.

It is a damp winter morning as we find him travelling through London's East End on the Docklands Light Railway to inspect successful British-Asian businesses – dressmakers, clothes shops and jewellery shops – in Newham. The staff are all thrilled to have a royal visitor and the Duke receives garlands and elaborate gifts wherever he stops. After lunch at West Ham United Football Club, he has a tour of Tate & Lyle's massive sugar plant next to the Thames. His hosts try to escort him down to the loading jetty but the wind is so strong that a gust knocks someone over. They all retreat indoors to watch a digger taking chunks out of a 27,000-ton sugar mountain. The Duke meets a man called Colin whose family have all worked here for as long as anyone can remember. It sounds familiar to the Duke. 'It's good to have family connections!' he says and everyone laughs.

His day among the East Enders has been positively glamorous compared to some of his trade missions overseas. These are coordinated by the British Government and they are hardly exotic. One conference room full of suits is much like another. On the rare occasions that his trips reach the British press, there is usually a photograph of a reception where the teetotal Duke will be portrayed as some sort of jet-setting party animal. But there is precious little hedonism here in Barcelona at 3GSM, the mobile phone trade fair. It is an area the size of an airport and it is full of earnest corporate types talking gadgets.

'Our mission today is to recognise and support British business,' explains the Duke as he prepares to embark on two days of handshakes and chat. 'Today we are with the mobile communications sector. The United Kingdom is one of the leaders in this particular area of endeavour so it's a no-brainer to come to an event like this.'

He moves from exhibition hall to exhibition hall, steered by a team of diplomats and civil servants and followed by a posse of photographers who are grateful to have a famous face amid all usual the industry types. 'There were 40,000 people here yesterday,'

Below: The Duke of York talks business in Barcelona.

he says. 'It's going to be one of those afternoons.' And it is.

There are 300 British companies here. At one stand, he finds fifteen of them and ploughs in with questions about digital technology. It's not easy. Asking a walkabout crowd how long they have been waiting in the rain is one thing. But it's another matter thinking up a useful question about data processing. Rather than get technical, the Duke sticks to the big picture. 'Where has the UK got its lead from?' he asks one executive. Eventually, he is shown some comprehensible technology – a coat with a waterproof keypad woven into the sleeve. 'This is the first time I have come near a keyboard which can accept coffee and water,' he says excitedly.

Some of these exhibitors have met him before. 'He does know his technology,' says Simon Cole of Unique Interactive. 'The number one thing when you're trying to start something new is the oxygen of publicity. It's a lot more effective to be with him than a politician.'

Needless to say, everyone here wants to find out what sort of mobile telephone the Duke uses himself. 'I do have a mobile on me but I'm not giving you my number!' he has to say more than once. From here, it is on to a reception for the British exhibitors where he makes a short speech without notes. 'It is very important that this community realises it is not only valued by the United Kingdom but that it is encouraged,' he tells them all. It is not the liveliest party. A man receives warm applause as he announces that his company has just opened its fourth call centre in Glasgow. But that is precisely what royal visits like this are about.

'It's not about brand endorsement. It's about doing the best thing for Britain,' says Sir Digby Jones, who acts as one of the Duke's advisers. 'Where Britain scores is we are very good at saying: "I don't care about the colour of your skin, the god you worship, the fact I can't pronounce your name. Come into Britain and do it." If you can add to that the magic dust the Monarchy brings, well – Made in Heaven.'

As a businessman, Sir Digby believes that royalty has one added marketing advantage. 'The best thing about the Monarchy,' he argues, 'is their greatest challenge. They are not like you and me.' Having a royal trade ambassador can certainly be useful in a country where the big decisions are taken by the local royal family. Shortly after his mobile phone excursion to Barcelona, the Duke embarks on a round-the-world trip via several Middle Eastern monarchies. The Duke is a regular in these states. Familiarity is a valued part of any trading relationship. This evening he is landing in Oman, which he has come to know quite well. 'His visit will open doors that I wouldn't normally get into very easily,' admits Dr Noel Guckian, the British Ambassador. The Duke will have just twenty-four hours here, starting with a gathering of local British businessmen. No sooner has he sat down than the curse of the mobile phone strikes at the end of the table. Astonishingly, the owner of the phone not only answers it but then stands up and leaves the table to continue the call. It is, by any standards, pretty bad manners. The Duke barely contains his lack of amusement. 'There's no need to answer it,' he says. 'Turn it off!'

Above: The Duke of York's visit to Oman.

Next stop is an embassy reception where the Duke meets 200 locally based British executives. Several are from a company called Serco which is bidding for several big contracts out here in the Gulf. The Duke has been busy promoting the British company at home and abroad 'There's no hard sell,' he explains. 'It is an opportunity to remind whoever that the United Kingdom is committed at every level within Team UK. It's what I would describe as a synergy of purpose.' The Duke did not go to business school but he is clearly picking up the jargon.

The next day consists of a series of meetings in dark conference suites interspersed with the odd police convoy. The only light relief is a visit to a British-backed holiday project where the Duke takes a keen interest in the golfing arrangements. The nearest he gets to a course is a plastic display model.

The Duke flies on to New Zealand via Saudi Arabia. Three months later, he gets an invitation to Serco's British headquarters. They want him to hear some good news. The company has just landed a huge contract in Dubai. The staff are adamant that part of the credit should go to the Duke. They cannot pay him, of course. So they give him a cup of tea.

THE EARL AND COUNTESS OF WESSEX

The Earl of Wessex learned long ago that there is no point expecting official engagements to follow the plan. 'I think we're constantly surprised by the people we meet,' he says at the end of a day in West Yorkshire. 'You can walk into one place and, on paper, it sounds brilliant. But when you get there, it's as dull as ditchwater. And then you meet some really extraordinary people.' He cheerfully admits that his hosts probably think the same about him, too. 'In terms of trying to judge the effect, it's very difficult. It's a bit like doing an exam. You've no idea whether you've scored ticks in the right boxes.'

Born in 1964, Prince Edward has grown up in an era of conflicting expectations for royal children outside the immediate line of succession. He was the first child of a Monarch to branch out and set up his own business (a television company). But he has also remained a senior member of the Royal Family and was made Earl of Wessex in 1999 on the day of his marriage to public relations executive Sophie Rhys-Jones. In 2002, after it became increasingly clear that royal and commercial imperatives were not really compatible, the couple decided to take up full-time royal duties in support of the Queen. Since then, they have quietly become a roving royal couple of the old school.

The two of them now undertake around 550 engagements each year. The Countess has taken on a broad portfolio of patronages related to children and disabilities. Much of the Earl's work is in the field of youth, sport and the arts. It has been agreed that, in due course, the Earl will inherit his father's title to become the Duke of Edinburgh, and he is already a very active trustee of the Duke of Edinburgh's Award Scheme. But whatever the engagement, it is that same old business: encouraging, congratulating, unveiling…

'The day depends hugely on the energy levels of the people who are around you,' says the Earl. 'If there's plenty of energy and they've got a good story to tell, then the day tends to work pretty well. The hard work comes when you're having to make most of the going.'

There is no shortage of energy here in West Yorkshire. The broad theme of this away-day is the performing arts. After a trip to a theatre workshop, he arrives at Litestructures, a Wakefield company which builds studios and stages in a former mining area. The Earl heard about the company during a previous visit and offered to open their new facility when it was completed. 'I was gobsmacked,' says managing director Adrian Brooks. As the Earl explains: 'You're looking at the whole regeneration of an area that's been hit by the end of the colliery. You've got to encourage business to come in and create the right environment.'

He chats to the staff before the mandatory plaque-unveiling. 'I want you to pretend it is the most exciting thing in your life so everyone outside will wonder why you're having so much fun in here,' he says. It turns out to be quite lively. Music blares out and three women in leotards start shinning up some velvet drapes towards the ceiling.

There is plenty of song and dance hundreds of miles to the south, where the Countess of Wessex is meeting charities in Berkshire. Pupils at the Mary Hare School for deaf children are keen to show her that deafness is no bar to musical ability and lay on a pop concert in her honour. It is a moving moment for the parents and staff. Afterwards, the Countess makes an impromptu speech of thanks before going backstage. 'I used to play the flute, too,' she tells one girl. 'But not for very long – and not as well as you!'

She climbs into the driving seat of her Audi – there's no chauffeur, she's doing the driving – with a detective in the passenger seat and a Lady-in-Waiting in the back. The final stop of the day involves more music at the Berkshire County Blind Society in Wokingham, where a large number of pensioners have gathered for tea and a sing-song. One of them, Maureen Nickless, launches into a spirited recital of the Carpenters hit 'On Top of the World'.

The Countess moves among the tables, meeting one woman who remembers her wedding – 'before I went blind'. A lady wants to know what

she is wearing. 'A pink coat, it's got pleats down the front. It's not too thick,' says the Countess, gently taking the lady's hand and helping her feel the material. Across the table, another woman, sitting with a blind man, introduces herself. 'This is my husband and I've been trying to describe you to him,' she says. 'I'll come over,' says the Countess, moving round. 'There's nothing worse than being told about someone.' There are children here as well. The Countess meets Charlie Strong, who wants to show her the tandem he rides with his father. As Maureen Nickless extends her considerable repertoire to Elvis Presley, it is time for the Countess to depart.

All day, there has been a distant echo of the late Diana, Princess of Wales, as the Countess moves around the room, crouching to the level of those who cannot stand, stroking frail hands and listening a lot. Both blonde, both born within a few years of each other and both from non-royal families, the two women have obvious similarities. But the Royal Family loathe comparisons with each other and are adamant about following their own instincts. The Duke of Edinburgh, for example, is brisk and quizzical, whereas the Prince of Wales conveys a warm and mildly concerned regard, rather like a family doctor. 'Every member of the family has a different way of going about what they're trying to achieve,' says the Earl, whose own style is to approach any event or greeting line with the overt cheerfulness of a television presenter.

In Yorkshire, his day goes on to include an unexpected walkabout among a crowd of schoolchildren outside a community centre. He is touched by the turnout but keeps his wits about him. 'There are always Smart Alecs in the crowd. Put a camera anywhere near a group of children and they will behave in a completely different way.'

Come the evening, he is at the Grand Theatre, Leeds for a performance of *A Sleeping Beauty Tale* by the Northern Ballet Theatre. The Earl is its proud patron. 'Anything I can do to help them, so much the better,' he says. Tonight's production is a science fiction version of the old fairy tale, and the cast are dressed as alien warlords and goblins. After the final curtain, the Earl goes backstage to meet the cast. 'I'm feeling distinctly incorrectly dressed,' he remarks as the aliens queue up for a handshake.

THE COUSINS

Bob Loveridge and Dr Dave Martill have spent their working lives pondering some of the planet's great prehistoric mysteries. What were the dinosaurs? When did they live? Today, the two academics from the University of Portsmouth have a more pressing question: how do you hang a dinosaur from the Queen's roof without causing any damage?

The Buckingham Palace Ballroom is a riot of activity. In one corner, a gigantic model of Albert Einstein's head is resting on its side. Two men are weaving their way through

a mess of packing crates carrying an enormous plastic mosquito. And Bob and Dave are crawling around in the attic trying to attach steel wires to the rafters so that they can dangle a replica pterosaur with a 37-foot wingspan above the Queen's head. It is all the fault of the Duke of Kent.

Back in 1998, someone had the bright idea of devoting an entire royal day to a particular British industry. The financial sector was chosen, and it was such a success that the 'themed day' has now become an established Palace event. From sport to the emergency services, different aspects of public life have been honoured over recent years. And it is thanks to the Duke of Kent that Bob and Dave have brought their pet pterosaur to the Palace. The Queen's cousin is a former Army officer, not an academic, but he is president of the Royal Institution and an honorary fellow of the Royal Society, Britain's two foremost scientific organisations. Eight months earlier, the Duke had noticed that there was no themed day in the pipeline. So he contacted the Palace's Co-Ordination and Research Unit (CRU) and suggested that the Monarchy should salute science. What's more, he had just the organisations to help. The Queen approved the idea and it was decided that the Palace should become an educational theme park for a day, followed by a reception for 500 eminent people from across the scientific spectrum. Obviously, the Queen and Prince Philip, as hosts, would be involved. But an event this size would need serious support. Step forward, the cousins.

For every major royal occasion which brings out the crowds, there will be dozens of other engagements all over the country. And, very often, they will be undertaken by

Left: Princess Alexandra meets ambassadors at the Diplomatic Reception at Buckingham Palace. Right: The Duchess of Gloucester.

the Kensington Palace team, the Monarch's cousins or, as the media are inclined to call them, the 'minor royals'. While it would certainly require a brutal twist of fate to elevate them to the forefront of the line of succession, there is nothing 'minor' about their work as far as their charities are concerned. The Duke of Gloucester (whose father was the third son of George V) undertakes around 230 engagements each year. His Danish-born Duchess performs around 120. The Duke of Kent (whose father was George V's fourth son) carries out around 230 engagements while his sister, Princess Alexandra, undertakes around 130. Between them, they account for roughly one fifth of the three to four thousand annual royal engagements and look after some 440 organisations and charities. All have reached pensionable age but, like their cousin Elizabeth, they do not discuss retirement. All have adult children with careers outside the Windsor pen so there is no younger generation to coach in the art of being royal. They simply continue to serve as a supporting cast where required, be it opening a scout hut in Dorset or attending a state funeral on the other side of the world.

Also involved are three royal cousins who seldom appear in the Court Circular. The Duchess of Kent devotes much of her time to her work as a music teacher and her own musical charity, Future Talent. Prince Michael of Kent – younger brother of the Duke of Kent and Princess Alexandra – is not on the official royal payroll because he is not in the line of succession. Under the rigid terms of the 1701 Act of Settlement – which Parliament has yet to repeal – members of the Royal Family who marry Roman Catholics are bumped off the list. So, when the Prince, a former Army officer, married

the Catholic Baroness Marie-Christine von Reibnitz, he was sidelined. A fluent Russian speaker, the Prince has many charity and Forces connections and still represents the Queen, at home and overseas, with Princess Michael.

'There are hundreds and hundreds of things the Queen could do, and she'd be exhausted if she did them all,' explains the Duke of Gloucester. 'It's not quite the same – us doing it. But, at least it's recognition. And I think that's what people like. I don't expect huge crowds or people lining the streets. It's as valid, even without a great deal of fuss.'

With just hours to spare, Bob and Dave have managed to hang their dinosaur in the Ballroom, narrowly avoiding snapping its head off. The time has come for 850 children – Britain's top science pupils – to pour into the Palace. It has been a tense couple of days for the Palace staff. 'We've had a maritime day, a music day and a design day,' says Tim Rolph from the CRU, 'but never a dinosaur.'

The Queen is away touring the Science Museum but the cousins are holding the fort. There are children everywhere. Some are handling insects. Others cluster round Professor Colin Pillinger, the man who sent a British probe to Mars. A group of girls from Norwood School in South London are enthralled by the dinosaur exhibition. But they are even more excited when they learn that there is royalty in the room. Three girls decide that a royal introduction is more exciting than a pterosaur so they start following the Duke of Gloucester. He cheerfully strikes up conversation on the translucent qualities of a piece of volcanic rock. The girls nervously wonder if he might give them an autograph. Rather like carrying cash, it's not standard royal practice, but the Duke obliges. 'I got my stuff signed by the Duke!' exclaims one of the girls as the teachers round up their pupils at the end of the day. 'I was looking forward to meeting Prince Harry,' sighs another. One pupil has been chatting to the Palace staff. 'If you get a job here, you get to live here so we're all applying,' she declares as they pile back on the bus.

Come nightfall it's time for the party, and the Queen leads the family among the guests. Among the first people she encounters is Professor Stephen Hawking, the great physicist. His journalist daughter, Lucy, does the talking on behalf of her father who has a form of motor neurone disease and speaks via eye signals and a computer. She explains that she and her father are working on a children's book about physics. 'We've had a lot of children through the house today, morning and afternoon,' the Queen remarks, 'but the House is still standing.'

Afterwards, Professor Hawking composes a summary of the encounter: 'This is a marvellous exhibition that should inspire children to want to study science. My father used to take me to the Science Museum, and that fired my desire to know more. Science and discovery are the most exciting things I know.'

Above: A pterosaur at the Palace.

Above right: The Duke
of Kent.

The Queen meets Bob and Dave plus their dinosaur. 'This is probably the best place I've ever exhibited,' Dave tells her. Bob assures her that her chandeliers are all intact. 'The children must have enjoyed it very much,' she replies. Afterwards, Bob is ecstatic: 'I think this is probably the greatest honour I've had since, well… being alive.' The Monarch retires for the night, but the cousins carry on mingling with the 500 boffins from across the academic spectrum. Baroness Greenfield, Director of the Royal Institution, salutes the organiser: 'It's suicide to live in a society dependent on technology when no one knows anything about it. The Duke of Kent is our president and he is assiduous in coming to our events. In the eight years I've been director, he's been wonderful.'

As the party draws to a close and the footmen gently perform their synchronised shuffle to usher the remaining guests to the doors, there is one question which no one is voicing aloud: what bright idea will the Duke of Kent come up with next?

While the cousins may not see many crowds 'lining the streets', their lower profile can be a blessed relief as they go about their duties. The Duke of Gloucester is certainly not complaining as he sits in a first-class seat on the train from London to Croydon. No one gives a second glance to the tall, studious man in glasses who is working his way through a large pile of documents. With just his equerry, Captain Ben Sempala-Ntege, and a plain-clothes protection officer, the Duke's lean entourage could be any bunch of executives en route to the London suburbs. The Duke likes trains and, with less security baggage than the more prominent members of the family, it is an easy option. Having turned 60 in 2004, he even carries a senior citizen's railcard.

Their journey has been seriously delayed because a man has thrown himself under a train at Purley. Some passengers are extremely cross. The Duke tries to lift the mood. 'If you want to commit suicide in Purley, I suppose you're near the *Pearly Gates*,' he murmurs. Suddenly, he realises that our camera is there. 'This isn't all being recorded, is it?' It is. 'Oh dear. I'll never be able to go to Purley again.' He comes across as an unassuming but thoughtful man who likes to say what he thinks. 'One can only be oneself really,' he says. 'There are lots of people, many of them volunteers, who do good work however you define it and they don't get much recognition. If I go along, it may not benefit them terrifically but, very often the local, or even the national press, are interested and it gives a greater opportunity to show what they're doing and to ask the public for money.'

A Cambridge-educated architect with a love of motorbikes, Prince Richard of Gloucester never expected to become either a Duke or a frontline member of the Royal Family. But the death of his elder brother in a flying accident in 1972, followed by the death of his father in 1974, suddenly placed him and his wife, Birgitte, in the spotlight. Since then, they have both taken on a broad cross-section of royal duties. The Duchess has a special fondness for charities which benefit children and the arts (she is a regular at the Royal Academy of Music). The Duke has made a particular point of supporting organisations with links to the building and design sectors.

As ever, his eyes latch on to every detail in the landscape. 'I'm always amazed by the number of chimney pots that London has,' he muses. Moments later, he ponders the design of the traffic on this line. 'They are hideous colours, these trains,' he says. 'Perhaps it discourages the graffiti writers. They wouldn't want to do it if they felt they were improving things.'

Below: The Duke of Gloucester on the London-Croydon line.

In Croydon, he insists on walking from the station to his first stop, a firm of management consultants who are doing charitable projects in the developing world. He has a limp from a recent motorbike accident, and it is a half-mile walk, but he enjoys taking in the buildings. 'Will that be demolished? It deserves to be,' he says, wincing at one. 'Oh, that's quite friendly,' he says of another. His hosts point out a famously inept branch of the Home Office which has just been refurbished and reclad. 'If only they could refurbish and reclad the people who run it,' he suggests.

From Croydon, a car takes him to Reigate School in Surrey where another of his organisations, the Construction Youth Trust, is promoting careers in the building industry. He discusses funding with the adults and safety gear with some boys. 'So the safety glasses have got more glamorous than they used to be? You don't want something that makes you look a prat.'

The Duke is glad that engagements have changed since his father's day. 'I remember seeing a film of my father going to a boys' club in the 1930s. First, nobody smiled and, secondly, everybody wore a hat.' As president of Clubs for Young People, he has strong views on the importance of youth charities, recalling his very first royal engagement. 'It was a boys' club in an old drill hall and I was really horrified because the city councillors said: "We've turned it over to these dreadful youths and I suppose it's a good idea keeping them off the streets." I thought that was absolutely the wrong way of looking at the problem. Here's a building which gives them an opportunity. Luckily, I haven't heard that concept very much recently.'

The Duke certainly doesn't find that mindset at the next stop, Reigate's Sovereign Youth Club. He came here to celebrate the club's fiftieth birthday. Today, it is celebrating sixty years, and the Duke is invited to cut the cake, which proves difficult. 'I've done the odd bit of knighting but always with the sword on the flat,' he explains as he attempts to slice it. Finally, he is driven on to Guildford to meet a human rights charity called Jubilee, which campaigns to protect abused children in the developing world. It is a small operation and they are delighted to have a royal visit. The Duke is impressed. 'They're spotlighting problems in murky corners that other people have thought it easier to ignore,' he says as a car drives him to the local railway station. On the train back to London, the Duke takes his seat next to a couple of football fans in Arsenal shirts and a Conservative MP. He immerses himself in a book and the other passengers do not bat an eyelid. None of them seems to have the faintest idea that the Queen's cousin is sitting next to them. After a day as a VIP, he has quietly merged back into the commuting masses. And that is just how the eighteenth-in-line to the Throne likes it.

CHAPTER THREE

FOUNTAIN OF HONOUR

Outside, it's pouring with rain, not that you would notice down here. We are in the basement of Buckingham Palace. Under the glare of strip lights and Anglepoise lamps, half a dozen smartly dressed women are reading and re-reading duplicate lists of names and delving into hefty reference books. Should a CBE precede a DSC? (Yes.) Should John Smith be 'Mr John Smith' or 'John Smith Esq.'? (It depends.) Can a woman have a different surname from her husband? (She can now.) These women invariably know the answer to such questions. But they still like to check. 'If we get it wrong, it would be in the papers,' says Mary Packham fearfully. The Dickensian atmosphere is even more pronounced at the far end of the table where two of the team are using ornate old pens, inkwells and blotting paper.

This busy dungeon might be the last place to inspire visions of sunlit chatter over iced coffee and strawberry tartlets but this is the office of the Queen's Garden Party Ladies. In three months' time, most of the people on these lists of names will be standing on a manicured royal lawn. Some will be talking to the Queen about the weather or war in Iraq. Pearl Mitchell, 49, from Belfast, will get the shock of her life – twice. And, whether they meet royalty or not, everyone will be treated to an endless supply of cucumber sandwiches (made with rock salt and dill but without crusts), strawberry tartlets and cups of the Queen's special Garden Party tea (a blend of Darjeeling and Assam). It will be a day which they all remember for the rest of their lives. And it all begins below stairs in this Palace backwater. Down here, among the Garden Party Ladies, we are at the true coalface of the honours system.

THE HONOURS SYSTEM

The Sovereign has always been the 'Fountain of Honour'. Once, this might have involved handing a medium-sized county to a Norman cousin or a gold chain to a particularly loyal medieval knight. Today, it underpins one of the most important and valued roles of the modern Monarchy: recognising and honouring service to others.

Every nation has its systems of reward and recognition. It might be the Order of the Aztec Eagle in Mexico or the Order of the Chrysanthemum in Japan. The United Kingdom has several orders of chivalry, some of which, like the Order of the Garter, date back to medieval times. Today, most people are appointed to one of the five classes of the Most Excellent Order of the British Empire. This was established, in 1917, as a means of recognising both sexes and all classes.

In addition to all these orders of chivalry, British citizens can also be made life peers – Baron (Lord) or Baroness (Lady). A peerage, however, is not an honour but an appointment to the House of Lords. As such, it comes in the post from the Prime Minister. An honour is a tangible decoration which is presented by the Queen.

Put together, this whole hierarchy is known as the honours system. These days, though, the selection process is left to the Government. The Monarch simply dishes out the decorations with as much fanfare as possible. Each year, around 2,500 people are informed that they have been put forward for a particular honour. The overwhelming majority of them are ordinary people honoured for a lifetime's contribution to a particular cause or institution. Most are thrilled, although a handful always turn down their awards. One former British ambassador, who has rejected two medals, says simply, 'My colleagues deserved it more than me.'

Any selective system which operates in conditions of close secrecy will have its critics. Many have asked how a country can hand a knighthood to a pop singer with a spectacular record of tax avoidance while simultaneously threatening a war veteran with prison because he cannot pay his spiralling council tax bill. These are all valid debates, but they have little to do with the Palace. As we shall see, the Monarch's duty is to make a fuss of those who deserve a fuss. Where the present Monarch differs from her predecessors is that she has extended the Fountain of Honour. There are only so many medals to go round in a normal year. To give out more would devalue the whole process. But there are many more deserving souls doing their bit for the country and the Queen likes to recognise them. So she has developed an extra system of her own. It does not come in the form of a medal. It comes on a plate.

Above: The Palace Ballroom on an investiture day.

THE LORD CHAMBERLAIN IS COMMANDED...

Every year, 2,500 names will appear on the two honours lists. But more than fifteen times that number are invited to one of Her Majesty's garden parties. In fact, in the course of the present Queen's reign, she has invited some two million people to these occasions. That is the equivalent of having the whole of Wales over for a cup of tea.

'It's a thank you for charity work, public work and so on,' says Anne Barton, the unflappable leader of the Garden Party Ladies, a part-time Palace team, who will check, double-check and then write out a personal invitation to every single one of the Queen's guests. There are much easier ways to send out invitations, of course. But what would most people prefer? An embossed, handwritten memento which will be framed and cherished for a lifetime? Or an email?

Until modern times, garden parties were an Establishment affair. Invented by Queen Victoria, they were originally known as 'breakfasts', despite a teatime start. The invitations seldom extended much beyond the nobility and officialdom. When the Queen came to the Throne in 1952, there were still 'presentation parties' at which eligible young ladies

– debutantes – were 'presented at Court'. The Queen decided that post-war Britain could survive without them. Presentations were scrapped to make way for an extended summer garden party season. There would be three at Buckingham Palace and one at Holyroodhouse in Edinburgh. The parties would be for ordinary people rather than the usual gathering of the great and good. To this day, most guests are invited just once. More recently, extra charity parties have been added to the schedule, the argument being that if the tents are up in the garden, then royal charities might as well make the most of them. Added together, an annual total of around 40,000 people will receive a royal summons courtesy of the Garden Party Ladies.

Each of the main parties is attended by roughly 8,000 people and the guest list is, in effect, a list of lists. The Services, Government departments, councils and professional bodies are allowed to nominate a certain number. The bulk of the names, though, are put forward by the Lord Lieutenants, the Queen's representatives in the counties. 'This is about unsung work,' says Anne Barton. 'It's nice after you've done thirty-five years of school dinners when someone says, "Why not send them along".'

Each invitation begins: 'The Lord Chamberlain is commanded by Her Majesty to invite ..... to a Garden Party.' The Garden Party Ladies must then fill in the names of the recipients and anyone who is expected to be accompanying them.

Here, again, there have been some radical changes during the Queen's reign. Traditionally, guests were only allowed to bring a spouse plus any unmarried daughters aged between 18 and 25 (a leftover from debutante days). Then, in 1993, it was decided that this amounted to sexual discrimination so unmarried sons were allowed along, too. It was also agreed that anyone without a spouse could bring a 'companion' of either sex. This could be a live-in lover, a carer or simply a friend.

Regina Bullough, the aptly named doyenne of the Garden Party Ladies, has been part of this team since 1986 and has seen plenty of changes. 'Guests came on their own for many years and then the Queen said that every guest invited on their own should have the opportunity to bring along a member of the family, a neighbour, a friend. It gives enormous pleasure. It's always lovely to talk about something you're enjoying if you've come all the way from Northern Ireland or Leeds or Truro and you're wandering round these lovely gardens.'

The dress code states that men should wear uniforms, morning dress or lounge suits. Women should wear 'afternoon dress' – the sort of thing they might wear to, say, a wedding – preferably with a hat.

Regina has noticed a major shift over the years. 'When I went to my first garden party in 1986, I remember it like yesterday, it was such a thrill. There were a lot of gentlemen in morning dress but today that isn't the case. More are now in lounge suits than in morning suits. Every lady wore a hat then. Now, you see a lot of elegant trouser suits and the odd lady who doesn't wear a hat.'

Sexual equality has even extended to the way in which invitations are written. These days, if the principal guest is a woman, she can decide how she would prefer to be addressed. 'The way to address the invitees has changed enormously and we have to be very careful about that,' says Regina. 'We do give the guests the title they ask for.' She points to a recent example which would have prompted howls of dismay among the Garden Party Ladies of days gone by. 'We have here an invitation going to a lady with one surname, a husband with another surname and a son with another surname.'

There are, however, no concessions when it comes to accuracy and consistency. For example, when addresses are written out on the envelopes, British men have 'Esq.' after their name – 'John Smith Esq.' – whereas all men from overseas are called 'Mr John Smith' (without the Esq.).

If a list refers to a 'Lady Jane Smith', she must be checked out. Only the daughter of a Duke, a Marquess or an Earl can call herself 'Lady' followed by her first name. If she is a 'Lady' because she is married to a man with a title, then her first name does not appear and she is, simply, 'Lady Smith'. And so it goes on.

Anne Barton also has to deal with some strange requests, not least people *asking* for invitations. 'I have had people ring up asking, "How does it work? What do I have to do to be invited?" and I always refer them to the Lord Lieutenant of their county,' she explains. 'They usually want an invitation for father or mother. Not many ask for themselves but one or two do. One person said, "I have paid a lot of tax"!' There is one category, however, who can invite themselves. All non-British residents in the UK can write to their London embassy or High Commission and ask for one of the batch of invitations allotted to each country. Every one of the 40,000 invitations is a task in itself. The invitation must be written out immaculately and checked by someone else. The words must be carefully spaced, too. This invitation will be a lifelong souvenir. It's got to look nice. Regina holds up a particularly challenging example from the Diplomatic List: 'His Majesty the Sultan of Brunei, Her Majesty the Duli Raja Isteri and Her Royal Highness Pengiran Isteri'. Regina explains that the tougher the challenge, the less the chance of a mistake: 'We don't get those wrong very often because we have to concentrate so hard.'

The invitation itself does not grant entry. Each guest must have a separate handwritten admittance card, and each envelope must also include security details, car parking badges, maps and even information about the London congestion charge. The bundle is packed in a large cream envelope which must also be handwritten and then stamped by the Court Post Office.

Whisper it softly in these parts but there are plans afoot to find a way of getting a computer to do the 'handwriting' part of the job, leaving the ladies to check all the spellings and addresses. For now, though, they are very happy doing the lot, because they love it. Regina likes to arrive early so that she can hear the Queen's Piper conducting his daily recital outside the Palace from 9 to 9.15 a.m. And when the garden parties are over, she will simply swap one palace for another. Come the summer holidays, she works as a tourist guide at the Prince of Wales's London residence, Clarence House.

So what tips do these experts have for the 40,000 novices who will be receiving invitations every year into the future? Regina has a few: 'At Buckingham Palace, the main entrance is the one to go for because you go through the Grand Hall and on to the terrace and… Wow! And when you get in the garden, go to the herbaceous border because it's quite beautiful in July. Although the invitation says "4 p.m.", they're allowed in at 3 o'clock and they've got an hour to look round the gardens.' Above all, guests should simply enjoy being there and forget about the etiquette. Wherever the party, Regina's advice is the same: 'Everything from the moment you enter is magic really.'

Right: The Queen and the Duke of Edinburgh arrive at a garden party, before taking separate paths through the crowds.

RSVP

ROYAL INVITATIONS

The Queen does not 'invite' people to anything. By tradition, she 'commands' her officials to do it. If it is a major Court event, then the invitation will come from the Lord Chamberlain and will state: 'The Lord Chamberlain is Commanded by Her Majesty to invite Mr and Mrs John X to a Garden Party at Buckingham Palace on July 1st from 4 to 6 o'clock.'

If it is to a more personal occasion, like a luncheon, it will come from the Master of the Household and will state: 'The Master of the Household has received Her Majesty's command to invite Mr and Mrs John X to a Luncheon...'

The accompanying blurb will usually let you know what to do next. If it is a garden party, no reply is necessary if you are coming. If you cannot attend, you are expected to return the admittance card. For other events a reply is expected. Contrary to popular perception, Royal Household staff are not very bothered by the format of replies. They just want a prompt answer. 'Frankly, whether it's fax, email, phone, carrier pigeon, whatever, we'd just much rather have a reply,' says Jonathan Spencer, Deputy Comptroller of the Lord Chamberlain's Office. 'We don't have some ancient rulebook.'

Many people, however, will always want to do the 'right' thing. If so, the 'correct' form of acceptance, according to the arbiters of etiquette at Debrett's Correct Form, should be written like this: 'Mr and Mrs John X present their compliments to the Master of the Household and have the honour to obey Her Majesty's Command to Luncheon on July 1st at 12.30 o'clock.' If you cannot attend, you do not need to give a reason, although, again, traditionalists disagree. According to Debrett's, a 'prior engagement' is not adequate grounds for refusing the Monarch's 'command'. So, a 'correct' refusal might read: 'Mr and Mrs John X present their compliments to the Master of the Household and very much regret that they are unable to obey Her Majesty's Command to Luncheon on July 1st due to the fact that they will be abroad/owing to the illness of Mr X...'

Other members of the Royal Family 'invite' rather than 'command' but, again, usually do so through an official. So, you might write: 'Mr and Mrs John X present their compliments to the Private Secretary to His Royal Highness The Prince of Wales and have the honour to accept his invitation to Luncheon...'

The 'traditional' rule is that a thank-you letter is only expected if the invitation requires a formal reply. Garden party invitations do not require a reply and so a 'thank you' is not expected. But many guests like to send one anyway. This should be addressed to the official who despatched the original invitation – 'Dear Lord Chamberlain' – and in it you should ask for your thanks to be conveyed to the royal host. 'We do get a lot of thank-you letters and the Queen likes to see them,' says Jonathan. 'It's a nice gesture and no one minds how they are written.'

The Lord Steward
has received Her Majesty's command to invite

....

....

to a State Banquet to be given at Buckingham Palace by
The Queen and The Duke of Edinburgh
in honour of
The President of the Republic of Ghana and Mrs. Kufuor
on Tuesday, 13th March, 2007 at 8.30 p.m.

A reply is requested to:
The Master of the Household,
Buckingham Palace,
London SW1A 1AA.

Guests

Evening Dress (White Tie),
Decorations,
Full Ceremonial Evening Dress for
Serving Officers, or National Dress

between 7.50 and 8.10 p.m.

The Master of the Household
has received Her Majesty's command to invite

....

....

to a Luncheon to be given at Buckingham Palace
by The Queen and The Duke of Edinburgh

on................ at 12.50 p.m. for 1.00 p.m.

Dress: Lounge Suit
Day Dress

The reply should be addressed to:
The Master of the Household,
Buckingham Palace, SW1A 1AA.

... AND HOW TO SEND A ROYAL INVITATION

Unless you know them personally, do not send members of the Royal Family
personal invitations. Instead, you should write to the private secretary of
the would-be royal guest explaining the nature of the occasion. The private
secretary's office will advise you how to proceed.

PIECE OF CAKE

The Band of the Coldstream Guards is beginning a repertoire of Beatles and Lloyd Webber tunes. A policeman is attempting a manoeuvre which was never on the training schedule for the Metropolitan Police's Royalty and Diplomatic Division: how to remove a very stubborn duck and her ducklings from the Queen's lawn.

The policeman is actually doing the duck a big favour. Any minute now, 16,000 well-shod feet are about to come clomping over this grass in determined pursuit of two things: a slap-up tea and a glimpse of the Queen. The guests have been hanging around Buckingham Palace long before the scheduled opening of the gates at 3 p.m. The final garden party of the season is about to begin. Hundreds are queuing on either side of the Buckingham Palace forecourt. Many are finishing off elaborate picnic lunches next to their cars in the Mall. It is not often you get an official pass to use Britain's grandest thoroughfare as a car park.

Inside the forty acres of Palace pond and garden, the lawns are ready, if rather parched. The temperature is a very un-British 90 degrees-plus Fahrenheit (in the 30-plus range in Centigrade). The Queen has been observing a regional ban on hosepipes, even though the Palace is exempt (and it has its own borehole). It would not look good if her gardens were ostentatiously lush while the rest of southern Britain looked like a desert. Just one small patch is kept dark green for reasons of visibility – the Palace helipad.

The clotted cream is on the scones and the brand new garden furniture has been laid out in immaculate lines. In the main marquee, the longest tea counter in Britain – a

400-foot non-stop stretch of buffet – is taking shape. It will require 110 serving staff, 40 clearing and washing-up staff, 30 chefs and 25 managers to feed the 8,000 people who will form 37 different queues. The Buckingham Palace guests will consume half a ton of sandwiches, 11,000 cups of tea and 8,000 glasses of cordial. No alcohol is served, although, over the summer, the guests will absorb around 80 litres of Balmoral whisky in the 25,000 slices of whisky cake served during the garden party season.

This is the final Buckingham Palace garden party of the summer but it is still a nervous moment for the caterers. The Queen is on her way to meet all the staff. She is no semi-detached hostess. She likes to check everything with Edward Griffiths, the Deputy Master of the Household and the chief architect of these events. These two make up just about the most daunting inspection team any caterer could imagine.

The Queen checks the entire menu and can already spot one potential problem for her guests on a hot day like today. Inspecting the chocolate brownies, she remarks: 'You can't take those away in doggy bags because they melt which is no good.' She likes the new touch involving the 'Gateau Opera', a rich chocolate cake drenched with coffee. Each piece has been stamped with the Crown. When the Prince of Wales had a garden party the other day, each slice had his feathers embossed on it. 'Oh, you changed the motif, that's very clever,' she says. On the whole, she has been pretty happy with this summer's events. 'Well, I've done a good deal of asking what the tea is like and I get very positive answers,' she says to the huge relief of the caterers who gratefully offer her a cup of tea.

'No thanks, I've just had lunch,' she replies. In the shade of the main tent, she foresees problems. 'I should think people will be very glad to get in here,' she predicts. 'But that makes it quite difficult working here because they all come in at once. They rush in!' The weather will also make it a busy day for the first aid team from the St John Ambulance and the Queen makes sure that they do not go unrecognised. It has been an extremely hot summer and she has detected certain trends among the guests. 'I've noticed twice that they've all gone to sit in the shade and the lawn's been more and more empty,' she says. 'They come too early and arrive boiling hot and exhausted.'

Edward Griffiths suggests that new shoes, bought specially for the occasion, might also be a factor. 'I don't agree with that!' the Queen replies, anxious not to deter her guests from buying new shoes. 'But people come so unsuitably dressed, that's the other thing. They're probably frizzled by the time they get here.'

She has been following events in the first aid tent closely. 'I think, last week, you had thirty-seven casualties,' she tells the ambulance team, who are pleasantly surprised to discover that she is watching their work so closely. The Queen has no doubt it will be the same story all over again this afternoon. 'You may be busy,' she assures the medics. Indeed, they will be.

The £600,000 cost of the garden parties is met by the Civil List, the annual £7.9 million grant received by the Monarch to perform her duties as Head of State. After some disappointing feedback in previous summers, the budget has now almost trebled from £6 per person to £17 per person in three years. When the Queen has finished her inspection, Edward Griffiths carries out his most important test – the sweetness of the iced coffee – and checks the most popular items – salmon sandwiches, 'Gateau Opera' and strawberry tartlets.

A quarter of a mile away, at their St James's Palace headquarters, another royal team is preparing for action. The garden party may be on royal turf but the Monarch's oldest bodyguard will still be in attendance during the garden party. The men of the Royal Body Guard of the Yeomen of the Guard – the oldest military corps in the land, if not the world – have been protecting monarchs since Henry VII appointed them in 1485. Based at St James's, there are seventy-one of them, all volunteers and all distinguished former Non-Commissioned Officers and Warrant Officers from the Army, the Royal Marines and the Royal Air Force (for archaic reasons, they don't recruit from the Royal Navy). And their uniform has hardly changed since Tudor times either.

Each man wears black buckled shoes, red stockings with red, white and blue rosettes, a scarlet doublet, a white ruff made of Egyptian cotton and a black

Below: The 'lanes' of garden party guests.

velvet hat with red, white and blue ribbons. They are well armed, too. Each carries a sword (which is never drawn) and a seven-foot halberd known as a 'partisan'.

They are often, wrongly, called 'Beefeaters'. This is the historic nickname for the Yeomen Warders, an entirely different corps with a similar uniform who guard the Tower of London. 'They are wardens and we are bodyguards,' says one Yeoman of the Guard firmly. 'Look at it this way, we wear stockings and they wear tights.' It is a surreal experience to receive a lecture on hosiery from a battle-scarred former Sergeant Major. But these things matter. Today, their main role is to mark out royal routes through the crowds, but they are always conscious of their bodyguard role. No one expects trouble at a garden party but these old soldiers will not flinch if they suspect their Monarch is in any danger – as the first garden party streaker discovered in 2003. The miscreant was the teenage son of a (very embarrassed) teacher who had been invited in recognition of his services to education. Quite why the young man wanted to run naked in front of the Queen is a mystery to this day but he was barely out of his trousers when Yeoman Ray Duffy, 56, a former Army rugby player, had flattened him on the lawn.

Before the Yeomen of the Guard go on duty today, they must receive their briefing from Messenger Sergeant Major Bill Davis, ex-Irish Guards. And he is not a happy man. Some of his men have let him down. A few days earlier, while guarding the Prince of Wales at a garden party in honour of his Prince's Trust, certain Yeomen were very obviously distracted by the sight of two former Spice Girls, Emma Bunton and Geri Halliwell.

Right: Messenger Sergeant Major Bill Davis and the Yeomen of the Guard prepare for duty. Far right: Eyes front and no ogling!

'They were looking absolutely gorgeous, gentlemen,' barks Bill. 'The trouble was you all were of the same opinion so, consequently, you started staring, leering, ogling! And you lost your concentration while you were on parade!' Mr Davis has firm instructions for today: 'Should there be any attractive ladies here today, by all means have a look but do not turn your heads. Concentrate on what you're doing.'

Furthermore, it turns out that one of his men had, himself, been the victim of some admiring glances at the same party. 'One Yeoman had his bum felt by a member of the public!' declares the Sergeant Major in shocked tones, even if his men are trying desperately not to howl with laughter. 'The chap who had his bum felt was under the impression it was a lady. Let's hope it was. But would you tell anyone who attempts to feel your backside today that being a guest at a garden party doesn't grant the privilege of feeling a Yeoman's backside.'

The guests are interested in other matters as they start pouring through the gates on the stroke of 3 p.m. For most people, it is the first time that they have seen beyond the Portland stone façade of the Palace's East Wing where the Royal Family appears on the balcony.

The inner quadrangle is a sight in itself, its reddish gravel crunching underfoot. The guests do not have long to look up and around, wondering who lives in which rooms of which wing, before they are steered through the Grand Entrance, into the Grand Hall and across acres of red carpet to the Bow Room. From here, the French windows open out on to the West Terrace and it is here, as the guests emerge from the fabulous portrait-

packed, marble interior into bright daylight and Edwardian elegance on the lawns that most of them do, indeed, utter the same word: 'Wow!'

Some head straight for the tea tents to bag a chair and a table. Others stride off to make the most of the gardens. After all, they only have three hours to absorb thirty-six acres of garden plus four acres of lake. The keenest guests will make it to the mulberry garden planted by King James I (and VI of Scotland) and the fifteen-foot Waterloo Vase, carved from a single piece of marble. Today's guests are from all over the country – and the social and political spectrum, too. Jean Watkins originally thought it was a hoax when her invitation came through the post. She thinks she was nominated either because of her work for the local police authority in Newport, Gwent or for her local charity work. Either way, she is thrilled to bits to be here and travelled up the night before with her husband – and two outfits – to stay in a hotel nearby. She will go to any lengths to see the Queen today. 'I'll punch my way to the front if necessary,' she says.

By no means all the guests are diehard monarchists. Ann Green, from Birmingham, says that she is an 'intellectual republican'. But she has always had a deep respect for the Queen and is delighted to have been invited in recognition of her work for the Chartered Society of Physiotherapists. Every year, the society receives four invitations in recognition of its royal connections and this year's quartet will also include Margaret Revie from Hamilton. She has flown down from Scotland a day early and has had a morning of intensive pampering at a hair and beauty salon. She is worried about her dress – 'when I bought my outfit I didn't think it would be 30-odd degrees' – but she is still extremely proud to have been chosen. 'I've had my invitation sitting up in my waiting area and the older patients are very excited,' she says. 'You look at the envelope and it says "Buckingham Palace", and that doesn't happen every week.'

Fergal McCormick and his wife, Anne, are both from Northern Ireland's nationalist community but Fergal, a chartered accountant, has been invited in recognition of his work for the people of Newry. He admits that it would have been unusual to see an Irish nationalist at the Palace fifteen years ago, but he has praise for the Queen's role in bringing Northern Ireland's two sides closer together. 'She has shown a level of maturity and leadership,' he explains. 'For that alone, she deserves much credit.' Anne says that it's a 'lovely honour' and that it is important for all sides of Northern Ireland to 'speak the language of other traditions'.

Another couple who have made the long journey across the Irish Sea are Pearl Mitchell and her boyfriend Gerry Crawford. Pearl runs a hotel in Ballymoney, Northern Ireland and has been invited for her charity work with the local branch of

Right: Royal introductions.

133

Left: The St John Ambulance team assembles. Right: The Queen inspects the volunteers.

Cruse Bereavement Care. The mother of two grown-up daughters, she admits that this is one of the most exciting days of her life. She had wanted to bring her elderly mother, Queenie, but the trip would have been too stressful so she has given her the original invitation card instead. 'She cried and proudly put it up for the world to see,' says Pearl, who has spent over £200 on a hat for this occasion. 'I am a huge fan of the Queen. I think she has done a fantastic service all through the years,' says Pearl. 'She hasn't had an easy life. There's got to be times she's got a headache but I've never heard of her cancelling anything.'

So, what would she swap her invitation for right now – £10,000, £20,000, £100,000? 'No. This is something that I really want to do and the opportunity might never arise again. Life's all about experiences.' Like most guests, Pearl and Gerry are overawed by the elegance, the scale, the sheer thrill of walking through the gates. She spots the Waterloo Vase. 'I've definitely decided we need a huge centrepiece in the courtyard,' she informs Gerry.

Fergal and Anne are equally impressed. 'It's a beautiful setting, quite awesome to see it in real life, seeing all the glamour and pomp,' says Anne, who has spent much of the morning at the hairdresser. Fergal bumps into a friend, a Northern Irish politician who gives him a tip on coping with the heat: 'The secret is never get a sweat up. Once you perspire, you're lost for the rest of the day.' Wise words.

Few are hotter than the Yeomen of the Guard who have taken up position on the lawn. They are all perfectly behaved today and there is no ogling of the guests as they carefully mark out the routes or 'lanes' down which the royal party will proceed. Today, the Garden Party Ladies have emerged into the fresh air. Anne Barton is on standby to

deal with those who have lost any or all of the documents they need to get through the door. 'People do forget their invitations,' she says. What? On a day like today? 'They pack up in a hurry, they forget their passports or ID but we have a system and it seems to work. A lot of them seem to lose things or the dog eats it, or the child scribbles on it. I get quite a few stories like that.'

Out on the terrace, the Queen's Senior Gentleman Usher, Rear Admiral Colin Cooke-Priest, is preparing to weed out guests for royal introductions. The Gentlemen Ushers are a collection of retired officers from the Armed Forces who help out at Court occasions, making sure everything runs smoothly, and the Rear Admiral has been doing this for thirteen years. Today, he will be working in the Queen's lane with three Gentlemen Ushers and their watchword is variety.

'We basically move down the lanes and try and find interesting people to introduce to Her Majesty. Part of the game is to make sure that we give a complete diversity. If one clergyman turns up and two down the lane is another clergyman, he's out of luck. If you get two servicemen, bad luck. We try and split it up.'

The Rear Admiral reveals a few other tips on how to get a royal introduction. 'We always try, if we can, to find a family – mother, father and one or two youngsters, that's great fun.'

Another rule is that the Queen does not want to see any familiar faces. They automatically go to the back of the queue. 'We do avoid those who, in their other lives, had a better opportunity to meet the Royal Family – mayors and people like that. We try and discreetly discover where they've come from, what they've done. It's only then, when that's worked out, that we actually let them know that they will meet the Queen.'

He, in turn, will hand over the chosen guests to the Lord Chamberlain, the most senior member of the Royal Household, who will introduce them to the Queen. Today will be the final garden party for this Lord Chamberlain, Lord Luce, before his retirement later in the year. He has always enjoyed this task, whatever the weather, and he will miss it.

'The most important thing is getting a cross-section of society – from all over the Commonwealth, the professions, different towns,' he says, adding that he relies on the Gentlemen Ushers to unearth the right blend. 'They have to pick up on an X-factor. My job is to make sure the Queen has a lead in the conversation.'

It is the job of the Queen, and any other members of the Royal Family present, to make sure that the people they meet are not overwhelmed. Royal officials call it 'putting people at ease'. The Prince of Wales has a tried and tested method of doing this. 'Do to others as you'd have them do to you. That's the way to do it,' he says. 'I always think: "What would I feel like if I was in that position?" And if that puts people at ease, I am thrilled.'

Ann and Margaret, the two physiotherapists, are just two faces among 8,000 candidates for an introduction. Ann is impressed that everyone has conformed. 'All the ladies are in hats, all the men are in suits,' she says. The two of them strike up a conversation with the Lord Mayor of Bradford who is standing next to them in full regalia.

Pearl is still wandering in a daze, stunned by the sights and the heat, though mildly perturbed to spot another woman wearing the same dress. 'I'm glad she's not tall and

willowy. I really can't believe someone can be wearing the same outfit.' But her luck soon changes. Suddenly, Pearl encounters one of the Gentlemen Ushers and she meets his diversity target. He has not met any other Northern Irish bereavement counsellors today. Before they know it, Pearl and Gerry are out in the royal lane waiting for a royal introduction.

The Gentlemen Ushers fill in introduction cards which the Lord Chamberlain will use to make the royal introduction. Pearl gives her name as 'Ms Pearl Mitchell'. The Gentleman Usher politely explains that it's a Miss or Mrs situation. 'The Queen doesn't recognise Ms,' he says. This is no time for an argument. Pearl happily opts for 'Miss'.

At 4 p.m., there is a sudden hush as the royal party emerges from the Palace onto the terrace and the band strikes up the National Anthem. The party really has begun. 'Oh look,' whispers Margaret, slightly overcome. Both physiotherapists stand to attention. Margaret is blinking hard. As the last notes disappear, she dabs her eyes. 'I thought: "I'm going to cry." It just felt different. I could feel my lip trembling. It was just so special.' The crowd applauds. 'You can see why people don't bring sandwiches out,' says Ann. 'You can't clap.'

The Queen then takes the left-hand lane, now lined by thousands of people, and the Duke of Edinburgh takes the right. The Duke of York and the Duke and Duchess of Gloucester perform a flanking manoeuvre around the outside of the main throng, meeting those at the back of the crowd. It might only be 250 yards to the end of this

Far left: Garden party guests Margaret Revie and Ann Green from the Chartered Society of Physiotherapists. Left: Ann eats a sandwich while Margaret surveys the garden party crowds.

'lane', but it is going to take the Queen and the Duke a full hour to make it across their own back lawn.

Ann and Margaret decide to go royal-watching instead of pushing through the crowd. They soon spot a cluster of people. 'The eagle has landed,' announces Ann triumphantly. It is the Duke of York. They both have a good long look and are impressed, professionally, by his posture. 'Must be that military training,' they murmur. 'I'm impressed how obedient the Queen's children are,' Ann reflects. 'If I said to my children, "I'm having a garden party, would you come," they wouldn't.'

They try for a closer look of the Queen. It's a constant struggle to see over all the hats but Margaret finds a peephole beneath a Yeoman's armpit. 'That hat is really lovely,' she reports back to Ann. What's more, as a physio, she is impressed that the Queen is standing correctly.

Right in front of her, out in the 'lane', Pearl and Gerry from County Antrim are still pinching themselves. They are going to meet the Queen. A succession of Gentlemen Ushers pause to offer them advice on what to say and do. Pearl asks one of them how many of the 8,000 guests will be introduced today. 'About a hundred,' he replies. 'I think I might pass out,' Pearl murmurs. What would induce her to part with her invitation now? 'I wouldn't sell it for a million.' Yet another man in a morning coat pops up.

'Are you the couple being presented? How wonderful. Over here,' he declares and

Above: Pearl
and Gerry's
royal encounter
– Lord Luce does the
introductions.

steers Pearl and Gerry over to one side so that they are at an angle to the Queen. 'We zig-zag her. One of the reasons we do that is it gives everyone an opportunity to see her.' There's yet another good-humoured mini-lecture on how to curtsy: 'Don't go too low because you may not get back up again and it's undignified to have a conversation lying on your back.' There's yet another reminder about what to say: 'Unless your false teeth are a problem, it's "Your Majesty", thereafter "Ma'am" as in jam.'

'Oh my goodness, my little tummy,' murmurs Pearl. Yet another courtier arrives. And this one introduces himself as Lord Luce, the Lord Chamberlain, no less. He goes through the etiquette once more. 'Oh, she's getting closer now, Gerry,' says a trembling Pearl. Her Majesty is indeed, just a few feet away, talking to another couple plucked from the crowd. Things are tense but it could be worse for Pearl. Next in line after her is Veronica Fennell from Oxfordshire. Standing with her nurse, Nanette Stephens, she is 'thrilled to bits' to be meeting the Queen. Is she nervous? 'No,' says Veronica at the very moment that a gust of wind removes her hat. 'Yes!' she says, quickly changing her tune as well-wishers pursue the runaway hat.

Finally, Pearl's moment has come. 'Your Majesty,' announces the Lord Chamberlain, 'May I present Miss Pearl Mitchell and Mr Gerald Crawford.' Sheltering beneath a parasol and smiling in the infernal heat, the Queen extends a hand. Pearl does a perfect curtsy. Gerry performs a very correct bow from the neck. Lord Luce explains the connection with Cruse Bereavement Care but the Queen, as its patron, is well up to speed on her charities.

'Yes, Cruse,' she says knowingly. Moments earlier, Pearl had been wondering what to say. She's certainly not short of words now.

Pearl: 'I'm the chairperson of the Causeway branch which is right up on the North Coast so it's a very busy office and area and we had 3,000 volunteer hours last year.'

The Queen: 'That's tremendous, isn't it? And do you have to train the volunteers?'

Pearl: 'There is quite a strict training, it's called support volunteers now and it's quite strict. We have fourteen new people who are training just at this minute.'

The Queen: 'So, there is a plentiful supply?'

Pearl: 'Oh yes, it's ongoing. Unfortunately for some volunteers, they have illnesses and their own bereavements, so we have to always recruit so we're very fortunate we can recruit so easily.'

The Queen: 'Lucky, isn't it?' She turns to Gerry. 'So what are you involved with?'

Gerry: 'I'm just along here as a friend.'

Pearl: 'We're delighted and very honoured to be here.'

The Queen: 'There are probably quite a few from Northern Ireland here today. Well, I hope you enjoy the rest of the party.'

Pearl and Gerry: 'Thank you, Ma'am.'

And with that, the Queen is gently steered on to Veronica (who has been reunited with her hat). She has learned a little more about one of her charities in a remote part of her Kingdom. For Pearl and Gerry, it has been the moment of a lifetime. 'I thought, "I am going to get tongue-tied," but she was easy, really easy to talk to,' says Pearl. 'Her skin is like porcelain. She's a fine-looking woman and I did remember "Ma'am". That has been just a fabulous, fabulous experience.' She's enjoyed meeting the courtiers, too. 'They're so lovely, aren't they? It's actually done terribly well.'

Pearl is astonished, on leaving the Queen's lane, to bump into the woman in the identical outfit. But this is her hour of glory, her moment of triumph. The other woman has not met the Queen, and Pearl is magnanimous in victory. 'You've got great taste,' she tells her with a big smile.

While the main tea tent hums with eaters, drinkers and shade-seekers, another set of invitees are slowly filling the two smaller tents on the north

Below: Two of the lucky ones plucked
from a crowd of 8,000.

side of the garden where the Queen will finally be given a cup of tea. To the right is the Diplomatic Tent; to the left is the Royal Tent which will contain a few eminent people from public life. Today, former Prime Minister Baroness Thatcher and Government ministers including Geoff Hoon are on the list.

Fiery Jean Watkins from Gwent has not met the Queen, but she has seen her up close. 'There was a lady in a silly big hat. I stood on her foot – I told you I'd fight,' she says. 'I've seen what I came for. The Queen. It was fabulous, really close, I had a really good look at her. She's fantastic for her age. Not a wrinkle. That's something to go down in history as far as I'm concerned. We can say we went to tea at the Palace and I had a cake with a Crown on it. And I ate it. It's been the best day of our lives – and I thought our wedding day was good.' Her husband, Trevor, knows better than to disagree.

The well-oiled catering machine rumbles on behind the scenes. The chefs are making the last 2,000 sandwiches in the enviable cool of an air-conditioned preparation unit. The worst job, in this heat, is being in charge of the tea urns. After every 100 cups of tea, these have to be refilled from four huge master vats which are steaming away in the sun. Every load also requires special royal-sized bags which each provide three pints of Darjeeling and Assam.

There is no slacking on detail. Even at this late stage, every tray of cakes is given a quick

Above left: Younger crowd – a garden party for children in honour of the Queen's 80th birthday. Above: Always popular – mini lemon tarts.

blast of air from a small bellows. The Queen does not like to serve her guests crumbs.

Finally, at 6 p.m., the Queen and Prince Philip make a quiet exit back to the Palace, via a line of some of the more infirm guests who have endured the day's heat. 'You've got an engine,' the Duke observes to a man in an electric wheelchair. 'Do you want a go on it?' the man asks. 'Haven't got a licence,' the Duke replies to all-round chortling.

Looking on, our two physiotherapists have their doubts about the Duke's posture. 'Rather stooped,' they both agree as the band thumps out old favourites from *Oklahoma!* Both women, though, have been enchanted by the day. 'It's like going to the best Society wedding,' says Ann. Finally, the National Anthem is the signal that the party is over. It has been a monumental catering exercise of epic proportions. Around 8,000 people have consumed some 65,000 scones and sandwiches. No one, though, is as happy as Pearl Mitchell, even though she hasn't tasted a single sliver of Gateau Opera. She is sitting on a chair on the lawn, taking it all in for the final time. 'I feel I'm really special today. It's been a special VIP type of day. I can't fault it in any way.' She is still so moved by the experience that she barely notices Gerry getting down on one knee. He has been unusually silent for much of the day. Now, on the Queen's lawn, in front of the Queen's house, he plucks up the courage to round off this day – and thirteen years of happy courtship – with a proposal of marriage. Pearl is – briefly – speechless. And then she orders Gerry to round it off with a kiss.

Getting on the List

The twice-yearly honours list is a list of lists. Of the 1,300 names on each one, around 300 will be from separate lists drawn up by the Foreign Office (usually diplomats), the Ministry of Defence (usually members of the Armed Forces) or the Royal Household (royal servants). The vast majority, around 1,000, will be on the main list which is drawn up by the Ceremonial Secretariat, a tiny Government operation inside the Cabinet Office.

Half of these 1,000 names will have been nominated by other members of the public. Anyone can nominate anyone and around 3,500 forms are sent in every year. All are studied closely by a team of sixteen and the whole process can take up to eighteen months.

At the same time, every Government department will be drawing up its own list of candidates within its particular fields. The Department of Health will have internal boards for nominating doctors, nurses and administrative staff. The Department of Culture will ponder which film stars are due for recognition.

All these nominations then leave Government hands and go to eight independent committees for filtering by a range of experts. One, for example, deals with economic activity. The largest handles community nominations. Each has a certain number of honours available each year and narrows down its field to fit. The heads of these committees then form the Main Honours Committee, chaired by the head of the Civil Service, Sir Gus O'Donnell, and they draw up the final list. After recent allegations of political favouritism, the Prime Minister no longer plays a part in this process. There is plenty of debate, though. A generous backer of the opera might have been nominated for a CBE by the arts committee. But the chairman of the economics committee might know that his business is about to go bust.

Two months before publication, the finished list is passed to the Prime Minister's Office which sends it to the Queen for approval. When it returns, Downing Street sends a letter to every nominee asking if they would like to receive the suggested honour. Only a handful decline.

Of the entire list, nearly sixty per cent will be nominated for community work but only forty per cent will be women. More than eighty per cent will be appointed to the Order of the British Empire. Whether they are a Member (MBE), Officer (OBE), Commander (CBE), Knight/Dame (KBE/DBE) or Knight/Dame Grand Cross (GBE), they will all be invited to receive their honour from the Queen. What's more, anyone from MBE upwards now has privileged access to a special place for family baptisms, weddings and memorial services – St Paul's Cathedral.

Right: The Victoria Cross, which takes precedence at any investiture.

Below: The Queen, the Lord Chamberlain (right) and the rest of the retinue arrive for a Palace investiture.

FIRST AID

THE INVESTITURE

This is not the Gordon Ramsay the public usually sees. Britain's punchiest television chef is not shouting at anyone. Dressed in a suit and tie, he is positively contented, exuding pride and humility. This is a man used to being the centre of national attention and making headlines – both positive and critical. This is a workaholic who likes to swear a lot. So what has brought on this gentle serenity?

The former footballer has just been made an Officer of the Most Excellent Order of the British Empire, becoming Gordon Ramsay OBE. And the award – in recognition of 'services to the hospitality industry' – has just been presented to him by the Queen. 'This is a huge honour,' he says. 'And it's something that my young daughter, Megan, will never forget for the rest of her life.'

Had he just won gold at the Food Olympics he could not be prouder. And he is not the only one beaming on this sunny morning. He is just one of nearly 100 people for whom this will be one of their proudest days. Most are not well known outside their particular fields. What brings them all here is that they have been singled out by the Government to receive the gratitude of their country. And what would be the point of an award without an awards ceremony? From school prize-givings to the Oscars, we like to salute excellence with a big occasion. So when a grateful country singles out someone for national recognition, it is only right that the State should present the award in person. And that is why honours are presented by the Head of State rather than the Head of Government. Besides, the Monarchy does it better than anyone else. And, as far as the Queen is concerned, few duties matter more than an investiture.

Every June, on the Queen's Official Birthday, and every New Year's Day, an honours list is published. The media will focus on the handful of celebrities on the list but most recipients will be ordinary people who have improved the public good in some notable way.

All their medals will come from a pretty but unobtrusive Georgian terraced house at the back of St James's Palace called the Central Chancery of the Orders of Knighthood. It sounds like an arcane court, perhaps, or a depository for old suits of armour.

Inside, we find a snug warren of rooms lined with portraits, prints and wood-panelled walls. But there is nothing olde worlde about the computers. This is the headquarters of honours distribution. The Central Chancery was created by Edward VII in 1904 to run all the orders of chivalry. To this day, it is the ultimate authority on the wearing of all medals. Worried whether your KB takes precedence over your KCVO? Then ask the secretary of the Central Chancery, Lieutenant Colonel Alexander Matheson, a former Coldstream Guards officer, and his team of experts.

They must organise the twenty or so investitures which will deliver the 2,500 honours awarded each year. Before each one, office keeper Simon Woods embarks on a two-day polishing marathon to ensure that everything is gleaming. These medals are not cheap. Some of the more popular medals cost around £100 each, while some of the grander decorations cost thousands. The Insignia Secretary, Jeremy Bagwell-Purefoy, has to account for every last gong. The really grand regalia which goes with the most senior knighthoods is so expensive that it must be returned after the recipient's death so that someone else can wear it. Because some collars and badges are worth hundreds of thousands of pounds, it is hardly surprising that some knights prefer to leave their decorations in Jeremy's vault for safe keeping until the next state occasion.

And it's not all about medals. The Central Chancery is also a database. If someone wants 'Sir John' or 'MBE' included on their passport, the Passport Office will check that the honour is valid. Every gong awarded in the last 100 years is logged here. Jeremy rummages through a filing cabinet and plucks out a yellowing card marked 'John Winston Lennon'. It carries the late Beatle's address, the date he was appointed an MBE, the date he received it (26 October 1965) and the date that he sent it back (in November 1969 – in protest against British foreign policy). He might have returned the medal, but he remained a Member of the Order of the British Empire to his death – which is also marked on the card. Once you're in the system, you stay in the system.

Anyone joining an order of chivalry (like the Order of the British Empire) must receive a Warrant of Appointment. This is an extremely ornate membership certificate which was once written by hand, signed by the Monarch and sealed in wax. These days, with nearly 900 OBEs and 1,500 MBEs awarded each year, a computer and a stamp do much of the work. But it's not a simple case of filling in a name, either. This is a royal document. An ordinary recipient is not just 'Joan Smith'. As far as the Monarch is concerned, she is 'Our trusty and well beloved Joan Smith'.

If the recipient has a title, the warrant is even more flattering. A baron or baroness is styled as 'Our Right trusty and well beloved…' A viscount is 'Our Right trusty and well beloved Cousin…' And so on, up the aristocratic ladder. When the Duke of Westminster received an OBE for his public works in 1995, his warrant called him 'Our Right trusty

and Right Entirely beloved Cousin the Duke of Westminster'.

Then there is the business of organising the ceremonies themselves. As soon as an honours list is published, assistant secretary Rachel Wells starts contacting recipients to invite them to an investiture. There needs to be a balance. You can't have twenty knighthoods at once – the Queen's arm would start to hurt. Nor do the recipients know who will be performing the investiture. It is usually the Queen, but it might be the Prince of Wales or another member of the Royal Family if she is ill or abroad. Staff know that the occasion will run late if the Prince is in charge. 'He always talks to the recipients for rather longer than planned,' says one.

The Central Chancery team must also brief the Queen. 'We do notes on each person,' Rachel Wells explains. 'So, besides the fact it's a headmaster, say, we tell her how many children are at the school, what the problems are and so on. She reads that through and marks the bits she wants to be reminded of.' The Queen will check her notes again over breakfast on the day itself. And nothing is left to chance. Every military recipient must be sent a letter detailing the correct mode of uniform. Each recipient is allowed to bring three guests and, these days, the dress code is much the same as that for a garden party. Men wear uniform, national dress, morning dress or lounge suits and women wear 'afternoon dress' – smart day clothes rather than evening dresses or gowns.

Delays and illness, inevitably, mean amendments. If someone is forced to miss their big day, Rachel Wells will ensure that they get another chance. 'About ten per cent of people have to change dates,' she says. They are all acutely conscious of the fact that it

Below and below left: The detailed preparations for an investiture.

Knights and Dames

Winston Churchill could have had any title he wanted. He was even offered a dukedom. But Britain's greatest wartime leader turned it down. For him, there was no greater honour than being appointed a Knight of the Garter. And so he became Sir Winston Churchill KG.

With its connotations of dragon-slaying and damsels, the knighthood remains the oldest and most romantic aspect of the honours system.

During her reign, the Queen has handed out more than 100 different varieties of decoration. Some, like the ISO (Companion of the Imperial Service Order), have not been given for years. Some, like the OBE (Officer of the Order of the British Empire) are presented every time. But it is the knighthood which goes back to the original age of chivalry (chivalry derives from the old French 'chevalier' or 'cavalier').

Medieval knights were holy warriors who followed a strict code of conduct. They were often knighted on the battlefield where the King or his lieutenant would use a sword to touch the candidate on the shoulder or the back or the neck with a few words along the lines of 'Arise, Sir Galahad.' This simple ceremony became known as 'the accolade' – from the Latin 'ad collum', 'to the neck'. It is the same ceremony which the Queen performs to this day – except she never tells anyone to 'Arise'.

These days, knights no longer have to be military. There are also a number of hereditary knights called baronets (these were originally sold to social climbers by James I as a money-making scheme). But the original concept of the knighthood as a one-off reward to an eminent individual remains the same today. In the early days, many knights were formed into bands of brothers or 'orders', rather like monks. The oldest is England's Order of the Garter (created in 1348 and limited to twenty-four) followed closely by Scotland's Order of the Thistle (limited to sixteen). These orders are always in the personal 'gift' of the Queen, as is the Royal Victorian Order, which honours royal staff. The other, larger orders are filled by the Government. The eighteenth-century Order of the Bath recognises success in the Armed Forces and the nineteenth-century Order of St Michael and St George honours diplomats. But by far the most important innovation has been the Order of the British Empire.

Born out of the First World War, it was the first order to which everyone could aspire. It also included the damehood, the first female knighthood. The order has two tiers of knighthood – a Knight or Dame Commander of the British Empire (KBE or DBE) and, for very senior recipients, a Knight or Dame Grand Cross of the British Empire (GBE for both sexes). Finally, there is the most common form

Above: The annual
procession of the Order
of the Garter, the oldest
order of chivalry in the
world.

of knighthood, the multi-purpose Knight Bachelor. These knights belong to no order
and so have no initials after their names. They are simply called 'Sir X'. Not every
knight, though, can call himself 'Sir'. Only those who receive the accolade (the
sword on the shoulders) can be 'Sir'. Because of the military symbolism of the
sword, Church of England clergymen cannot receive the accolade (although clergy
from other religions can). Nor can foreign subjects. So, these people will usually
receive a KBE which means that they can, at least, have some initials after their
name. Their wives, however, do not become 'Lady'. Equally, the husbands of Dames
do not become 'Sir'. But if chivalry was pure logic, what would be its attraction?

is never 'just another investiture' and that, for every single medal on the tray, there is a story which could fill a book.

The Queen has held investitures all over the world, from an open-air public investiture in the Bahamas to a cosy ceremony in the drawing room of the old Royal Yacht. Most honours are presented in the Ballroom at Buckingham Palace but the routine seldom varies.

No sooner have people arrived than they are split up. Those in line for decorations are led off to prepare for the big moment. Their guests are sent the other way where Gentlemen Ushers show them to their seats.

There is a timeless atmosphere as the Yeomen of the Guard protect the royal dais and a medley of musical favourites wafts down from the military band. The music is there to make people less nervous. Shortly before kick-off, a senior member of the Royal Household issues a polite reminder of three strict rules: no mobile phones or cameras, no standing up and no applause. The first two are obvious. The third, officially, is because the award is applause in itself. But it would also be a slow and tedious process if everyone had to clap everyone else for an hour or more. Inevitably, the later awards would receive pretty feeble applause.

Backstage, every recipient is equipped with a little tag from which the Queen can hang the medal. Medals have not actually been pinned to chests for many years. Queen Victoria is the last Monarch who drew blood from a loyal subject (he was an unflinching recipient of the Victoria Cross). Lieutenant Colonel Andrew Ford, the Comptroller and the Queen's master of ceremonies, runs through the ritual several times. Everyone will be lined up in an ante-room according to their category of honour, CBEs followed by OBEs and so on. 'Over the public address system will come your surname,' he says. 'And that is your cue to move. If you don't, you'll get a sharp prod from the Gentleman Usher.'

He adopts a friendly, light-hearted tone. For some people, the occasion is daunting enough as it is. 'Your toes should be pretty much at the edge of the dais. Please don't climb onto it. It's crowded enough. But don't stand so far back that the Queen nearly falls off.' He also gently explains that all the women present are going to lose their bags which often get in the way of medal-hanging. 'Ladies, we'll take handbags off you,' says Andrew. 'And, depending on the quality of your curtsies, we'll give you these back afterwards.'

He explains that the Queen will talk to every recipient and then shake their hand. The handshake is the time-honoured signal that time is up and that

they should reverse and move on to the next room. There, they will be given a box for their decoration, and ladies will be reunited with their handbags. They are then ushered back into the Ballroom to watch the rest of the proceedings.

'It's a very simple, well-oiled mechanism. People are quite nervous, understandably so,' Andrew Ford explains. 'It's my job to relax them a little and get them comfortable in front of Queen. I try to remove the thought that they're in a palace. We're full of grand surrounds and that can put people off a little.' As the former Lord Chamberlain, Lord Luce, explains, the Queen takes all this extremely seriously. 'Investitures are one of the most important things the Queen does,' he explains. 'She is recognising great deeds on behalf of the whole country.'

The Insignia Secretary, Jeremy Bagwell-Purefoy, is still counting his trays of medals, which he will hand to his boss, Alexander Matheson. 'Alexander will pick up the right piece in order, put it on the cushion so the Queen doesn't even have to look at it. She will just, literally, turn round, grab it and pin it on the next recipient.'

The Page of the Chambers, Ray Wheaton, has his own routine too. Just behind the Queen are two switches and a telephone. He disables the telephone – nothing must interrupt an investiture – and he checks the switches. These turn on two coloured lights in the Ballroom balcony where the band will be playing. Red tells the band to lower the noise and green tells them to raise the volume. 'Needless to say, we never use the green light,' says Ray.

Today's recipients include actress Penelope Keith (CBE), footballer Steven Gerrard (MBE) and sheep farmer George Hughes (MBE). But the ritual is always pretty much the same.

At 11 a.m., the Queen appears, escorted by two Gurkha orderly officers, following

Below left: Footballer Steven Gerrard receives his MBE. Below: The Page of the Chambers, Ray Wheaton, prepares the Ballroom for the investiture.

a tradition started by Queen Victoria in 1876. No sooner is the National Anthem over than the ceremony is underway. A senior official, usually the Lord Chamberlain, reads out the class of award, the name of the recipient and a brief summary of the reason – 'for service to the community in Norfolk' and so on. The only exception is if the Queen is presenting one of the two senior decorations for gallantry, the Victoria Cross or the George Cross, which take precedence at any investiture.

On these rare and deeply moving occasions, the Lord Chamberlain will read out the entire citation for the award. It is a humbling moment to hear the exploits of a man like Private Johnson Beharry VC being recited in calm, understated tones. He was the young driver of a Warrior troop carrier who twice rescued his unit from lethal ambushes in Iraq. Even the battle-hardened old generals present at his 2005 investiture found themselves blinking hard as this modest recruit from Grenada stood to attention before the Monarch, his scars clearly visible, while his heroics were recounted: '... Beharry displayed repeated extreme gallantry and unquestioned valour in the face of relentless enemy action...'

He might be fearless in battle but, as he admitted later, he found the investiture terrifying, since he was first in line. 'There was no one in front I could follow.' It was quite a novel experience for the Queen, too, since she had previously awarded the VC to only three living recipients during her entire reign. As she told Private Beharry, 'It's not very often that I am able to present this honour.'

At most investitures, the first awards will be the knighthoods and damehoods. The knight or dame is already Sir John X or Dame Jane X from the moment the honours list is published. They come to the Palace to 'to receive the Honour of Knighthood'. Each knight kneels with the right knee on a velvet 'knighting stool' to receive the 'accolade'. The Queen taps him lightly on the right shoulder and then the left with her late father's sword but, contrary to popular belief, she does not say 'Arise, Sir John.' The knight then receives his insignia, a badge that hangs around the neck on a riband. Dames are not tapped with a sword (the reason being it is a men-only medieval warrior ritual) and are just given their insignia like everyone else. And so, the process carries on through the various classes of the various orders.

When it's all over, there is a mixture of relief and pride. Several official portrait photographers are lined up outside. Recipients can order an official video of their big day. The press office will also have a roped-off area where photographers and reporters will interview the celebrity element of any investiture – 'How does it feel to be Sir Mick?' and so on.

There is no pecking order among a crowd like this. The teacher with the MBE for 'services to the community' stands in the same line as the expat star who has flown in

from California to receive a knighthood for 'services to the entertainment industry'.

Perhaps the most scenic investitures are those which take place at the Palace of Holyroodhouse in Edinburgh. It is here that we find a nervous Gordon Ramsay waiting in line with everyone else outside the Picture Gallery where he will receive his OBE beneath 110 portraits of Scottish monarchs. The celebrity chef is one place ahead of John Ramsay who is being honoured for 'services to Training and Lifelong Learning'. The two men have never met but start discussing the Ramsay clan tartan. 'I've got the kilt but I'm slightly concerned how my legs are these days,' says Gordon.

Each time they hear a name announced, they shuffle a little nearer the door. In the Picture Gallery, every name prompts one trio of guests to sit bolt upright in proud anticipation of their loved one meeting the Queen. A mother and two daughters appear to be suffering from mild electric shock as they hear Dad summoned to be a Member of the Most Excellent Order of the British Empire for 'services to the community in Glasgow'. When a famous name, like Gordon Ramsay, is called, there is plenty of discreet nudging and everyone peers past the hat in front. But all recipients get the same 'quality time', the same attention and the same valedictory handshake from the Monarch.

Outside, beneath those stirring hills and stern old turrets, everyone is as important

Above: Gordon Ramsay, his OBE newly awarded for 'services to the hospitality industry'.

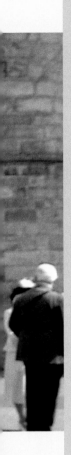

as everyone else. Sir William Gammell, newly knighted chairman of Cairn Energy and childhood chum of both Tony Blair and President George W. Bush is in the same queue for an official photograph as Margaret Shuttleworth. She has just received an MBE for her services to the visitors' tea bar at Dumfries Prison.

Marina Dennis has been awarded an MBE for her services to crofting in Strathspey. Crofters – who run small farms in the bleaker bits of Scotland – are not always diehard monarchists. But this occasion means so much that her daughter and granddaughter have flown right around the world from Borneo. Singer Eddi Reader has just received an OBE: 'The sense of history's amazing, just shaking her hand and knowing her genetics go way, way back and we all know the stories,' she says. 'It must be a quite bizarre lifestyle. I found her really lovely, she's just like any other Mammy, you know.'

Gordon Ramsay is still bowled over by it all. 'Today symbolises the importance of staying very much traditional,' he says, almost lost for words. 'This is going to continue for, I hope, hundreds of years. The set-up is extraordinary. We're steeped in tradition, we're steeped in culture.' He recounts his chat with the Queen – they discussed his restaurants around the world. Despite living in London, he is proud of his Scottish roots and was determined to receive his award in the land of his ancestors. 'To come here, to be part of this, is extraordinary. My Mum has just stopped crying which is great news so no need for the armbands.'

HONOUR BOUND

For some, an investiture is more than a 'thank you' from a grateful Monarch. It is the start of a bond which will last for a lifetime. Monarchs have always remained close to their bravest, their most loyal and their most distinguished subjects. It is royal common sense. In centuries past, a Sovereign unwise enough to fall out with the great men and women of the day could lose the Throne.

Today, the relationship between the Monarch and her most illustrious cohorts – the members of the Order of the Garter, the Order of the Thistle, the Order of Merit and so on – is more relaxed. But it is as valued as it ever was. And, from time to time, the Monarch likes to have a reunion. With the Garter and the Thistle, it is an annual occasion – in Windsor for the former and Edinburgh for the latter. It always involves a lot of ritual, a church service and a very jolly lunch. Restricted in numbers to twenty-four and sixteen respectively, these orders are made up of eminent public figures (retired prime ministers, for example) and a few public-spirited aristocrats. The Queen is the first Monarch in history to open up both these orders to women (who are officially called Lady Companions).

All orders need to replenish the numbers from time to time. The Knights of the Thistle have gathered in Edinburgh in their green velvet robes, and this year's church service will include the 'installation' of two new Knights. Lord Steel of Aikwood, the former leader of the British Liberal Party, is in his Thistle regalia for the first time. It includes a priceless chain called the 'Thistle Collar with Badge Appendant'. He has already told his son that it must go back to the Queen on his death. 'He's got to hand it back if I snuff it tomorrow,' says Lord Steel. 'These are kept in a bank vault because they're so expensive that nobody could afford to insure them.'

His fellow new boy is Lord Robertson of Port Ellen, the former Secretary-General of NATO. 'I came back from NATO to get this letter saying, "The Queen wants to appoint you a Knight of the Thistle." For a Scot, there's nothing better. It's quite interesting that the Queen has opened up the ranks of the Order to people who are not part of the ancient aristocracy. I was born in a police station on the Isle of Islay. So, if you were born in a police station, look where you can end up.'

He admits that he feels 'slightly awkward' dressing in medieval costume and a floppy velvet cap in front of other people. 'This is breaking the great political rule: Never wear funny hats.' He is very proud, though, of his new coat of arms, which features the Port Ellen lighthouse. Once all are assembled in the Signet Library, ahead of the service in St Giles's Cathedral next door, the Queen arrives for the formal photograph. 'What a pretty sight!' she declares as she sees them all lined up in their finery.

While they process to church, where they swear to be 'loyal and true to my Sovereign Lady the Queen', the Queen's Chef, Mark Flanagan, is preparing a lunch of Scottish crab gateau and Scottish fillet of beef. He likes the Order of the Thistle, solid types and not a single fussy eater. 'We've got no alternative diets today, which is very unusual. The people that are here tend to be more traditional people who are used to eating good local produce.'

Once they have changed out of their velvet robes, the Knights and the Ladies follow the Queen back down the hill to Holyroodhouse. Most are in morning dress. Lord Steel is in startling tartan trousers. The atmosphere is thoroughly informal, but this will still be a proper royal production with five glasses laid for each guest – champagne, red wine, white wine, sherry and water. It will be a convivial lunch.

The Queen seats the two new boys next to her, Lord Steel on her right and Lord Robertson on her left. The band strikes up next door and everyone talks incessantly right through to coffee. The Queen quizzes Lord Steel on his dogs. Lord Robertson enjoys a very detailed discussion on the reorganisation of the British Army, a sensitive subject in these parts. 'She's got a huge knowledge of it,' he says afterwards. Everyone leaves feeling a valued part of an ancient and extremely exclusive club. But the effect is the same as it was in medieval times. The Monarch has reinforced the links between the Crown and her most trusty lieutenants.

Below: Private Johnson Beharry, outside Buckingham Palace with his VC, upstages the most senior soldier in the British Army, General Sir Michael Jackson.

It is the same sentiment which brings the boldest of the bold to Windsor Castle. The spotless chairs and sofas in the Green and Crimson Drawing Rooms are usually roped off. This morning, the guests are very welcome to sit on them. They are led by Colonel Stuart Archer, the chairman of the most exalted band of brothers and sisters in the honours business, the Victoria Cross and George Cross Association. Colonel Archer himself was awarded one of the first George Crosses of the Second World War for calmly defusing a huge unexploded bomb in the bedlam of a blazing Swansea oil refinery in 1940. His near-suicidal achievement revealed vital secrets about a new German fuse mechanism and saved countless lives.

The members of this tiny club have always enjoyed a special relationship with the Royal Family. The Queen is their patron and the late Queen Mother was a very active president, a link gladly continued by the Prince of Wales.

Every two years, the members meet in London for a three-day reunion. This year, eight of the twelve living VCs and twenty-one of the twenty-four living GCs have made it. But, for this year's gathering, the Queen has invited them all with their spouses to a special birthday drinks at Windsor Castle. Not only is it the 150th birthday of the Victoria Cross but it is also the 50th birthday of the VC and GC Association.

They have come from all over the world. Captain Lachhiman Gurung VC of the 8th Gurkha Rifles has had an epic journey from a remote hill village in Nepal. He won his VC in Burma for single-handedly fighting off 200 Japanese troops in May 1945. Despite losing an eye and an arm, he stood his ground for four hours before help arrived. Others

have come from Australia, New Zealand and South Africa. Getting them here is one thing. Getting them all to sit down in the right order for their official photograph with the Queen is quite another.

Colonel Archer hands over command to Didy Grahame, the long-serving secretary of the association. She keeps the whole organisation ticking over and maintains a constant check on the welfare of her more elderly members around the world. This morning, though, she has to adopt the persona of a sergeant major. 'They're a very good family and they don't mind me being bossy on these sorts of occasions,' she explains. They have no choice.

'Will you sit down NOW because I've got to get everybody in!' she shouts above the banter of thirty-one old chaps all gossiping and all standing in the wrong place. It's rather like watching a school outing.

'John! You're four in from the end,' shouts Didy, and Flight-Lieutenant John Cruickshank VC shuffles into position. In 1944, he sank a German U-boat with his badly damaged Catalina aircraft, sustained seventy-two wounds and still managed to get plane and crew back in one piece. He is, self-evidently, a very brave man. But he doesn't dare answer back to Didy.

At last, they are all in place. It's time for the final briefing. 'When you stand up,' Didy announces, 'people on the back row, for goodness sake stand up gently or you'll knock the vase off! All right?'

The Monarch enters and all thirty-one are suddenly on their best behaviour. Those that are able to, stand up. All then sit, the official photographer takes his photographs and then Colonel Archer presents the Queen with a small bronze statue of Queen Victoria at the first VC investiture in 1857. The gallant guests then shuffle through for a reception. Jim Beaton GC does the royal introductions. The Queen knows him well since he is the retired protection officer who was awarded the GC for fending off a kidnap attempt on Princess Anne in 1974. He was shot three times and still carries fragments in his hand.

As the Queen moves around the room, the atmosphere is that of a family gathering rather than a state occasion. People want to gossip and catch up, not talk about near-death experiences.

'The Queen Mum used to call us "My boys and girls",' explains Keith Payne VC, a former Warrant Officer in the Australian Army. In 1969, badly injured in Vietnam, he launched a solo charge into enemy fire to rescue forty new recruits from an overwhelming enemy assault.

'I know Her Majesty and when she gets to an occasion like this, she talks freely rather than being official. She's with a family and she enjoys that.'

No sooner has the Queen met Joe Lynch GC than the conversation switches to hip replacements. 'I've got a crazy cousin,' the Queen remarks. 'She's done both hips.' Meeting Bill Speakman-Pitts VC, she observes that it's been a hectic reunion: 'You've had a busy couple of days.' 'It's wonderful to see you again,' says Mr Speakman-Pitts, a towering former Black Watch private who won his VC in Korea in 1951. Wounded and short of ammunition, he launched repeated attacks on the enemy using bottles and stones.

Right: Holders of the Victoria Cross and the George Cross are lined up for a royal photograph at Windsor Castle.

The Queen is full of sympathy when she meets the newest member of the club, Captain Peter Norton GC. He was decorated for leading his bomb disposal unit out of an Iraqi ambush in 2005 despite losing his legs in the attack. Talk turns to physiotherapists. 'Are they beastly?' asks the Queen. 'They're very pleasant but they're not called physioterrorists for nothing,' replies Captain Norton. Afterwards, Captain Norton is typically modest about his own deeds – 'I just did something that needed to be done on the day' – but, as the new boy, he brings a fresh eye to this event. 'We have something we're fighting for which represents hundreds of years of history and when you're fighting for that, you're fighting for a whole ethos, a whole country. There are people here who took knowing decisions to put themselves in harm's way and the fact that the Queen is so happy to meet and gather these people means a lot.'

Every nation, of course, produces countless courageous men and women. And it is not a respect for hierarchies which makes ordinary people do extraordinary things. Lance Corporal Chris Finney GC, badly injured in Iraq while dragging wounded comrades out of the line of (friendly) fire, puts it very succinctly: 'To be completely honest, when you're there, that Queen-and-country stuff goes out the window and you're doing it for your mates.' Realising that this might sound a bit worthy, he adds: 'And for a good suntan and a bit more money.'

Neither age, rank nor background counts here. 'I'm just a 22-year-old lad who went to some state school and now I'm at Windsor Castle eating cakes and drinking tea with the Queen,' says Chris Finney. 'And it's just brilliant to meet these guys. We're all in the same boat – forget about ranks and what you've done and all that crap. Just sit and have a drink and a laugh.'

And they do – both with their mates and with their Queen. Eventually, they bid her farewell with three cheers. 'That was marvellous. This is one big happy family,' says Anthony Gledhill GC, a former policeman decorated for his pursuit, under fire, of an armed gang in 1966. He looks up, his eye catching the portrait of the late Queen Mother on the Crimson Drawing Room wall, just along from George VI, creator of the George Cross. 'That's a lovely picture,' he says, recounting a long-ago reunion lunch in Central London when a bomb scare had blocked all the roads; how the Queen Mother had simply turned up on foot; how she learned that he had been following a particularly important cricket match and had ordered her most senior official to find a radio to relay regular updates 'because Mr Gledhill wants to know'.

Outside, in the Quadrangle, Didy Grahame and Jim Beaton are herding their charges onto a fleet of coaches. 'As soon as they knew they were meeting the Queen, they were busting a gut to get here,' Jim explains. 'Some of the ones from Nepal, they've got to fight officialdom to get here. They're all absolutely determined to come.' When this lot want something, who would dare stand in their way?

CHAPTER FOUR

HEAD OF STATE

Ask any child to paint a picture of the Queen and the result will probably involve a crown, a throne and a carriage. This is the fairy-tale depiction of the Monarch, unchanged for centuries. It is remarkable that it is so firmly entrenched in the modern public mind, given that the Queen appears like this for only a few hours of one midweek morning once a year. But it is understandable. Because if any image sums up what the Monarch's job is all about it is this one: a spectacular and symbolic manifestation of power.

The Queen's duties as Head of Nation are relatively modern. Walkabouts, ribbon-cuttings and garden parties have evolved. They are, if you like, 'optional'. Other duties, though, are 'compulsory'. They go with the territory of being Head of State. Chief among them is the appointment of Prime Ministers and, thus, Governments. Before Gordon Brown could take over from Tony Blair, the Queen had to ask him first. Having appointed a Prime Minister, the Monarch will expect to see him or her every week for an hour-long audience. The preliminaries are the same, whoever is in 10 Downing Street. The Prime Minister's car pulls up on the Palace gravel and he enters not through the Grand Entrance but through the Monarch's private door. He is ushered upstairs, past the 'Watch Out! Corgi About!' sign and into the Queen's Private Audience Room, a cream-coloured combination of the stately and the homely with every available flat surface covered in picture frames.

There are pictures of the Queen's parents, of herself as a young Monarch and of Prince Philip and the children at every age. An arty black and white shot of an impish Prince Harry sits alongside a picture of the Duke of York having hysterics on a hill above Balmoral. The grand piano is virtually unplayable, being covered in pictures of foreign royal cousins. The one piece of furniture without photographs is the Queen's desk on which sits a metal ruler – in metric and imperial – detailing every Sovereign from Roman times to the present. In here, with no private secretaries and no record-keeping, the

Above: Former Prime Minister Tony Blair at his annual Balmoral audience of the Queen.

Monarch and her Prime Minister discuss anything.

'There's absolutely nothing you can't say,' says her tenth Prime Minister, Tony Blair, a few weeks before his farewell audience. 'I've told her about lots of things in my time – everything from Cherie being pregnant with Leo through to major decisions. Because the one thing you know is that she will never divulge anything to anyone.'

Apart from total discretion, he says, there is no set routine to these meetings. 'The amazing thing about the Queen is that, because Winston Churchill was her first Prime Minister, she has got an absolutely unparalleled amount of experience of what it's like to be at the top of a government. She has a very shrewd and intuitive sense about politics with a small "p". She's very informative and really quite analytical about some of the difficulties and challenges that the Prime Minister faces. She's someone who actually understands part of what you go through, the pressure of it. And she has an immense amount to give in a situation like that, certainly to someone like me who was not born when she came to the Throne.'

If the Prime Minister is detained elsewhere, he will make a point of talking to the Queen on the telephone. And during the summer holidays he will usually spend a night at Balmoral, where there is more of a family atmosphere. Spouses come too and, depending on the weather, everyone is treated to one of Prince Philip's barbecues. However, the primary purpose of the Prime Minister's visit to Royal Deeside is the audience and the rules are observed just as firmly here in the Highlands as at the Palace.

Above: New Prime Minister Gordon Brown also had regular meetings with the Queen when he was Chancellor of the Exchequer.

The only obvious difference is the prevalence of tartan and the fact that the Sovereign is wearing a kilt. It's late afternoon when Tony Blair arrives for his last prime-ministerial stay at Balmoral. The sun is streaming through the windows onto a copy of *The Field* magazine. 'You've just been having tea with Charles,' says the Queen, greeting Mr Blair, who has flown by helicopter from the Prince of Wales's residence at nearby Birkhall. 'Very nice,' says the Prime Minister. 'The garden's looking very nice isn't it?' she continues. 'On a day like this, it's wonderful,' Mr Blair concurs.

'I can assure you it wasn't like this this morning,' says the Queen. 'Very grey and threatening.' They talk about the weather and their respective Scottish duties. 'I gather Mrs Blair was doing Barnardo's yesterday,' says the Queen. 'Edinburgh was looking nice, I'm sure.' At this point, our exclusive glimpse is curtailed.

The Prime Minister is a regular visitor all year round but he won't be the only one. As Queen of fifteen other countries, the Queen has fifteen other prime ministers. Some will ring for a chat. When in Britain, they will drop by in person. In any given month, an extraordinary range of people pass through the Private Audience Room. As Head of the Commonwealth, the Queen often receives its Secretary-General, New Zealand's Don McKinnon. Today, he drops in to discuss the upcoming Commonwealth Summit in Uganda. The Queen has just been reading his latest speech to the University of the West Indies. 'I thought it was rather long,' she teases him. 'But it was very interesting about small states.'

A few days later (and just a matter of weeks before his elevation to the office of Prime Minister), it's the turn of the Chancellor of the Exchequer, Gordon Brown. He is about to announce the Government's Budget for the year ahead. It's a subject so secret that even the Prime Minister has yet to learn some of the details. But the night before every Budget speech, the Chancellor comes to tell all to the Queen. She has chucked the corgis out for the occasion. 'The noise level's getting higher and higher,' she tells her equerry as the dogs are expelled and the Chancellor comes bounding up the stairs.

'Well, it's come round again awfully quickly,' says the Queen when Mr Brown appears. He begins with a subject particularly close to the Queen's heart at present. 'I've got some good information for you about how we're trying to support the troops. I know there's a family interest,' he says. 'Harry,' replies the Queen fondly. Her grandson is preparing to head overseas with the Army.

'He's a very brave young man and we'll certainly do everything we can to support him,' says Mr Brown. 'The first thing I'll do in the Budget is put more money for our troops.' 'Of course, they're very pushed now, in so many places,' the Queen gently reminds him. Mr Brown explains that he has recently paid his first visit to Iraq. 'I thought the morale was very high,' he says. Talk turns to royal visitors to the war zones. 'Anne has just been in Iraq,' the Queen notes. 'She does a wonderful job,' says Mr Brown, adding hastily: 'So do all of you.'

'Andrew went to look at the helicopters,' adds the Queen, noting that her second son used to fly the things. 'We're doing some investment in helicopters,' says Mr Brown, a tad nervously. 'It would be good if the helicopters we bought actually could work,' the Queen says crisply. The Government is thus left in no doubt that the Head of the Armed Forces is not happy with her choppers.

The conversation continues at length in complete privacy. Afterwards, Mr Brown says it has been enjoyable and lively. 'Obviously it's a little less formal when the cameras are not there and one of the things people don't realise is she's got a tremendous sense of humour and she'll be talking about things that make both her and me laugh.' Military matters, he says, always pop up. 'There are so many members of the Royal Family who've actually served in the Armed Forces.' But after ten years of pre-Budget audiences, he appreciates their value. 'She knows over the years what works and what doesn't. Sometimes you go back and change a bit of your speech.'

Right: The Queen and her Privy Council prepare to swear in two
new members at a monthly meeting.

Most of the time, the Queen is kept up to date by her private secretaries and the contents of her red boxes. And, once a month, she presides over the oldest legislative assembly in Britain. The Privy Council dates back to the days when the King and his Council ran the nation. These days, much of its work concerns institutions governed by Royal Charter – the BBC, for example, or certain charities or universities. There are 400 Privy Councillors, but only four are usually called upon to attend meetings. Standing up (to ensure that meetings are brief), they will approve decisions which have already been approved by the Government. But these measures still need the formal approval of the Monarch before they take effect. Thus a random 2007 meeting includes amendments to the charter of Leeds University, an order concerning Royal Navy pay and even the go-ahead for the wedding of a very distant cousin of the Queen. Amelia Beaumont, 24, wants to marry a young man called Simon Murray but, because she is a great, great, great, great granddaughter of Queen Victoria (albeit via an obscure German route), she still needs permission under the Royal Marriages Act of 1772. Many people will find it bizarre that, in the twenty-first century, an ordinary wedding should require the attention of four Government Ministers and the Head of State. But if the Monarch's constitutional role seems rather complicated, it is neatly summed up every year by that image of the woman with the crown and carriage in the child's picture.

Red Boxes

Short of marooning herself on a desert island, the Queen can never shake off those famous red boxes. At seven o'clock every night, wherever she is in the world, she will be presented with a battered, leather-covered metal container bursting with bits of paper. By eight o'clock the next morning, she will have processed the lot.

Red boxes come in two sizes. The smaller is the 'reading box', a shoebox-sized thing which one of the Queen's private secretaries will prepare for her each evening during the week. This will contain an account of the day in Parliament written by a senior Government whip (the Queen does not expect her whips to go beyond a closely typed single side of A4). There might also be a top copy of the Cabinet's latest minutes, classified security briefings and several Foreign Office telegrams (embassy reports report about anything at all – from the situation in Afghanistan to an election in Mexico). Also in the mix will be one or two of the weekly summaries which the Queen is sent by the Governors-General of her fifteen other realms – from Belize to Australia. If it's from Canada, some of it will be in French. In total, there might be around sixty sheets of paper rolled or folded into a box.

At weekends, the Queen is given a larger 'standard', briefcase-sized box. It will have at least two days' worth of reading material and documents which require a signature and, therefore, cannot be folded. There are just four keys to all the Queen's red boxes. She has one and her three private secretaries have the others. When the lid comes down on each box, two metal teeth clasp a white label which sticks out at the side. An incoming box has 'The Queen' on the label. When she has been through it, she turns the label round so that it protrudes with the name of the relevant private secretary to whom it must be returned. That way, a red box is never lost. Perish the thought.

The Prince of Wales maintains a similar arrangement with his own private secretaries. There is no chance of anyone confusing his boxes with the Queen's, however. His are green.

THE BIG SHOW

Alexander de Montfort gulps and then signs his name in the register. This is not a task to be undertaken lightly. With one scribble of a pen he has just assumed responsibility for the largest white diamond on the planet. The register in question is the Tower of London's Jewel House Book. And Alexander, 28, has just signed out the Imperial State Crown and the Sword of State – two of the most sacred symbols of British democracy. They are not insured.

As Secretary of the Lord Chamberlain's Office, it is his job to take them from the Tower and back to Buckingham Palace for their annual appearance at the State Opening of Parliament. Such is their importance in the ritual that they will have a carriage procession of their own. And until they return to the Tower, they will be replaced by a simple sign: 'In Use'.

The jewels are in safe hands. Alexander is not even allowed to touch them. That privilege belongs exclusively to the man alongside him, David Thomas, who rejoices in the title of Crown Jeweller. He is holding the Imperial State Crown in an old wooden box.

After a journey cloaked in understandable secrecy, the two men and their priceless cargo arrive at the Palace. David takes the old box upstairs to the Queen's private quarters. The Queen has worn this crown many times before but it weighs two and half pounds and she still needs time to get used to it before tomorrow's big event. She has cancelled a few engagements in recent weeks due to a bad back so it is essential that the head which wears the Crown is comfortable with it.

The State Opening of Parliament is the moment when all the important elements of the British constitution remind each other – and the outside world – where they stand. The Monarch comes to Parliament in a fairy-tale carriage, puts on a crown and summons the elected representatives from the House of Commons to the unelected House of Lords where she announces her Government's plans for the year ahead. But it is the elected lot, squashed in at the back of the room, who have written her script. The message is very clear: Parliament derives its authority from the Queen, but the Queen abides by its democratic decisions. In other words, the Queen is in charge. The people are in control.

This dazzling spectacle is pure theatre, of course, but the play goes to the heart of British democracy. 'People know it's a ceremony,' says former

Prime Minister, Tony Blair. 'They're not seriously thinking that the Queen's sat down and written out the Queen's speech herself, but what's wrong with that? It's one of the things that people love about this country. I think that's true also of a lot of the ceremony that surrounds the Royal Family. If you use it in the right way – and I think they do it quite skilfully – it actually is a good thing.'

The man responsible for this production is Lieutenant General Sir Michael Willcocks, otherwise known as Black Rod. The 'Gentleman Usher of the Black Rod', to give him his full title, has been keeping order at the Palace of Westminster since the days when monarchs lived on the premises. They moved out long ago, but Black Rod has always stayed put as the Monarch's representative. His symbol of authority is still a black ebony rod tipped with gold. These days, he also runs 110 parliamentary staff and a £70 million budget.

After a distinguished Army career, Sir Michael saw the job advertised in the papers. He knows Parliament better than some of the longest-serving politicians but he takes no chances in his preparations for the biggest day in the Parliamentary calendar. It will all be televised on live television and any mistakes could expose a sacred constitutional ritual to ridicule.

'The ceremony remains broadly the same but, if you take that approach, it's fatal,' he explains. 'You have to have an eye for detail. This morning, we spotted a carpet snagging where the Queen comes in. It's now being stitched by the seamstress. The Queen has an eye like a hawk and she does notice.'

Sir Michael begins a fresh inspection, following the Queen's route from the Sovereign's

Left: The Australian State Coach.

Entrance, up the stairs, into the Robing Room (where she puts on her crown and ermine) and right through to the Lords. Her throne always sits a couple of inches taller than Prince Philip's. 'You can't sit higher than the Queen,' Black Rod explains.

Once the Queen has taken her seat, she gives a signal to the Lord Great Chamberlain who, in turn, waves a white stick at Black Rod – the signal to fetch the MPs. Then she has to sit back and wait for several minutes. Like most of us, she does not particularly enjoy sitting in silence, twiddling her thumbs, while being stared at. So, the onus is on Black Rod to collect the MPs as quickly as possible. Sir Michael is always trying to shave a few seconds off the proceedings. In a traditional show of strength going back to the days of Charles I, the MPs always slam the door in his face. He admits that it is his secret ambition, one day, to catch them by surprise. 'I always try to get through without them closing it. I speed up without them noticing,' he says impishly. 'Last year, I very nearly did it and there were cries of "Shut the ****** door!"'

Once the MPs have let him in, he has to process into the Commons, bowing and enduring a gauntlet of jeers, notably from Dennis Skinner, the Labour MP and anti-monarchist whose annual barbs are now part of the ritual.

Sir Michael fondly recalls his own debut: 'My predecessor was much taller than me and Skinner said, "We've been short-changed. They've sent a midget." And, of course, I collapsed laughing and couldn't remember what I was supposed to say.'

Once he has made it up to the Despatch Box, Black Rod then declares: 'Mr Speaker, the Queen commands this honourable House to attend Her Majesty immediately in the House of Peers.' Slowly, the MPs do as they are told. 'They don't rush,' Sir Michael

Right: The Imperial State Crown arrives at Westminster.

Right: Sir Michael Willcocks (Black Rod) prepares for the State Opening of Parliament. Far right: Black Rod in the House of Lords ahead of the State Opening.

observes. 'They amble, they talk, they make a noise.' He always relishes the moment as the elected rabble surface in the robed splendour of the Lords. 'Finally you walk into the chamber and: Wow! Bang! There's the Throne, solid gold with the Queen sitting on it!' This will be an occasion when all sorts of traditional quirks will spring to life from the history books. It is a celebration of democracy but the man in overall charge of the ceremony is the hereditary Earl Marshal who is always the Duke of Norfolk (it will be the fifth State Opening for the present Duke, now 50). We will see the Queen's Watermen, professional boatmen on the Thames who have escorted the Crown Jewels since Tudor times and still wear Tudor uniforms at state occasions. The royal coachmen will wear 100-year-old coats woven with gold thread and worth £15,000 each. Inside Parliament, the Queen will be protected by two bodyguards, the Honourable Corps of Gentlemen at Arms and the Yeomen of the Guard.

The Yeomen like to point out that they are the Monarch's oldest bodyguard, having been founded by Henry VII. The Gentlemen at Arms, who were founded twenty-four years later by Henry VIII, like to point out that they are called 'The Nearest Guard'. At state occasions, they will be closest to the Monarch and, before royal funerals, they will stand guard over the coffin. They never flinch. 'During the lying-in-state for Queen Elizabeth the Queen Mother, there were quite a few moments when feathers

were blowing about in the wind and, indeed, a rather persistent bee,' recalls Colonel Sir William Mahon, the Adjutant of the Gentlemen. 'Nobody moved. Because you don't move.'

They are all retired officers of a certain age and their pay has not changed for two centuries (it's £75 a year). But they still regard themselves as bodyguards and each carries a long spiked staff called a poleaxe. 'You've heard the expression "to be poleaxed"?' asks Sir William. 'Well, if you were hit on the cranium with that poleaxe, you'd go at the knees.'

The Yeomen are very proud of their supporting role. Ever since the Gunpowder Plot of 1605, when Guy Fawkes and his gang planned to blow up the King in Parliament, ten Yeomen have processed through the Commons cellars with lanterns before every State Opening. It is a quaint and entirely ceremonial procedure. There will be 1,200 soldiers, 1,500 police, 300 parliamentary staff and a team of sniffer dogs to do the serious security checks. The Yeomen are not expected to look too closely.

Black Rod likes the ritual but he cheerfully admits that it is in the wrong place. 'The Yeomen go down into the cellars and, these days, it's all machinery. Where the plotters actually put the gunpowder was where I park my car. It wasn't even in the cellars. It was in a ground-floor storeroom.'

Before the big event, the Earl Marshal stages a full rehearsal. His wife, Georgina, otherwise known as the Duchess of Norfolk, stands in for the Queen. The Monarch is always attended by four pages who carry her train. They are schoolboys – they have to be shorter than the Queen – and are usually the sons or grandsons of royal chums. It's a daunting task for any 12-year-old. 'You'll be fine,' the Duchess assures them before the run-through. 'You'll be brilliant.'

Having reminded the State Trumpeters not to blow their trumpets too close to the Queen's ears, the Duke of Norfolk gives them the nod. A mighty fanfare announces the start of the rehearsal and the procession sets off with the Duchess moving at a regal pace through to the Lords. She takes her seat on the Throne and the Duke reminds everyone that there will be a long wait until the MPs arrive.

It is then the turn of the Lord Chancellor, Lord Falconer to walk slowly up the few short steps to the Throne, kneel down and hand the Queen her speech. He gives it a go. Just as the Duke of Norfolk tries to point out that he is kneeling on the wrong step, both Lord Falconer's knees go at once and he collapses amid hoots of laughter from everyone else. 'Just kneel on the top step,' the Duke advises helpfully.

Lord Falconer is the most prominent legal figure in the land, a man of huge intellect who is used to extreme pressure. And yet he finds this simple ten-second ritual more daunting than any judicial appearance. 'It's the most nerve-wracking event you could possibly imagine,' he explains. 'It's a fantastically visual demonstration of all parts of the constitution but the eyes of the world are upon you.'

At least the Queen has recently scrapped the ancient rule that Lord Chancellors should walk in reverse. 'The first time I did it, you had to go backwards. Round the corner is a toilet with steps up to it which I went up and down backwards 55,000 times. I'm now allowed to do it going forwards but it's still utterly nerve-wracking.'

It has not been a great day. Black Rod is delighted. 'If you get a perfect rehearsal you get a disastrous performance.'

A day later, there are only a couple of hours to go before the big event and, in the Palace Billiard Room, the Crown Jeweller, David Thomas, is laying out all the regalia for the day. It is a custom that Buckingham Palace staff are allowed to view these great national emblems before the procession. A queue is already forming.

David started working for a firm of London jewellers at the age of 17 and, in 1991, he was appointed Crown Jeweller, a post created by Queen Victoria in 1843. 'There's only one Crown Jeweller in the land,' says David. 'It's everybody's heritage. The jewels cannot be moved or touched unless the Crown Jeweller is there to do to it.'

He begins by removing the Cap of Maintenance from its box. Unlike the Crown and the Great Sword of State, this symbol of spiritual power lives in the safe here at

the Palace. David places it firmly on a supporting staff to ensure it doesn't fall off.

Much care must also be taken with the Great Sword of State, the intricately decorated symbol of the Monarch's might. Some of its tiny appendages have an annoying habit of falling off. 'You have to be careful with the unicorn because his horn unscrews,' says David, checking the detail. 'It was just made that way. There's no reason. I always tell the person carrying it: "Please don't fiddle".' Today's bearer, Lord Boyce, former Chief of the Defence Staff, has been warned.

David has retrieved the Crown from the Queen who has spent the previous evening getting used to its weight. Very carefully, he slides it out of its box and places it on the cushion which will support it on its journey to Parliament.

It is decorated with 2,868 diamonds, the largest of which sits at the front. This is the whopping 317-carat Second Star of Africa which was cut from the Cullinan Diamond, the largest pure white diamond ever discovered, a 3,106-carat South African monster presented to Edward VII as a birthday present. The Crown also contains the Black Prince's Ruby (actually a spinel), worn by Henry V at Agincourt, and pearls from a necklace of Elizabeth I. Older still is the sapphire from a signet ring worn by Edward the Confessor at his death in 1066. A thousand of years of history will sit on one head.

The Crown Jewels set off in a two-carriage procession of their own – complete with full military escort – at 10.37 a.m. on the dot. The Queen's Procession then arrives from the Royal Mews to pick up the Monarch. The military entourage includes the Princess Royal, the Colonel of the Blues and Royals, who will be part of the Sovereign's Escort. She is here as one of the Monarch's protectors, not as her daughter.

The Queen emerges from the Palace looking timelessly regal. Dressed in a long white gown and wrapped in white fur, she would not have looked out of place in a procession 200 years back. She does not yet have the Crown on her head but, for now, she is wearing Queen Victoria's diadem and it certainly looks the part. Accompanied by the Duke of Edinburgh, the Sovereign climbs into the Australian State Coach. The new Lord Chamberlain, Earl Peel, waves her on her way. He will hold the fort until her return.

On the stroke of 11 a.m., Head Coachman Mark Hargreaves commands the six grey horses – McCarthy, Daniel, Flagship, Cloud, San Anton and Britannia – to start the journey to Westminster. It will take exactly fifteen minutes.

The traffic is not all one-way. By tradition, when a Monarch goes to Parliament, Parliament must provide a hostage, usually a Government whip. It is the second time that John Heppell, Labour MP for Nottingham East, has acted as a Queen's ransom. He rather enjoys it: 'I'm not chucked into the dungeon. I nip up and have a cup of coffee with the Lord Chamberlain and the odd gin and tonic comes into it. I think the British public like to see these things maintained.'

The Queen arrives at the Sovereign's Entrance bang on time and processes to the Robing Room, where there is no time to admire an interesting exhibition of parliamentary

Below: Black Rod and the Earl Marshal (far left and left) bid farewell to the Queen after the State Opening.

curios ranging from a copy of Charles I's death warrant to an old scorebook of the Lords and Commons Cricket Club.

In the screened-off area, she puts on the same crimson Robe of State which was made for her Coronation in 1953. Decorated with gold thread and small ermine tails, it is over eighteen feet long and nearly four feet wide. Then she places the Crown on her head and, at 11.27 a.m., the doors of the Robing Room swing open and State Trumpeters announce her appearance (but not too close to her ears). The Duke of Edinburgh holds her left hand. The fairy-tale procession begins.

Immediately in front of her, the Cap of Maintenance is held aloft by Baroness Amos, the Government Leader in the Lords, and Lord Boyce remembers not to fiddle with the Sword.

They all process through the Royal Gallery, beneath portraits of monarchs past, through the Prince's Gallery, beneath a huge statue of Queen Victoria, and into the Chamber of the House of Lords where the Sovereign takes the Throne.

Black Rod is sent off to summon the House of Commons, and the door is slammed in his face. Dennis Skinner offers his customary jibe (this year, it's a joke about actress Helen Mirren who has just played the Queen in a film), and the MPs eventually arrive making the usual din.

Lord Falconer does not fall over. The Monarch recites her Government's programme for the year ahead and, with that, Parliament is open for another year. The entire procession is then conducted all over again in reverse and the Queen leaves the Palace of Westminster for home. All the elements of Britain's unwritten constitution have reasserted their correct position in the political universe. John Heppell MP is released from his well-upholstered captivity to return to his desk. The Crown Jewels can return to the Tower. Alexander de Montfort, who has spent the last twenty-four hours being entirely responsible for the most precious jewels in the world, can sleep once more.

COMMANDER-IN-CHIEF

Like her relationship with Parliament, the Queen's connection with the Armed Forces goes to the heart of what constitutional monarchy is all about. The Queen is their Commander-in-Chief. They are serving 'Queen and country', not 'country and Queen'. They receive their orders from the Government. They owe their allegiance to her. But this is also a very human bond.

The Queen's grandfather, father, husband and two sons all served in the Royal Navy. Two of her grandsons have joined the Army. She wore uniform herself in the Second World War. All members of the family are very proud of the Services links they maintain on her behalf.

Left: The Head of
the Armed Forces
– with some of them.

The Crown Jewels

A synonym for the best of anything, the Crown Jewels have lived in the Jewel House of the Tower of London since medieval times. The collection consists of crowns, orbs and sceptres packed with some of the finest gems in existence. It would consist of a lot more if most of the first set had not been dumped by a fugitive King John in 1216 and most of the second set had not been melted down by Oliver Cromwell.

With the exception of the thirteenth-century Coronation Spoon, three swords and a few gems, today's Crown Jewels have all been crafted since Charles II restored the Monarchy in 1660. Many items have not left the Tower since the Queen's Coronation in 1953. Among the most important emblems is St Edward's Crown, made of gold in 1661, which is lowered onto the Sovereign's head at the climax of the Coronation Ceremony. But the best-known symbols of the Queen's authority are the three pieces which play an annual role in the State Opening of Parliament. They are deemed so important that they warrant their own carriage procession to and from Westminster.

- The Imperial State Crown. First created in 1838 for Queen Victoria, it was rebuilt for the Coronation of George VI and then altered for the Queen's own Coronation. Although she had the arches lowered, for a more feminine look, it still weighs two and a half pounds, which is why Her Majesty likes to get used to it before public outings. It contains the 317-carat Second Star of Africa, cut from the greatest white diamond ever discovered (the 530-carat First Star is in the Sceptre which the Monarch holds at Coronations). The Monarch only wears the Crown inside Westminster. On the journey there and back, she will wear a smaller crown – or diadem – while the Crown travels separately.

- The Cap of Maintenance. Made of red velvet and ermine from the winter belly of a stoat, the Cap represents the spiritual power of the Sovereign. Originally designed as inner linings for crowns, such caps were once a customary gift from the Pope to a Monarch.

- The Great Sword of State. Forged in 1678 for ten guineas, it symbolises the might of the Sovereign. It was never meant for combat but was designed to be held upright, which is why all the writing and engraving goes vertically, not horizontally.

The Prince of Wales is extremely proud of his honorary commands in all the Services, which he likens to a collection of extended families. 'It matters to me a lot, particularly now when the British Armed Forces are so heavily involved in different parts of the world.' The Prince regards his own years in the Royal Navy as a defining period of his life. 'It's *service*, that is what I think matters so much about it. In the Navy, it's a bit traumatic to start with until you find out how to do it. But it's very good for one to have to do these things. It provides a certain amount of discipline in one's life, which is the only way you can survive in this world.'

As far as the Queen is concerned, the veterans of the Second World War are her father's men, just as the veterans of the First World War were her grandfather's men. Today's forces, in the same way, are her men and women.

That is why the second Sunday of November, known as Remembrance Sunday, never needs marking in royal diaries. It is the day Britain honours its war dead. And, on Whitehall, between Parliament and Horse Guards Parade, the Queen always leads the central event at the Cenotaph, the simple Portland Stone monument to 'The Glorious Dead'. 'It is a wonderful, dignified, simple, very moving occasion,' says the Prince of Wales, who is also a devoted patron of the War Widows Association. 'The wonderful thing about it is that it's always the same. At a certain time of the year, we always remember in the same, solemn, dignified way. We sing the same hymn – "O God Our Help In Ages Past". It doesn't need to be changed. It's like walking down a country lane that you've known ever since you were small.'

As usual, the temperature is close to freezing but the old soldiers, sailors and airmen are not complaining. Many have not seen each other for years. There is plenty of banter and retelling of old stories as they form up on Horse Guards. This will be an event of two parts. First, the Queen will lead the formal commemorations at the

Above: At the Cenotaph for Remembrance Sunday.

Cenotaph. She will then withdraw to leave the stage free for the less formal Royal British Legion Parade. More than 10,000 former servicemen and servicewomen will march, walk or wheel their way past the Cenotaph laying wreaths of paper poppies. Within an hour, one of London's busiest thoroughfares will be a carpet of red. This year, it is the turn of the Royal Marines Association to lead the parade. Donald Denby, 84, has been chosen to lay the association's wreath. He spent the Second World War fighting in North Africa and northern Europe. 'Once a Marine, always a Marine,' he says proudly. Marching next to him will be fellow-Marine Arthur Ansell, 84. Arthur always spends this day thinking of his younger brother Charlie, killed in action aged 19. 'He should never have been in the front line because he wore glasses and the sun reflected off them. He was easy meat for a sniper.'

Massed bands play sombre classics – 'Flowers of the Forest', 'Nimrod' and so on – as the Prime Minister and other VIPs collect their wreaths and proceed outside to their allotted places. With one minute to go before the hallowed hour, the Queen leads the Royal Family out of the Foreign Office to their spots on the northern side of the Cenotaph. Her position is a pace ahead of the rest of the family.

On the stroke of 11 a.m., the King's Troop Royal Artillery fires a single round to mark the start of the silence. All over Britain, millions pause. Only birds and the distant hum of ignorant traffic can be heard above Whitehall. Donald Denby is thinking of old pals. Arthur Ansell is remembering his brother. Who knows what is running through the mind of the Monarch? She lost an uncle and many friends in the Second World War. Her

mother's favourite brother was killed in the First.

Finally, the silence is shattered by a second blast from the King's Troop. The Queen places her wreath in the centre of the northern face of the Cenotaph. The Royal Family and VIPs follow suit. A short service is conducted for those of all faiths and none. There is nothing remotely triumphal about this most sombre and simple of ceremonies. The National Anthem marks the end of the formalities and the Queen leads the VIPs off parade via the Foreign Office. It is the turn of the veterans to take their place. The Bands strike up jaunty old marching tunes like 'It's A Long Way To Tipperary', and it is time for Donald Denby and the other 10,000 marchers to get in time. Thousands of spectators clap them all the way down Whitehall, through Parliament Square and back round to Horse Guards Parade, where they are saluted by a member of the Royal Family. This year, it is the turn of the Duke of Kent.

One of Donald's old comrades collapses but refuses to be stretchered away because members of his family are lining today's route. The old man wants to march past them. Somehow, he gets back on his feet, determined to make it to the royal finishing post. And, like a true Royal Marine, he does.

HAPPY BIRTHDAY

To the untrained eye, it is all rather baffling. Not only does the Sovereign's Birthday Parade always fall months after her actual birthday (to make the most of the weather) but it involves a huge and seemingly incomprehensible military ceremony. Otherwise known

Far left: Members of the Royal Family on Remembrance Sunday. Left: The Queen lays her wreath at the Cenotaph.

as Trooping the Colour, the Birthday Parade has its roots in the mid eighteenth century. Back then, it was the tradition to present or 'troop' the regimental colours to soldiers on guard duty so that they would recognise their own side in the chaos of battle.

Today, the ceremony is a tribute to the Sovereign from the seven regiments who make up the Household Division. When not on duty somewhere in the world, these are the soldiers who stand outside – or ride past – the Palace. They are one of the iconic sights of Britain, even if marching up and down outside royal residences is probably not why they joined the Army. 'I think they probably look back on it with a certain degree of pride and nostalgia,' reflects the Prince of Wales, who certainly enjoyed watching the guards as a boy. 'The pubic duties side is incredibly important. Nobody else does it like we do. But perhaps, at the time, it can get a bit dull.'

Every year, to mark the Monarch's official birthday, they troop a colour from one of the regiments. For her 80th, it is the turn of the Welsh Guards. It will be a proud moment for the man supervising the parade, London's Garrison Sergeant Major Billy Mott. He is from the Welsh Guards. He is also one of the most respected soldiers in the Army, feared by generals and squaddies alike. At any state occasion, his word is law. And he is planning an unusual closing touch in honour of this birthday – a 'feu de joie' or 'fire of joy'.

This ancient form of celebration involves ranks of soldiers firing a single shot, one by one, in rapid succession. The problem is that the British Army has not performed one of these for many years.

So he has summoned his men to Windsor for rehearsals. 'Now, just to give you a little

Preparations for the Birthday Parade. Far left: The Guards rehearse the 'Fire of Joy'. Left: The briefing for the Royal Air Force flypast.

bit of history,' he begins, 'the feu de joie is fired by the British Army in a ceremonial manner, not like cowboys in Bosnia or in Afghanistan.' In case anyone is wondering why it has a French name, Billy offers a historical perspective. 'It was fired as a symbolic gesture at the end of the battle. When we beat up people like the French, that's how we got it and that's why it's got a French name. That's where we inherited it from.'

The first attempt is, to put it mildly, disastrous. 'No, no!' screams Billy. 'A ripple! I want it to be a ripple – short and sharp!' One of his drill sergeants mutters that it sounds more like breaking wind. Billy's patience is wearing thin. They try again. It is dismal. 'No! No!' shrieks Billy. Once more. It's even worse. The Garrison Sergeant Major looks positively ill. He is, temporarily, speechless.

Some 150 miles to the north, another uniformed group are rehearsing the big day – in their heads. After the main parade, the Queen and the Royal Family will come out onto the Palace balcony for the traditional Royal Air Force flypast. This year, it will be one of the largest since the war – forty-nine aircraft spread over a twenty-four-mile distance. Wing Commander Bob Judson, the station commander at RAF Coningsby in Lincolnshire, will be in charge. It could be a scene from a war movie in his huge briefing room. Earnest young men in flying suits sit in large armchairs talking pilot-speak. 'We're trying to go over Buckingham Palace at 1200 Zulu, I repeat Zulu,' says the Wing Commander. 'Weather limits? They are absolutes. Get your prayer mats out and hope that the weather is good for the day. A diamond nine going AMC is not a clever thing to do…'

Left: 'Beating Retreat' with the Household Cavalry.

The formation will include everything from the very latest Typhoons to the old warhorses of the Battle of Britain Memorial Flight. It is a safe bet that the biggest cheers will greet the Lancaster bomber, the Hurricane and that eternal crowd-pleaser, the Spitfire.

The Official Birthday brings perfect flying weather. Tens of thousands fill every vantage point around Buckingham Palace. Round at the back, the staff of the Royal Mews have been preparing horses and carriages since dawn. The Queen will travel in Queen Victoria's phaeton (an open carriage). She rode for many years and, in 1981, famously carried on riding when a man in the crowd started shooting at her with an air pistol. But when her beloved Canadian mare, Burmese, retired in 1986, the Queen decided that no other horse would do and switched to a carriage instead.

Some members of the Royal Family, like the Prince of Wales, have military roles today and will ride on horseback. He has every faith in his trusty mount, St James, who 'just stands there, doesn't fidget and tries to eat my boot'. Others will travel in carriages like the Queen. She is the last to leave, pulled by two trusty Windsor Greys. In a corner of the Palace Quadrangle, a soldier talks into his handset: 'All stations, this is 33. Flag down. Two-Four. Over.' It is the signal to lower the Royal Standard. The Queen is leaving the Palace. Across London, everyone knows that the Birthday Parade is under way.

On Horse Guards Parade, the 'Trooping' is as slick as ever. The Queen takes her seat in the Parade Chair and all eyes are on Second Lieutenant Simon Hillard, 25, the Ensign who has to carry the Colour. He doesn't drop it. The other Guards then march past the Queen before she returns to the gates of the Palace at the head of her soldiers. There, she climbs on to another dais to watch the parade file past all over again. By now, a Royal Family party is under way in the Centre Room, the ornate Oriental dining room just behind the Palace balcony. A large television relays proceedings to the rest of the family. 'Wide screens make everybody look fat,' the Duke of Gloucester observes. Prince Harry, in his Blues and Royals uniform, is already peckish and makes for a table where the royal chefs have prepared a spread of sandwiches (turkey, lettuce and mayonnaise on brown; cream cheese and tomato on white; prawn and chive on granary and much else besides).

This will be a gathering of the wider Royal Family, cousins and second cousins who may not have seen one another for months. 'It's obviously very jolly seeing everybody,' says the Prince of Wales. The only notable omissions are Prince

Guarding The Queen

By tradition, the honour of guarding the Monarch falls to seven regiments which, collectively, are called the Household Division. Two of them, known as the Household Cavalry, are on horses. Five of them, the Foot Guards, are infantry soldiers who wear the famous scarlet tunics and bearskins.

THE HOUSEHOLD CAVALRY

- The Life Guards were a band of 'loyal gentlemen' who stood by Charles II during his exile after the Civil War.
- The Blues and Royals are an amalgamation of the Royal Horse Guards – known as 'the Blues' because of their tunics – and 'the Royals' (the 1st Royal Dragoons). Prince William and Prince Harry are among their latest recruits.

THE FOOT GUARDS

To the untrained eye, they may all look the same but they are all very proud of their own identities and regalia.

- The Grenadier Guards have single buttons on their tunics and their collar badge is a grenade.

- The Coldstream Guards wear their buttons in pairs and their collar badge is the Garter Star.

- The Scots Guards wear their buttons in threes and their collar badge is a thistle.

- The Irish Guards wear their buttons in fours and their collar badge is a shamrock.

- The Welsh Guards wear their buttons in fives and their collar badge is a leek.

CHANGING THE GUARD

The Foot Guards provide the Queen's Guard which stands on duty (officially it is 'mounted') outside Buckingham Palace, St James's Palace, Clarence House, the Tower of London and Windsor Castle. In London, it changes every day in summer and every other day in winter. At Windsor Castle, it only changes on certain days. The Household Cavalry provide the Queen's Life Guard. It is 'mounted' outside Horse Guards every morning.

Right: On guard at the Palace.

William, who is in training at Sandhurst, and the Duchess of Cornwall, who is mourning the death of her father. With a large bar, it will be a convivial affair.

One non-royal member of the party is Air Vice-Marshal Christopher Harper from RAF High Wycombe which is coordinating the flypast. He is in the Centre Room to make sure that the Queen is kept fully up to speed on the progress of the airborne tribute. The last time the Air Vice-Marshal was here was to be awarded the CBE. 'It's totally different today,' he says. 'There's a much more relaxed atmosphere.'

He cannot relax just yet, though, because he cannot get through to his man at headquarters. 'He's engaged!' he says in disbelief, putting down the telephone. He tries again. An outburst of RAF jargon follows: 'That's extremely good news. Is AOC 1 Group in good heart? If he's chipper, I'm chipper.'

The Queen and Prince Philip finally arrive in the room. This is an informal gathering, so there is no great fanfare. The Queen's 4-year-old great niece, Margarita Armstrong-Jones, offers a little curtsy. The Queen, enchanted, performs a curtsy back. The Prince of Wales has fond memories of being a child at this event. 'I was always looking up at people with wonderful uniforms and breastplates and wanting to pull their swords out,' he recalls. 'It's so funny seeing it happening with other generations all wanting to do the same thing.' Prince Harry kisses the Duke of Edinburgh (British royal men kiss each other). The Queen makes for the television screen to watch the King's Troop Royal Horse Artillery fire their last salute of the day in Hyde Park. Clearly, the troops and Her Majesty's watches are synchronised to a different time. 'Go on!' says the birthday girl, looking at her watch. 'Shouldn't he be looking at his watch?' Even after eighty years, being saluted by the King's Troop has lost none of its excitement. Finally, they fire their guns.

The cheering of the crowds suggests that the RAF are on their way and the Royal Family move out onto the balcony, with the Queen centre stage. The police have let the thousands of spectators from all over the world fill the entire concourse in front of the Palace. Right at the front are Claire and Brian Hill from Surrey. They have been here since 9 a.m., looking out for their son who is among the Guards. 'I'm the proudest mum in Britain,' says Claire. 'It's very moving and you feel proud of everything.' British-born Stuart Riley travels from his Australian home to watch the Birthday Parade every year. What does the Queen mean to him? 'Stability, stable government, the British way of life.'

Messrs Lancaster, Spitfire and Hurricane all arrive on time. Watching through the gaps in the curtains (only members of the Royal Family are allowed on the balcony itself), the Air Vice-Marshal counts the aircraft down the Mall. 'This couldn't be better. We should be seeing the Typhoons exactly one minute behind…' Sure enough, there they are.

Out on the balcony, there is sudden hilarity as Prince Harry sneezes noisily, prompting the Duke of Edinburgh to swivel round and Prince Harry to lapse into

giggles. On and on come the planes, the C17, the Tristar and its Typhoon escorts, a pair of Jaguars, a Nimrod…

In the crowds, there is so much to take in. Megan O'Brien, aged 6, is utterly enthralled. 'Are they going to do that again,' she asks her father, Danny, as the Red Arrows swoosh overhead with their signature of red, white and blue smoke. Next year, perhaps.

The time has finally come for Billy Mott's men to let rip with their 'ripple'. It is feu de joie time. The first burst is immaculate and catches many people by surprise. On the balcony, the Queen takes it in her stride although Princess Beatrice is startled. One down and three to go. Round two is pretty impressive, too. The rat-a-tat-a-tat-a-tat goes almost seamlessly down the line. There is another cry of: 'Guards, reload!' Round three goes off without a hitch. 'That was wonderful!' the Queen exclaims, coming in from the balcony and pulling off her gloves for a spot of lunch.

Down below, at long last, the Garrison Sergeant Major allows himself what might almost qualify as a smile.

STATE VISITORS

In the Buckingham Palace kitchens, pastry chef Kathryn Boyden and her team are making hundreds of chocolates by hand. They are even painting some of them to make them look like cocoa beans. And they have been very particular about the ingredients. Only chocolate from Ghana will do. The Queen does not cut corners with fellow heads of state.

When one nation wants to make the ultimate gesture of friendship to another, then its head of state invites his or her opposite number to stay. It is called a state visit. The

Below: Chocolates prepared in the Palace kitchens for the state banquet.

Queen has been at it longer than anyone. But even the most experienced head of state on earth is not immune to the unexpected.

In a few days' time, the President of Ghana, John Kufuor and his wife, Theresa, will be arriving at Buckingham Palace (hence, Kathryn's hard work with the chocolates). It is fifty years since the former West African colony achieved independence. Britain is Ghana's largest trading partner and the British Government wants to salute its stability and economic progress. 'The visit recognises that something positive is happening in Ghana,' says Annan Cato, Ghana's High Commissioner to Britain. 'The Queen is saying to us: keep it up, you're making it and we're proud of you.'

The President will have meetings with the Prime Minister and financial leaders. There will be visits to the British Museum and to Liverpool (where he will receive an honorary degree). But the high points will be the carriage procession to the Palace with the Queen and the state banquet.

Former Prime Minister Tony Blair knows the impact of these occasions. 'If you said to them: "Let's scrap all that and we'll go down to the local bistro or even to Downing Street for a dinner," it wouldn't be the same to them. They love the fact that they're there in Buckingham Palace with the Queen of the United Kingdom.'

Mr Cato and his staff join the Royal Household team to rehearse every moment. The home side reassure the Ghanaians that nothing can go wrong. 'Everybody is always escorted,' explains Edward Griffiths, Deputy Master of the Household. 'No one will have a chance to get lost.' The Queen's Senior Page, Philip Rhodes, conducts final checks of all the visitors' accommodation. The President and his wife will have the Belgian Suite, overlooking the gardens, a sumptuous ground-floor corner of the Palace with two bedrooms, two bathrooms, the 1844 Room for audiences, the Carnarvon Room for dining (the Shah of Persia allegedly sacrificed a sheep in here in 1873) and the 18th Century Room for relaxing. The President's small retinue of eleven will be divided between the old suites overlooking the Mall and the new set of rooms in the former hospital wing, newly renamed the 'Ambassadors' Floor' to make it sound more appealing.

Philip and his team ensure that every suite has the correct supply of flowers, drinks and even smoking apparatus. 'If you want to smoke here, you certainly can,' he explains. All the guests will have their own valet or lady's maid. All their clothes will be unpacked, pressed and placed on hangers the moment they arrive. The Yellow Drawing Room, an important Palace conference room, will be transformed into a hub of ironing and shoe-polishing. 'It's one great way of showing how well we do our entertaining,' says Philip. 'If we can make anything easier for them, we do it.' Palace housekeeper Linda Saunders conducts a final check of the rooms. She does her best to make the bomb-proof net curtains look as pretty as possible. 'I'm afraid they're a necessity,' she explains. Edward VII never had that problem.

A team of footmen are crawling over the furniture, dusting and measuring every inch of the U-shaped dining table now erected in the Palace Ballroom. There will be 169 guests for dinner, and every place setting must be precisely eighteen inches apart. In the Palace vaults, the Queen's sommelier is counting out the bottles for the banquet. Robert Large, the Yeoman of the Cellars, is in charge of the 25,000 bottles of wines and spirits stored here. Some, like four bottles of 1850 Malmsey, may never be touched. Another batch gathering dust is the wine collection of the Duke of York. It includes a wedding present, a Nebuchadnezzar (twenty standard bottles in one) of Moët & Chandon champagne signed by Sean Connery and others. Since the Duke doesn't drink alcohol, it hasn't been touched for twenty years. In another corner of the cellars is an exhibition of all eighty-nine different beers and wines created for the Prince of Wales's first wedding in 1981.

The cellars are split into carefully defined sections. One is for private supplies. Another is for Civil List wine – the wine which the Queen serves on Government business. For this banquet, Robert has chosen state-owned wines – a white Burgundy (a Chassagne-Montrachet 2000), a claret (Chateau Montrose 1986), a Louis Roederer 1996 vintage champagne and port (Warre 1977). But this will not be an excessively boozy affair. Robert allows for two bottles of wine per ten guests.

The big day dawns and the Mall is sealed off to traffic as crowds arrive. The grand old road is fully dressed, Union flags alternating with the flag of Ghana. Britain's Ghanaian community is here in force. Many are in the national colours of red, yellow and green. There is a party atmosphere but a sense of history, too. 'Democracy triumphs in Ghana,' shouts one man in the crowd. 'On behalf of all Ghanaians,' declares another, 'we are proud of the Queen, we are proud of our President, we are proud to be Ghanaians.'

Cheers and anthems greet President Kufuor and his wife as they arrive on Horse Guards Parade for the formal welcome by the Queen and her Government. The two heads of state climb into the Australian State Coach and six horses pull them to the Palace. After lunch, the royal party move through to exchange gifts in the Carnarvon Lobby. The Queen gives President Kufuor the traditional gift of the Order of the Bath with its ceremonial red sash and collar. 'I'm afraid there's always a photograph to add to it,' she says, presenting him with an official picture. 'I'm going to cherish it,' he replies. There are personal gifts, too. 'This is for you yourselves,' says the Queen, presenting a pair of engraved goblets. 'You might be able to do some toasts.' 'I will be tempted,' he replies. For Ghana's First Lady, there is something else. 'This is a box which was made by my nephew, David Linley,' says the Queen, tapping it firmly. 'Ah, yes, we've read about him,' says the President. 'He's a very good craftsman,' says Lord Linley's proud aunt. The President, in turn, offers the Queen a gold necklace engraved with prayer symbols – she is fascinated and instantly requests a translation – plus a length of Ghana's prized

kente cloth. For Prince Philip, there is a pair of huge gold cufflinks. 'Oh, that's very kind,' he says. 'I'll have to be careful about wearing these.'

President Kufuor is delighted. 'Her Majesty and her Government are quite modern,' he says afterwards. 'They may use traditional trappings – riding in a horse-drawn coach and all that – but there is real meaning to the invitation.' And the Monarchy? 'Their forebears have been able to lead a powerful nation for so long. So this must be a particularly gifted and smart family. Their genes must be good.'

The Kufuors spend the afternoon visiting Westminster Abbey and the British Museum before meeting various British dignitaries in their suite back at the Palace. David Cameron, the Conservative Party leader, arrives for the customary teatime meeting between the state visitor and the Leader of the Opposition. 'It was a very interesting half-an-hour get-to-know-you chat,' Mr Cameron says after a conversation which has covered Zimbabwe, Sudan, debt relief and football. The Tory leader certainly sees the merits of occasions like this. 'Okay, there's a lot of flummery, but actually in terms of making sure that nation shall talk unto nation, that heads of state will get to know each other, the Monarchy has a huge role in all of those things. And I bet people quite like coming here.' He shares President Kufuor's admiration for the Queen. 'She seems to be someone who just defines public service and never slips up. Her first Prime Minister was Winston Churchill, so she's seen them come and she's seen them go.' He will be back shortly for the banquet once he has squeezed into the regulation evening dress and a stiff-fronted shirt. 'It's like a dinner plate,' he groans.

Below: The Duke of Edinburgh escorts the President of Ghana on his inspection of the Guard of Honour. Below right: The exchange of gifts.

Above: Conservative
Party leader David
Cameron after
his meeting with
Ghana's president.

In the Ballroom, where florist Sharon Gaddes and her team have prepared twenty-three vast arrangements, the staff have lined up for the moment of truth – the Queen's inspection. She never hosts a banquet without checking it all in advance and is intrigued by a new battery-operated lighting system for the flower displays. She is informed that each battery will last four hours. 'We won't be here for four hours,' the Master of the Household, Air Vice-Marshal David Walker, assures her. 'I hope not!' the Queen replies. Something would need to go badly wrong for any banquet to last that long. The Queen does not like long meals. 'Have we got enough food?' the Queen asks mischievously. 'I think we'll be all right, Ma'am,' the Master replies with a smile.

There is, indeed, no shortage of food – or drink. The Yeoman of the Cellars, Robert Large, is decanting the wine and listening out for the correct glug-glug-glug 'singing noise' which denotes a contented wine. 'There you go,' he says, pouring another bottle of the Warre 1977. 'That is the singing noise. So this is a happy port!' He talks his team of footmen through the evening's schedule. He has even printed a special diagram to show the correct choreography for all 1,014 glasses. Each guest will have one glass for white wine, one for red wine, two for champagne (one for toasts, one for pudding), one for water and one for port. Robert also has a list of special instructions. The Duchess of Gloucester, for example, is not drinking white wine this evening. And no more than two glasses are to be cleared at any one time.

Nigel McEvoy, the Palace Steward and the man in charge of all the waiting staff, reminds everyone of his traffic light system. A discreet blue light means 'stand by'. A subsequent green light means 'serve the food'. In addition to his resident staff of forty-four, Nigel has hired fifty trusted casuals for the evening. All guests should have reported any dietary requirements. But Stephen Murray, who rejoices in the title of Yeoman of

the Plate Pantry, knows from long experience that some will not have done so. 'The first course is sole served with a white wine sauce,' he tells the footmen. 'But if one of the guests suddenly elects to become a vegetarian tonight, we do have a vegetarian course.'

The guests, who include politicians, diplomats, business people and many eminent British-based Ghanaians, are soon arriving for drinks in the Picture Gallery. Each is given a personalised booklet with a menu, a guest list and a seating plan featuring a coloured blob marking their seat. As usual, the Queen despatches the Duke of Edinburgh down to the Belgian Suite to collect the state visitors and bring them up to the White Drawing Room where she will introduce them to the rest of the Royal Family. Tonight, though, there is a problem.

With no sign of the Duke or the two most important guests, nervous staff scuttle back and forth in a state of mild panic. There is clearly something wrong. Much to everyone's consternation, the Queen suddenly comes marching out of her private apartment to take stock of the situation. 'Lift's down!' she mutters. 'What a life!' It turns out that the Duke, the President and Mrs Kufuor have got in the lift which will make the short journey from the Belgian Suite up to the royal apartments. But the lift will not budge. And Mrs Kufuor is unable to use the stairs.

The guests in the Picture Gallery carry on drinking, unaware of the drama backstage. The guest list includes many eminent Brits with Ghanaian connections. Ghana-born British actor Hugh Quarshie is one of them. The dress code is white tie (tailcoat, white waistcoat and white bow tie) or national dress. John Prescott, attending his last state banquet as Deputy Prime Minister, has done his own thing, opting for a dinner jacket (which demands a black bow tie) with a white bow tie. No one at the Palace says a word. His choice, though, will be the source of a certain amount of bemused discussion among

his Cabinet colleagues the next day. Some politicians take this stuff *very* seriously.

Back in the royal apartments, the Duke, the President and the First Lady of Ghana are out of the lift, but it hasn't moved so they are still on the wrong floor. How will Mrs Kufuor get up to the state rooms? The Queen reappears to monitor events through the banisters. 'Ahh! The staff lift!' she says triumphantly as the Duke ushers the Kufuors into the luggage elevator. It is not the most dignified start to the evening but it serves its purpose.

To everyone's delight, President Kufuor has decided not to wear white tie and emerges in his finest robes of Ghanaian kente cloth. He makes a splendid contrast to the Queen in her classic white evening gown with Queen Mary's tiara and the family diamonds. She leads the Kufuors through to the White Drawing Room where the other royal guests are lined up. The Prince of Wales is wearing the full red, yellow and green regalia of the Order of the Star of Ghana, which he received in 1977. 'I'm sorry you got stuck in the lift,' he tells Mrs Kufuor, who is certainly seeing the funny side of the delay. 'It wasn't my fault!' The hold-up has proved a blessed relief in the kitchens. 'They're running twenty minutes behind time which, to be perfectly honest, suited us just fine. It took us a bit longer to do the first course than we anticipated,' says the Queen's Chef, Mark Flanagan.

The Queen, the Duke and the two state visitors take up position in the Music Room where every guest is formally introduced. That means 165 handshakes each. Finally, the guests are ushered through to dinner. The Royal Household team usually rely on the Archbishop of Canterbury to go first, thus encouraging others to follow, but, tonight, he is elsewhere. It is going to take even longer.

The Lord Chamberlain finally leads the royal party through to dinner while all stand for the national anthems. At the top end of the U-shaped table, the Queen has the President on her right, followed by the Princess Royal. To her left is the Duke of Edinburgh followed by Mrs Kufuor who has the Prince of Wales on her other side.

Above left: Preparations for the state banquet.

Right: The Queen and President Kuofor enter the state banquet.

The rest of the Royal Family are scattered around the table. The Duke of Gloucester sits between Cherie Blair and the President's press secretary. The Prime Minister sits between the Rector of Exeter College, Oxford and the Ghanaian Foreign Minister – who has been heckled at a student meeting earlier in the day. 'It's a hazard of public speaking now. There's always someone who wants to make a scene,' sighs Tony Blair.

Speeches always come before dinner here, starting with the host. 'Ghana today is a progressive, open society,' the Queen declares, saluting Ghana's political and economic progress. 'Our histories and our people have long been woven together. As we mark the completion of Ghana's first half-century, we look forward to accompanying you on the journey of the next fifty years.'

President Kufuor is equally gracious in reply. 'Ghana is proud and grateful for the personal interest you have taken,' he tells the Queen. And he has high hopes for future links: 'There is no doubt that the full terrain of opportunities for investment is yet to be fully explored.' Down in the kitchens, the phone rings. 'OK, guys,' Mark Flanagan shouts at his team. 'The President of Ghana is starting his speech.' There is a fresh urgency amid the steam. The 'roulade of sole royale' starter is ready to go. Mark's team can now start measuring out the main course, lamb with Normande potatoes and panache of vegetables. Finally, the President toasts the Queen and the people of Britain. Nigel McEvoy's blue light switches to green. Teams of footmen march forth with the sole starter. State banquets are always slick but the footmen take their cue from the top end of the table. The Queen does not want to stare at an empty plate for long. Steve Marshall, the Yeoman of the Glass and China Pantry, is running the plate clearance team tonight. He sends his young charges on their way with a favourite motto: 'Don't

Below left:
Painting the
handmade
chocolates.

wait for a straggling plate!'

The footmen follow his instructions religiously all evening. Slow eating means no eating. Suddenly, the distant sound of bagpipes grows ever louder as a dozen pipers from the Scots Guards appear. There may be no after-dinner speeches here but the Queen likes after-dinner piping. It signals that the formal part of the banquet is over. Once the pipers have finished, the Queen leads her guests back through to the state rooms for coffee and Kathryn Boyden's hand-painted chocolates. When the Kufuors are ready, the Queen escorts them back to the Belgian Suite.

'It was actually quite relaxed,' says Hugh Quarshie. The actor is still chuckling at the speed of the service. 'They are brisk eaters, the Royal Family. If you left your food on a plate, someone whipped it away.' His favourite memory of the evening will be the immortal lament of a Lady-in-Waiting: 'Food always tastes cold when it's on gold plate.'

President Kufuor will certainly not forget the Queen's hospitality either. 'I couldn't believe that she was so on top of world affairs,' he says as he leaves. 'Given the very special connection between my country and Britain, this visit becomes like a jewel in the crown for my tenure of office.' There is no mention of the troublesome elevator.

Below: Actor Hugh Quarshie, a guest at the state banquet.

THE COURT OF ST JAMES'S

No city on earth has a larger diplomatic corps than London. More than 150 countries have a mission in the capital. But these nations do not, officially, despatch their diplomats to Britain. They send them to the Court of St James's, the historic address of the Head of State (even if she no longer resides at St James's Palace and lives down the road at Buckingham Palace). And no matter how mighty or tiny a country may be, no matter how friendly or chilly its relations with the British Government, the Queen treats them exactly the same. Well, almost.

Right now, two Royal Mews carriages are drawing up in the Buckingham Palace Quadrangle, each one drawn by two horses. Out of the first carriage steps the new Ambassador for Chad, Mr Ahmat Haggar. Two of his staff emerge from the second. All are in the national dress of long white robes. Britain and the ex-French colony in Central Africa have few trading or political links. The country is so poor that Mr Haggar is actually ambassador to several countries as well as Britain, and he speaks little English. However, he is his country's newly designated Ambassador to the Court of St James's and he is made as welcome as anyone else as he comes to introduce himself to the Head of State. Whether it's Chad or the USA, the Queen always sends one carriage for the ambassador and another for the senior embassy staff. The only – very subtle – difference is for High Commissioners (Commonwealth ambassadors). Because the Queen is Head of the Commonwealth, she pays them an extra compliment. They have four horses pulling their carriages. Non-Commonwealth envoys get just two. It's a tiny difference.

The Commonwealth

It is still the case (just) that 'the sun never sets on the British Empire'. With fourteen overseas territories from Bermuda to Gibraltar to Pitcairn, Britain still has a clutch of what used to be called 'colonies'. The Queen herself has a good deal more land to her name. She is Queen not just of Britain but of fifteen other realms, including Australia, Canada and New Zealand (where she is also known as 'Kotuku' or 'The Great White Heron'). But she has a direct link with almost one-third of the world's population. When the Empire ceased to be, the Commonwealth came into being. Today, it thrives as a voluntary 'club' of fifty-three nations, sharing history, legal systems, educational structures – and the English language. And its titular head is the Queen.

She does not have any executive powers but is an honorary figurehead. Even so, she takes the role extremely seriously and knows almost all the leaders – from India to Vanuatu. She meets them every other year at the Commonwealth summit and makes a point of attending the Commonwealth Games every four years. At home, the Queen maintains close contact with the Commonwealth Secretariat which is housed in palatial royal premises at Marlborough House (next door to St James's Palace). Every March, she attends the Commonwealth Day service at Westminster Abbey and she treats the organisation's Secretary General like a surrogate Prime Minister. If anyone can name the capital of Kiribati or recognise the flag of Dominica, it will be the person who has met more Commonwealth leaders than anyone else on earth.

The Queen's Realms: Antigua and Barbuda, Australia, the Bahamas, Barbados, Belize, Canada, Grenada, Jamaica, New Zealand, Papua New Guinea, St Christopher and Nevis, St Lucia, St Vincent and the Grenadines, the Solomon Islands, Tuvalu and the United Kingdom.

STATE BANQUET
IN HONOUR OF

THE PRESIDENT
OF
THE REPUBLIC OF GHANA
AND
MRS. KUFUOR

BUCKINGHAM PALACE
TUESDAY 13th MARCH 2007

Above: The Queen's Chef, Mark Flanagan, gets the cooking under way.

But protocol is all about little gestures.

'The Ambassador of Chad,' announces the Marshal of the Diplomatic Corps, and Mr Haggar steps forward to meet the Queen in the blue and gold splendour of the 1844 Room. In quiet, nervous French, he explains that he has come to present his credentials. The Queen immediately picks up the conversation in French.

'A ce moment vous êtes à Bruxelles?' she asks. Mr Haggar nods. Yes, his main office is in Brussels.

'Vous voyagez ici de temps en temps?'

'Oui,' says Mr Haggar. He does indeed come here from time to time. It looks like it is going to be a fairly slow-moving twenty minutes but the Queen ushers him to a chair and the conversation proceeds.

After a quarter of an hour, the doors open and Mr Haggar's two assistants are ushered in for an introduction. When it is over, they all emerge smiling broadly, evidently delighted with the way the encounter has gone. The new Ambassador is now a fully paid-up emissary to the Court of St James's.

Ambassadors have been accredited to St James's Palace since Tudor times. No sooner have they arrived in Britain than they will be invited for a cup of tea in a spacious but homely ground-floor drawing room on the northern side of St James's, next to the Prince of Wales's former study. This is the headquarters of the Marshal of the Diplomatic Corps – the link between the Queen and the 2,382 diplomats officially based in London.

The diplomats are drawn from 157 missions, a mission being either an embassy or, in the case of a Commonwealth country, a High Commission. At present, London has 112 of the former and 45 of the latter. In 1960, the total was just 70. The end of Empire and Cold War has more than doubled that figure and even the smallest states usually want a foothold in London. Despite his grand title, the present Marshal of the Diplomatic Corps, Sir Anthony Figgis, runs a compact operation. His department occupies just two rooms and his staff consists of himself, his secretary, Laura Howard, two Border terriers called Lottie and Daisy and two West Highland terriers called Molly and Teazle.

If this place has the feel of a cosy country house, it is deliberately so. Any diplomats with serious political issues will deal directly with the British Government. Sir Anthony and his 'team' are here, on behalf of the Queen, to make the diplomats feel a welcome part of the Court and the royal scene. No one wants an ambassador reporting home that the Monarchy is a hostile institution. The Marshal knows that it can be a testing experience to be a newcomer in a big city.

'If they want a chat, they can come to me,' he explains. 'They often have domestic problems and aren't sure who to go to. For example, a young ambassador arrived recently not speaking much English. His wife had no English, they had a very small embassy, she was seven months pregnant and they wanted to know where she could have the baby and get antenatal care. For them, it was a huge issue occupying all his time. For us, it was a twenty-minute phone call.'

Sir Anthony also arranges social and sporting events – a tour of Big Ben or a golf tournament. The new Ambassador of Kazakhstan is a demon tennis player so Sir Anthony has put him in touch with the powers that be at Wimbledon. 'Many of them want to go riding but they don't have a horse, so I can put them in touch with the Household Cavalry,' he says. 'We would usually trust an ambassador with a horse.'

Before they do any of that, they will meet the Queen in the carefully prepared ceremony which Sir Anthony has supervised more than 250 times. This must be just as polished for every new arrival. The latest is the new Polish Ambassador, Barbara Tuge-Erecinska, who has just dropped in for tea. Sir Anthony reminds her of some of the complexities of British officialdom, not least the fact that London has two mayors.

He turns to the pressing matter at hand: Barbara's presentation of credentials to the Queen. Barbara is handed a programme of the arrangements, detailing everything from the necessary amount of curtsying (two on the way in, two on the way out) to the names of the horses which will pull her carriage (Pearl and Merlin). Sir Anthony explains that Barbara and her staff will also be expected to wear national dress or evening dress (a long gown for ladies, white tie for men).

This ambassadorial business is not all work and protocol, though. He produces a list of upcoming events. Barbara will be invited to everything from the Royal Agricultural Show to a royal garden party. He runs through some of the other perks of ambassadorial life. There is Royal Ascot – 'if you're interested in horseracing or the fashion display'. Barbara is not. 'Are you a golfer by any chance?' No, she is not. 'Tennis?' There are regular diplomatic tennis tournaments but Barbara politely declines those, too. Sir Anthony tries a different tack. He mentions that there is an annual ambassadorial trip to

Below: The new Polish Ambassador makes her way to the Palace to meet the Queen.

Stratford-upon-Avon on Shakespeare's birthday, taking in a lunch, a lecture, a wreath-laying and a play. 'I would love to,' says Barbara. A few days later, at the allotted time of 11.43 a.m., there is the clatter of hooves outside the Polish Embassy in London. It is the signal that the new Polish ambassador is being summoned to present her credentials at the Palace. Dressed in a new evening gown, made by a local Polish girl, she pulls on her long white gloves.

These occasions are usually a family day for ambassadors. Barbara's son is taking exams in Denmark, her elderly mother is stuck in Poland and she has no husband to accompany her, but her sister Iwona, an artist, has travelled from her Amsterdam home for the big occasion. Iwona is astonished by the level of detail from the Palace. 'We even know what the horses will be called!' she exclaims. In unison, the sisters recite their names: 'Pearl and Merlin.'

Outside, two carriages are drawing up. While her four most senior staff climb into the second one, Barbara climbs into the first, behind Pearl and Merlin. She is asked if she wants the roof up or down. Given the light December drizzle, she opts for cover. A footman hands her a hot water bottle to put on her lap. Embassy staff clap her on her way, while a sightseeing bus pauses to allow tourists to film the occasion. Why is a woman in a ball gown getting into a horse-drawn carriage at 11.43 in the morning? Who cares? It looks good.

A police escort speeds the carriage procession through London's West End. At Marble Arch, the carriages divert through Hyde Park and take the scenic route on to the Palace. At the Grand Entrance, Barbara is ushered into the Bow Room, where she is steered towards a sofa and a welcoming posse of ladies-in-waiting, equerries and the Marshal. Sir Anthony ushers her to the double doors leading into the 1844 Room. The Queen is waiting inside, beneath the gold and blue decor and Albert Cuyp's 'Trooper With a Grey Horse', along with Sir Peter Ricketts, the Permanent Under Secretary at the Foreign Office. The buzzer goes, two pages open the doors, and Sir Anthony steps forward with

Barbara. 'The Ambassador of Poland, Your Majesty,' he declares and withdraws.

Barbara has remembered the routine to a tee. She bobs, walks forward, bobs again and holds out her state documents. 'Your Majesty, I have the honour of presenting the letters of recall of my predecessor and my own credentials,' she says. 'Thank you very much,' says the Queen, handing the letters to Sir Peter for safekeeping. Barbara responds by conveying the thanks of the Polish President, Lech Kaczynski, who met the Queen a month earlier during a visit to London. 'He was going up to Edinburgh after I'd seen him,' the Queen remembers. 'There are such a lot of links between Scotland and Poland.'

Barbara agrees, pointing out that her President spent many years in a part of Poland known as 'New Scots' because of the number of Scottish tradesmen. 'New Scots? How very nice,' says the Queen. A Scottish-Polish theme is clearly developing. 'The Polish Division was stationed in Scotland for a long time,' the Queen continues, harking back to the Second World War, 'and married lots of Scottish girls!' There is going to be no shortage of conversation points during this audience. After fifteen minutes, Barbara's staff are summoned inside for a handshake. At the end of the allotted twenty minutes, the Queen bids her farewell. 'I hope you enjoy your time in London,' she concludes.

Barbara walks to the door, turns around once more and performs a final bob. The Marshal of the Diplomatic Corps is waiting outside to escort her home. 'Many congratulations, Ambassador,' says Sir Anthony. 'You now need to take the important decision: whether you would like the carriage open or closed? It's a little bit cold.' 'Open,' says Barbara firmly. 'If you promise it's not going to rain.'

At the Polish Embassy, staff have prepared silver trays of carrots for the horses and shots of Polish vodka for the coachmen. Inside, leading members of London's Polish

community have gathered for a small reception – or 'vin d'honneur' as it is known in diplomatic language. Barbara is thrilled by her experience at the Palace, especially by the Queen's detailed knowledge of Polish affairs. 'I didn't have a feeling that the Queen was briefed. She didn't need a briefing. She knew.'

The Marshal interrupts the proceedings to give a short speech and a toast to Barbara. Her staff break into a song of celebration. 'Sto Lat!' they sing. It means '100 years'. It's a nice thought. But no ambassador has ever lasted that long.

'THE DIP'

Buckingham Palace is no stranger to dressing up. But even by its own standards of unusual outfits, there is nothing to match the costumes at the largest indoor event in the royal calendar, the Queen's Diplomatic Reception. It is anything but a reception. Around a thousand ambassadors, High Commissioners, senior diplomats and spouses are invited to drinks, dinner and dancing.

In the basement of the Palace, Mark Flanagan and his team are preparing their biggest dinner of the year. He has devised a menu with three principal dishes – guinea fowl, salmon and vegetarian tart – but this will be a buffet, which means everyone must be able to eat it with just a fork. 'Guinea fowl's very popular in France,' he says. 'It's along the lines of chicken but a bit more interesting. The type of people we're feeding eat out an awful lot. The last thing we want to put in front of them is another rubber chicken dinner.' Every culture is duly observed, too: 'No alcohol, no bacon, no pork products. A lot of people come to these things year in, year out so we have to be non-offending and interesting every year.'

His boss, Edward Griffiths, the Deputy Master of the Household, arrives to check all the dishes. Dorchester-trained Edward is as concerned as Mark to get this right. The 'Dip', as it is known here, has one dubious distinction. It is the only party given by the Queen at which glass brackets are used so that people can attach their glasses to their plates. There simply isn't enough table space, even here at the Palace, for a thousand people to park their plates and glasses. Certain rules, however, stand firm. 'Champagne is served in goblets, not flutes,' says Edward firmly.

Everyone will be in their very grandest kit. The dress code for men is national dress, evening dress or Court dress (knee breeches) with full decorations. For women, it means long ball gowns and no stinting on the jewellery. The lady members of the Royal Family will be wearing tiaras. More eye-catching than any tiara, though, is the gold-spiked cap of the Mongolian Ambassador who arrives to the sound of the old Beatles hit, 'When I'm Sixty-Four'.

There will be rigid protocol tonight. To avoid offence, diplomatic precedence is governed by the length of time in office. The greeting line will be arranged according to when people took up their posts. The longest-serving London diplomat – known as the Dean of the Diplomatic Corps – will be Khaled Al Duwaisan, the Kuwaiti Ambassador, who has been here for thirteen years. He needs no directions as he arrives through the Ambassadors' Entrance and heads for the Picture Gallery where he grabs a glass of orange juice and hails his fellow ambassadors. Talk turns to his upcoming trip to India and his daughter's university career in America. This is not an evening for politics.

A fanfare of trumpets announces the arrival of the Monarch, who arrives in a tiara worthy of the Statue of Liberty and the full regalia of the Order of the Garter.

The great diplomatic handshake begins, starting with Kuwait. Other members of the Royal Family follow the Queen. Mr Al Duwaisan congratulates the Duchess of Gloucester on her recent performance at a diplomatic tennis tournament. 'Flattery will get you a long way, Ambassador,' she laughs. The Queen meets the Nigerian High Commissioner, Dr Christopher Kolade, and discusses a forthcoming visit by the Prince of Wales. Moments later, Princess Alexandra's eyes light up. 'Good evening,' she says, shaking Dr Kolade warmly by the hand. 'I know your country!' Dr Kolade looks flattered but unsure. 'I gave it independence in 1960!' the Princess explains. 'Yes, of course,' Dr Kolade replies. The Princess was there to represent the Queen. 'I've never been back, but I'll never forget it,' she says, reeling off a list of all the people she met there. 'You have a fantastic memory,' says the High Commissioner. 'Lovely country,' says the Princess.

At the other end of the room, the Queen meets the most recently arrived heads of

mission. One of them, the new High Commissioner for Cyprus, George Iacovou, has only been in the job a few days. He has not even had time to present his credentials to the Queen. But he and his wife have lived in Britain on previous occasions. 'We are newcomers and old-timers in England,' says George. 'Old timers?' asks the Queen. 'It's fun to come back. It may be very different now.' 'How are things at home?' asks the Duke of Edinburgh, before noticing the High Commissioner's row of medals. The Duke is quite an expert on decorations and observes that none of George's medals is from Cyprus. 'Diplomats are like prophets. They're never honoured at home,' the Duke reflects, as he enjoys trying to identify the High Commissioner's different medals: 'This is German. Mmm, this is Austrian… That one – I can't remember!'

Next up is the Duke of Gloucester who asks about the state of the Cyprus sherry industry. 'Lamentably, we don't produce sherry now,' says the High Commissioner, pointing out that European Union rules have stopped Cyprus sherry from being called sherry. 'Really?' asks the Duke in disbelief. 'Sherry has to come from Jerez,' George points out. The Duke is surprised. 'Really? It must be the same stuff!' The High Commissioner assures him that Cyprus sherry is no more. Princess Alexandra joins in: 'I was in Cyprus a few years ago to visit the military. It's such a lovely island. Do you enjoy being in London?' Within a few minutes, the new High Commissioner has met half the Royal Family.

Once the Queen has met all the British VIPs and has covered all her state rooms, she makes a discreet exit. Like the parents at a teenage party, she wants her guests to be able to let their hair down a little – in as much as diplomats ever let their hair down. The band strikes up a selection of safe disco favourites in the Ball Supper Room and Buckingham Palace's biggest bash of the year shuffles and gyrates to an elegant close.

Below: 'The Dip'. Below right: 'The great diplomatic handshake' continues.

CHAPTER FIVE

OVER LAND AND SEA

THE QUEEN IN AMERICA

You are one of the most famous women in the world. And you have met most of the others. You are used to people doing things your way and you travel the world with a large entourage who ensure that, on the whole, you get what you want. This has usually worked for Annie Leibovitz – until now. Her reputation as America's must-have portrait photographer might dazzle most celebrities and any self-respecting politician. At Buckingham Palace, however, Annie and her vast entourage of a dozen assistants have just stumbled across a subject who is not overly impressed.

The photographer has been allocated a considerable chunk of the Queen's morning to produce several historic photographic images. Annie has asked the Queen to wear her Garter robes, the intricate and cumbersome regalia of the oldest order of chivalry in the world. Putting all this on has not been easy, and the Queen has had to postpone some engagements. When she is informed that Annie has a few other outfits in mind, the Sovereign is not amused. 'I'm not changing anything,' the Queen informs her press secretary, Penny Russell-Smith, as she sweeps into the state apartments, a faithful page trotting behind with her velvet train. 'I've done enough dressing like this, thank you very much. I've had enough!'

Her mood is not improved by the size of Annie's team. She has never encountered an operation this big just to take a photograph. Annie has also brought along her young daughter, Sarah, who presents a bouquet. This does little to improve the royal frame of mind.

'I'm sorry, I can't stay very long,' says the Queen firmly. 'It's taken me such a long time to put all this on.' Annie has spent days planning this shoot and had been hoping to photograph the Queen in the garden, too. It now looks as if this could all be over in a matter of minutes. She needs to move fast. She steers the Queen to a chair near an open window in the White Drawing Room for the first picture.

'I'm so sorry,' she tells the Queen. 'Your Majesty, if you sit here like this, I'll do the rest.' Before taking a single frame, though, Annie decides to rearrange things. She wants the Queen to remove the dazzling diamond-packed tiara which is sitting on her carefully prepared hair. This is going to require some serious tact. 'I think it will look better without the crown,' Annie says boldly. You can sense the collective stiffening among the royal staff. The needle on the regal pressure valve is already in the danger zone. Annie presses on, piling on the flattery. 'I've heard you do your own hair, which I believe is so amazing. Can we try it without the crown? It will look… less dressy.' Everyone has a fuse, including monarchs.

'Less dressy?' the Queen asks in exasperated disbelief. 'What do you think this is?' she adds, pointing to her Garter robes. Short of putting on her Coronation kit, this is, indeed, about as dressy as the Queen could be. 'If you take the crown off—' Annie begins. The Queen breaks into a mirthless laugh as her dresser explains the problem. If the tiara – it is not a crown – is removed, then it cannot go back on, because the Queen's hair will be out of place. 'You can't… OK… erm… well…' Annie is searching for the most diplomatic solution to this. 'I have an idea,' she says. 'Let's take a couple of frames with it on, then we'll take it off for the rest of the shooting.' 'Well, I'll have to go back and tidy my hair,' says the Queen, mellowing slightly.

And so the photo shoot begins. From a near-disastrous start, it gets better. The Queen does indeed remove her tiara and, in due course, her Garter robes. Annie gets her photographs and, by the end, the Queen is smiling as she departs for her engagements. There is huge relief all round.

'I was worried when it took so long for her to come out. I knew there was some problem,' Annie admits afterwards. 'At first I wasn't too sure if she was kidding or not. And then I realised she wasn't kidding.'

Annie has seldom had a morning like this, but she has enjoyed the experience. 'I just liked her feistiness. It made me admire her even more. I thought she totally pulled herself back together and started to enjoy herself. She was funny.'

Above: The Queen sits for a portrait by photographer Annie Leibovitz.

It has been a challenge to find a fresh perspective on someone who has been on the stamps and coins of many countries for more than half a century, a person who is instantly recognisable around the world. The Queen sits for an average of four painted portraits each year and a similar number of official photographs. But this shoot has been different. Annie Leibovitz has not been here to photograph just another Christmas card or birthday portrait. Her images will serve as a curtain-raiser to one of the Queen's most important tours of recent times. It is sixteen years since she last set foot in the United States of America, and President George W. Bush has invited her to return. There is an important anniversary to mark – 400 years since the founding of Jamestown, Virginia, the first English colony on American shores. With it came the English language and the rule of law, although there is much more to this visit than that. The precise dynamic of the 'special relationship' between Britain and the USA may be a subject of endless debate, but the two old allies have so many common bonds of language, history and culture that they are often taken for granted. Every now and then, these need to be held up and celebrated. In political and diplomatic terms, there can be no greater sign of friendship between two countries than a state visit. 'It's a symbol of the closeness of the two countries,' says the British Ambassador, Sir David Manning. 'It gives people a sense of the importance of that relationship.' Annie's photographs will be distributed to publications all over America to kick-start the publicity for the visit. It is unlikely that anyone will need to be reminded who the lady in the pictures is.

State Visits

No Sovereign in history has seen as much of the world as the present Monarch. Queen Victoria may have been an Empress in nominal charge of much of the planet, but she herself never ventured much beyond the Alps. Unlike her predecessors, of course, the present Queen has enjoyed the advantage of the jet engine. But of the three monarchs in British history who have turned 80 – Victoria and George III are the others – she is the only one who continues to do the job just as she always has. As Head of the Commonwealth, which covers nearly a third of the world's population, and as Queen of sixteen countries in total, she continues to clock up hundreds of thousands of miles each year. That is why her holidays are always spent at home.

From time to time, her subjects might turn on the television and wonder what the Queen is doing beneath a swaying tropical palm. Wherever she happens to be, though, it is not because she fancies a change of scene. It is because she has been invited by the host nation and because her Government has asked her to go.

The Queen can only spend so much time abroad so other members of her family deputise for her abroad. As every Foreign Secretary soon discovers, the royal connection helps Britain stand out from the rest of the diplomatic herd. Former Prime Minister Tony Blair has seen it time after time. 'People love the Monarchy around the world. It's part of what they perceive about the country,' he says. 'It doesn't mean that people don't think that Britain is a modern country. But they recognise that this is a part of our tradition and our history.'

A state visit is the ultimate diplomatic tool for any country. In the case of the Queen, there is also the 'Elizabeth II factor'. Foreign hosts increasingly regard a visit by the British Monarch as something very special. It is partly because she is a queen and not yet another politician. It is partly because she is the most famous Sovereign on the planet. It is also because of her experience. Here is a head of state who began the job with Churchill and has waved farewell to Blair. She grew up at the feet of George V, absorbed the mistakes of Edward VIII and learned her job from George VI. Her reign has spanned the cold war, the end of Empire, rock 'n' roll, the Beatles, the Space Age, the Internet and the war on terror, and she is still going strong. She is, quite simply, modern history in human form.

THE PRESIDENT
AND MRS. BUSH
WELCOME
HER MAJESTY
QUEEN ELIZABETH II
AND
HIS ROYAL HIGHNESS
THE PRINCE PHILIP
DUKE OF EDINBURGH

The White House
Monday, May 7, 2007

THE BRITISH ARE COMING

The most powerful nation on earth is not easily impressed by visitors from overseas. But even the 43rd President of the USA acknowledges that this will be a very special visit. With one exception (Lyndon Johnson), the Queen has met every American President from Number 33, Harry S Truman, right up to the present.

'Behind an important title is a very kind and compassionate woman,' comments President Bush, as his White House staff prepare for the most elaborate state visit since, well, 1991 when the Queen last came to Washington.

'She's got a neat twinkle in her eye,' says Mr Bush. 'She's very savvy and she makes you feel at ease.' And he should know. President Number 43 first met the Queen at the White House during the 1991 state visit when his father, George Bush Senior (or '41' as he is known in the family) was US President. The Queen duly entertained Number 42, Bill Clinton, during his various visits to London. And, in 2003, she welcomed 43, Bush Junior, to the Palace.

'My memories are of landing on a beautiful lawn in a helicopter,' he recalls. 'I'd met Her Majesty when Mom and Dad were here at the White House. She was easy to talk to. I found her to be a warm, kind person. I remember sitting down in the Palace and it was a very relaxed environment. I wasn't nervous. She's not the kind of person that makes you nervous. That's one of the things I liked about her.'

Even the presidential dogs will get involved in the occasion (one of them will change colour in the process). Mr Bush has vivid memories of meeting the Queen's pets at the Palace in 2003. 'I know she loves her dogs and I love dogs. Sometimes you learn something about someone in how she treats the pets.'

The President admits that he is a somewhat secondary figure in the preparations. It is the First Lady, Laura Bush, who is calling the shots round here. 'Laura will be making the decisions about how we handle all of this,' he says. 'I'm just an ornament.'

Mrs Bush has very fond memories of her stay with the Queen. 'It's probably every little American girl's dream to go to Buckingham Palace and a dream none really believes would ever happen,' she explains. All state visits are special, no matter who the guests may be. Even so, an extra effort is being made for this one. Mrs Bush has been studying the archives to make sure that the correct items from the White House Collection are in pride of place. 'In the yellow Oval Room, the two candelabras that are on the fireplace mantel were gifts from Her Majesty when she came in 1951,' the First Lady explains. She leads us through to the rose-coloured Queen's Bedroom, so named because the Queen stayed there on that first tour – even though she was Princess Elizabeth at the time. The mirror which she presented on behalf of George VI back in 1951 still hangs on the wall of her old bedroom. For this visit, as a head of state, the Queen will stay over the road at Blair House, the official guest quarters for visiting leaders.

The most visible tribute to the Queen will be the grand state banquet in her honour. It will be a white-tie affair – long gowns for ladies; evening tails, stiff shirts, wing collars and so on for men. There has been nothing like it since the President took over at the White House in 2001. 'I'm not looking forward to white tie, I must confess. I'm kind of a casual guy,' Mr Bush says, half-joking. 'Laura convinced me. This will be the only time in my presidency that we have hosted a dinner in white tie and I think it's a great tribute to Her Majesty. I really do.'

Admiral Steve Rochon sums it up. He is the Chief Usher of the White House (if he was at the Palace, they would call him Master of the Household). And he has a new motto for his ninety-four staff: 'Pristine for the Queen!'

So why the fuss? After all, the Queen has been here many times before. Having made three state visits, two official visits and four unofficial visits to look at horses, this will be her tenth trip to America. And wasn't the USA the product of an anti-British revolution? Didn't the Brits torch the White House in 1814? This, though, will be about marking events long before and long after those hostilities. This is a very simple, very personal reaffirmation of the solidarity between two old allies. Add to the mix the fact that the Queen has just been the subject of an Oscar-winning movie, then throw in the Elizabeth

Below and right: The First Lady, Laura Bush, inspects preparations for the Queen's visit to the White House.

II factor and, suddenly, you have the makings of a very substantial event.

And if Washington is excited, then Virginia is positively fizzing. After all, this is a state which calls itself a 'Commonwealth' and is named after Elizabeth I, the Virgin Queen. What's more, Elizabeth II came here in 1957 for the 350th anniversary of the Jamestown landing. Now she's doing the 400th and, once again, will spend a night in the old state capital of Williamsburg. Clearly, she has happy memories of her 1957 visit because she has elected to stay in exactly the same hotel.

So when Bill Leighty, the Governor's chief of staff, gathers a small army of state employees for the big pre-visit briefing in the present capital, Richmond, he does not begin with platitudes. He lets out a loud whoop and launches into an old James Brown hit, 'I Feel Good'. 'A head of state visiting Virginia's general assembly is not something which happens even every century,' he says. 'People will be talking about this for the rest of their lives.' His phone, he says, has not stopped ringing for weeks, as people he forgot he even knew have been begging for royal invitations. He also has a great excuse for any disappointments: 'It's been good to have the Secret Service to blame everything on.'

She may be 81 but the Queen will be getting straight down to business from the moment her chartered British Airways plane arrives from London at Richmond Airport. The royal convoy will take her to the 194-year-old Governor's Mansion for a small reception with Governor Tim Kaine. This has been allotted exactly twelve minutes in

the schedule. Even so, the Old Governor's Bedroom has been lavishly redecorated just in case the Queen needs 'some quiet time'. She will then walk the short distance to the State Capitol building past a crowd that has been selected by lottery. Every day, many of them call Bill's office asking for tips on dress codes and etiquette. Newspapers and bulletins all over the country have been offering detailed advice on the 'correct' way to behave in front of royalty, despite repeated pleas from the British side that it really isn't necessary. 'We are not telling Americans how to behave in their own country,' insists Steve Atkins at the British Embassy press office.

Of all the changes which the Queen will observe since her previous visit, the most obvious will be multiculturalism. During her 1957 visit, the state authorities segregated the crowds into black and white, ignored the Native American Indians and billed the Jamestown anniversary as a 'celebration'. This time, the event will be a 'commemoration', which reflects the bad as well as the good things which resulted from empire-building, not least slavery and land grabs. The chiefs of Virginia's eight native tribes will welcome the Queen formally to the assembly building, the State Capitol. There, the Queen will meet legislators as well as students from Virginia Tech, the local college where thirty-two people were murdered by a gunman in the month before her arrival. 'We've had a very, very hard few weeks here,' says Governor Kaine. 'These communal experiences where we rally together are real high points and we could use that right now.'

The tragedy will, doubtless, feature in her speech, and the staff want it to be remembered for all the right reasons. They have contacted the British Embassy to confirm the correct height for the royal microphone (four feet and six inches). The Queen's previous state visit to America is best remembered for the moment when she delivered her arrival speech on the White House lawn and the lectern obscured all but her hat. Wherever she goes on this tour, the local organisers will be paranoid about a repeat of what became known as 'Podiumgate'.

From Richmond, the Queen will spend the night in the 'Colonial' quarter of Williamsburg, where a horse-drawn carriage will take her to the historic Williamsburg Inn. This huge, white, period piece is also where she stayed in 1957. The Queen's team have chosen Suite 3269, rather than the 'Queen's Suite' that she occupied last time, because it has more adjacent rooms for Royal Household staff. What, one wonders, will the Inn call Suite 3269 in future? 'The Queen's Other Suite'? The Palace staff have made a few modest requests: a chair, a full-length mirror and some carpet in the royal bathroom (one slippery tile could scupper an entire tour) and a small dining table in the main room. They have also asked that any towels and linen should be washed four times in advance. This request is somewhat academic since the hotel has purchased new towels and new Egyptian cotton sheets (these have been washed four times, anyway).

Below: Bill Leighty, the Governor of Virginia's chief of staff, checks
the Queen's 'quiet time' retreat.

There is also a new lavatory seat for the Queen. Only the bathrobes are 'pre-worn', and executive housekeeper Ines Almeida has washed them herself. There is already healthy competition among all the housemaids as to who will be closely involved. Two veterans of the 1957 visit have even volunteered to come out of retirement for the occasion.

In the kitchens, executive chef Hans Schadler is well aware of things to avoid – spicy food, large portions and so on. Besides catering for the Queen's personal needs, he must prepare a royal lunch for 400 – Virginia ham salad, local rockfish and 'lemon cloud' tart. He has even prepared a complex wall chart with every detail right down to the fact that the Queen will start her salad by 1.09 p.m. and that she has ten minutes to eat it.

Just down the road is the catalyst for the entire visit: at Jamestown, the Queen and Prince Philip will visit a remarkable spectacle which simply wasn't there on their previous tour. It had long been assumed that the original Jamestown fort had been washed away by the river, but it was discovered in 1994 by Dr Bill Kelso, a revered local archaeologist. 'When people say "the Queen is coming", there's only one Queen, OK?' Surveying his collection of a million-plus ancient artefacts recovered from the site, he points out that the anniversary is as significant for the visitors as for the hosts. 'What makes this visit so important from the British standpoint is that Jamestown is the beginning of the British Empire.'

Right: Richmond's checklist for the royal visit. Far right: Final touches to the decor in the royal suite.

PACKING THE BAGS

At Buckingham Palace, there is similar excitement. Everyone is conscious that the Americans are going out of their way to make this an exceptional visit and the Queen's team want the warmth of the state visit to radiate on both sides of the Atlantic. A week before her departure, the Queen invites 350 of the 500,000 British-based American citizens to a reception at Buckingham Palace. The American Embassy has helped draw up a list which includes financiers, celebrities and even the American oarsmen in this year's Oxford v Cambridge Boat Race.

Also on the list is Mary Jordan, the London correspondent of the *Washington Post*. There is already great interest in the White House preparations for the state banquet, so Mary has been allowed to see how the Queen organises hospitality at her place. The Palace is many times larger than the White House (with 550 employees, it also has more than five times the staff). Mary is surprised by some of the kit in this place. There is the latest high-tech kitchen equipment, but some of the copper pans are engraved with royal cyphers going back to Queen Victoria and they are still in use. Her parting impressions are of a pretty contented staff in a huge house working for a much-loved enigma. 'Americans are endlessly fascinated,' she explains. 'We went to great efforts to get out from under the Monarchy, we don't like inherited titles, and we can't read enough about the Queen.' So, what is it about the Monarch that fascinates her readers? 'They see her as sure and steady. And I think that's how a lot of people see England herself.'

The same sentiments are echoed soon afterwards at the big reception. The state rooms

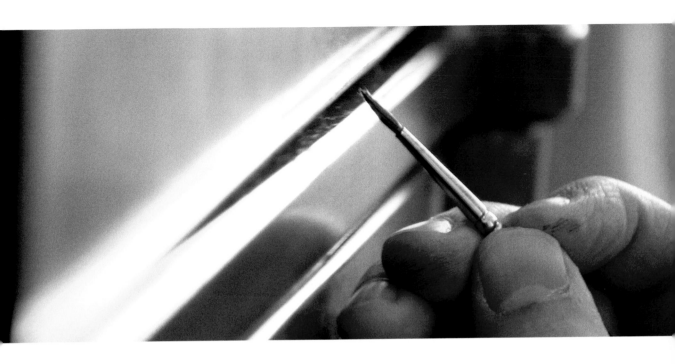

include an exhibition of photographs of the Queen's encounters with all the American Presidents she has known. The Queen and Prince Philip stand at the entrance to the White Drawing Room and greet every single guest, from bankers and teachers to the model Jerry Hall. Also in the line is television presenter Ruby Wax. Afterwards, Ruby mocks the British public's need for a 'nanny' figure, but then admits that nothing would have kept her away: 'We're all here, we've all shaved our legs and I'm wearing shoes that are killing my feet. I could almost confess war crimes I'm in such agony.'

'A smile comes over my face when I think back to the American Revolution,' says US composer Stephen Montague. 'In the American psyche is a desire for a monarchy. Deep down, most Americans are monarchists.'

As she leaves, the Queen thanks the American Ambassador, Robert Tuttle, who has helped with the guest list. 'It's delightful to meet them all,' she tells him. 'There were lots of people from Virginia here this evening and they'd no idea we were there fifty years ago.' They will certainly know about the next visit.

The next afternoon, the tour is top of the agenda during the Queen's weekly audience with the Prime Minister. She tells him how much she is looking forward to returning to Jamestown. 'We were there for the 350th anniversary and now it's the 400th,' she tells Tony Blair. 'I don't suppose I shall recognise it, although I don't suppose Williamsburg's changed much because it's a site of historic interest. Have you ever been there?' Mr Blair has not. 'People say it's wonderful,' he replies. 'It's absolutely lovely,' the Queen assures him. 'Very pretty and colonial.'

When most heads of state arrive in Washington, they have a White House press conference but the Queen does not do press conferences. She is not an executive politician. She makes speeches instead. And, on this trip, she will be required to make at least five in as many days. By constitutional convention, they must all be checked with her ministers.

With just a day to go before her departure, the Queen's Private Secretary, Sir Robin Janvrin, wants to make a tiny change to the text of her speech to the Virginia Assembly but it must be approved by the Queen. 'You've changed one word?' she says, scanning the alteration. 'That looks all right.'

She has also decided that she wants to mention the Northern Ireland peace process in one of her Washington speeches. It is her idea, but it still needs the approval of the Government. 'We're still waiting for clearance of all the speeches,' Sir Robin explains. 'But I'll get the final version of the Virginia one in the box tonight, Ma'am.' In other words, it will be waiting for her, like homework, in her next Red Box. 'I can practise it in the aeroplane, too,' says the Queen. So, it doesn't sound like she will be checking out the in-flight movies.

TOUCHDOWN

Palace veterans have learned that it is often the simplest things which can cause problems on a royal tour. You can spend weeks fine-tuning an important speech only to find that the microphone fails. You can come to open a world-class building and then the scissors don't work. And so the Queen's fourth state visit to the mightiest country in the world begins with a comedy foul-up straight out of Laurel and Hardy. No fewer than 800 members of the world's media have been accredited for this tour. A large number of them are on the tarmac to record the moment when the Queen arrives in the USA – and is then marooned on her own plane. For some reason, neither the aircraft steps nor the red carpet are ready. It is 'Podiumgate' all over again, and the Queen has not even set foot on American soil.

The chartered jet glides to a halt with the Royal Standard flying from the cockpit. But the carpet is folded up, members of the honour guard are pulling it in various directions and the operator of the mobile steps seems to have fallen asleep. After several minutes, a set of steps is attached to the rear door which opens like a jack-in-a-box. Out bursts an irritated stream of Palace staff – protection officers, footmen and officials – all of whom dash to their pre-assigned places in the convoy. But they are wasting their time. Nothing is happening at the front of the plane. The carpet is still being shuffled this way and that. No one has had the bright idea to roll it up, move it and then unroll it. Sir

David Manning, the British Ambassador, and his counterpart, Robert Tuttle, the US Ambassador to London, stand helplessly on the runway.

All royal schedules have a delay factor of a few minutes built in to them but it is usually assumed they start on time. Ten minutes after this farce has kicked off, the front door of the plane opens to reveal a very frustrated Group Captain Tim Hewlett, the Director of Royal Travel. He shouldn't even have opened the door as there is nothing between him and the ground but he wants to see what is happening. He shakes his head and rolls his eyes as the steps and the carpet meander aimlessly below. The Duke of Edinburgh cannot resist a glimpse and appears rather amused as he watches it all.

Finally, twenty minutes after what should have been a mere formality, the Queen and the Duke are able to leave their plane, and the convoy departs for Richmond. Overnight downpours have softened to drizzle, which is still irksome for the 7,000 people waiting outside the State Capitol in Richmond as they have been banned from carrying umbrellas for security reasons. Huge video screens relay the Queen's every move to the crowds who cheer her in and out of the Governor's Mansion. There is to be no 'quiet time'.

Below: The Queen visits Jamestown.

The chiefs of the eight tribes perform their dance of welcome outside the Capitol. Prince Philip is much taken by the snarling wolf head carried by the Chickahominy tribe. On the steps, the honour guard includes a contingent of cadets from Virginia Tech. There should be a dozen of them. But there are just eleven. They have left a gap in honour of Matthew La Porte, a victim of the shooting.

It is the first subject on the agenda of the Queen's speech to the members of the State Assembly after a rapturous standing ovation. 'As a State and as a Nation you are still coming to terms with the dreadful events at Virginia Tech,' she says. 'My heart goes out to the students, friends and families of all those killed, and to the many others who have been affected.' There is also a sombre note to her reflections on the Jamestown settlers 400 years before. She salutes 'the ingenuity, the drive and the idealism of that group of adventurers' but admits that opinions have changed since her last Jamestown visit. 'Fifty years on,' she adds, 'we are in a position to reflect more candidly on the Jamestown legacy. Human progress rarely comes without cost.' Slavery, she says, has been part of that legacy. She concludes by reflecting that the bonds of friendship 'are far stronger than any temporary differences of opinion'. The US-UK relationship, she says, 'is one of the most durable international collaborations anywhere in the world at any time in history, a friendship for which I have had good cause to be thankful.'

Her words are cheered to the Capitol's dome. Before leaving, she meets some of the injured students and bereaved families from Virginia Tech. British-born Colin Goddard, who is in a wheelchair after being shot in the leg, insists on standing up to greet her.

Right: Preparing the royal carriage in Williamsburg.

Outside, as the royal convoy takes off for Williamsburg, most of the crowd feel that it has been worth the wait. 'It's been the experience of a lifetime,' says William Smith, executive director of Virginia's heritage music trail, who has driven 400 miles to 'see that smile'. Bill Leighty, who earlier enjoyed a chat with the Queen, is whooping all over again. 'Whohoo! Great party!' he declares. 'I'm very happy and very pleased for both sides of the Pond.'

As the Queen arrives in 'Colonial' Williamsburg, there is another unexpected glitch. A police horse – minus its rider – comes charging through the royal convoy as it reaches the middle of town. However, if there is one world leader who is unlikely to be bothered by a difficult horse, it is the Queen. The royal couple climb into their horse-drawn carriage and, despite the persistent drizzle, leave the roof open as they process down streets which have been lined with steel barriers for the first time in history. An armour-plated convoy several hundred yards long growls along behind the carriage as it makes the ten-minute journey to the well-scrubbed luxury of the Williamsburg Inn. By now, it is nearly midnight British time. If the Queen is suffering from jet lag – and she has not given any indication that she is – she can finally enjoy some 'quiet time'.

The crowds are out early for a glimpse of the royal party the following morning. One eighth-grade schoolboy, dressed in a suit, has travelled all the way from Maine to wave the British flag in front of the Queen. 'It's a sign of respect towards her and her husband,' he explains. There is a choice of two enormous convoys waiting outside the royal hotel. One is made up of limousines, the other of all-terrain 'SUV' vehicles. The sun is out but it is still damp underfoot. Royal aides opt for the SUVs.

At Jamestown's replica fort, the royal couple are greeted by the Vice President, Dick Cheney, and treated to a very carefully balanced anniversary pageant, which gives equal weight to the English, Native American and African-American contributions to modern America before culminating in a eulogy to shared democratic values. The royal couple tour the impressive educational site. It is bustling with historical 'interpreters' dressed in period costume and tourists who, for now, are rather more interested in the walking piece of history in the turquoise hat than in the replica seventeenth-century stuff. Prince Philip goes aboard a life-sized model of one of the settlers' ships, the *Susan Constant*. The royal group is informed that only one of the colonists died on the arduous crossing 400 years before – and that was a case of sunstroke. 'That won't happen to us today,' says the Vice President's wife, Lynne Cheney.

As the Queen looks on from the quayside, the *Susan Constant*'s replica guns fire four rounds in tribute. The sound is certainly authentic. 'It's quite a noise,' the Queen observes. In royal speak, that means: 'Ouch!'

Dr Bill Kelso takes the royal guests to his archaeological vault, where the Duke of

Edinburgh is intrigued by a collection of old Indian pipes, especially when he is informed that the American Indians were smoking tobacco before anyone else. 'Better get an apology from them,' he observes drily. An entertaining debate then breaks out about the presence of horses in early Jamestown. Dr Kelso argues that horses were a colonial import. The Duke insists they were here already. Dr Kelso diplomatically decides not to pursue the point. The Queen, meanwhile, spots an iron spatula labelled 'for severe constipation – a disease that killeth many'. 'David!' she says, summoning her travelling doctor, Commander David Swain. 'You should have some things like that.'

Staff and supporters line the route down to the site of the real fort. The Duke takes the opposite side from the Queen and helps children climb under the tape barrier to meet her. He even beckons across an adult woman with her flowers. The woman is almost speechless. 'Welcome to Jamestown,' she gasps, thrusting forth her flowers. 'Are these from your garden?' the Queen asks her. But there is no response.

Further down, the Queen passes Frances Davis of the Colonial Dames of the 17th Century, a national society for women who can prove that they had adult ancestors in America prior to 1701. Members wear an 'ancestor bar' for each known descendant. Frances has seventeen. They certainly know their history in these parts.

At the local church, the Queen presents Governor Kaine with an intricately crafted replica of a seventeenth-century English high-backed chair made from American cherry

Above: Inside the Governor's Mansion in Richmond.

and Scottish elm. 'Would you like to sit down?' she jokes. 'Why not?' Mr Kaine replies and promptly tries out the gift to loud applause.

In Williamsburg, executive chef Hans Schadler is starting the countdown to his royal lunch in the huge marquee attached to the old Governor's Palace. He is already in a very good mood. The previous evening, the Queen had asked him to cook a dinner of lightly sautéed shrimps which had travelled from Britain in the royal plane. 'She cleaned her plate and that made me very proud,' he says. 'The page pointed out the plate and said: "That's a thumbs up".' It was the same story at breakfast. 'This morning, I made her very, very soft scrambled eggs, three rashers of bacon – very well done – and some toast. She ate that too!'

The Queen takes her seat next to the Governor and opposite the Vice President. Normally, a lunch like this would not command a royal speech, but this is not a normal visit. 'The Jamestown landing is not just a historical fact,' she declares, 'but a symbol of the convergence of civilisations, of the spread of the rule of law, of the growth of representative democracy and also the symbol of the deep and enduring friendship between the United States and the United Kingdom.'

After being made an honorary graduate of the College of William and Mary, the Queen flies on to Lexington for a private weekend at the Kentucky Derby. At the Williamsburg Inn, there is no time to celebrate. The royal entourage have only just

Above: Making Virginia's State Capitol fit for a Queen.

Right: A day before the Queen's arrival in Richmond, the rain comes down.
Far right: Painting the White House in 'Whisper'.

checked out and the next occupants are already at reception. It's all very well having the Monarch to stay. But the members of the Raleigh Tavern Society are rather keen to begin their three-day conference, thank you very much.

VENI, VIDI, DC

The White House can seldom have been whiter. The smell of emulsion wafts around the corridors of power as the presidential decorators touch up every mark and scratch before the Queen's arrival. 'Pristine for the Queen!' declares Admiral Steve Rochon, Chief Usher, for the umpteenth time. 'Everything that's not moving, we're painting.' Rommel Robinson, one of the painters, reveals a lesser-known state secret as her brush glides delicately over one of the royal entrances. Technically, the White House isn't white at all. 'There's a lot of whites – "China" white, "Navaho" white,' she explains. 'Everybody thinks the White House is white but it's really "Whisper".' No sooner has Rommel slapped another coat of 'Whisper' on the South Portico, though, than there is the first casualty of the state visit.

Miss Beazley, one of President Bush's two black Scottish terriers, decides to stretch out against the fresh paint and go to sleep. She awakes with two white ears and a white streak down one side. Dale Heaney, the White House gardener, carries her off for a bath before she can brush against any VIP legs.

While the Queen has a lively day with 156,634 other race-goers watching Street Sense win the Kentucky Derby, Washington is starting to sweat. For Admiral Rochon, these are sleepless times. He has only been in the job a few weeks and he is in charge of one of the biggest events in years. 'We do have a high standard normally but we've definitely kicked

it up a notch,' he says, repeating his 'pristine' mantra again. Every chandelier has been taken down and cleaned. And he is applying the First Lady's white-tie decree to all the staff. On the night of the state banquet, everyone will be in tails, even the plumbers and electricians. 'For an electrician used to wearing a blue shirt and open collar, that's a big ordeal,' he admits.

During her 2003 stay with the Queen, Mrs Bush saw what goes into a Buckingham Palace banquet and she wants the same standards here. 'We got to see the dining room as the butlers were setting the table,' she recalls. 'It was very interesting to see how precise they were, even using a ruler to make sure every place was exactly the same distance apart. We don't do that here but I do think I should suggest it!'

Executive chef Criseta Comerford is chopping up the chive buds which will go with the opening dish at the banquet, spring pea soup. 'It's very classically made and then garnished with lemon mascarpone and little cones with American caviar,' explains Cris.

White tie is not the only novelty at this banquet. White House dinners are normally four-course affairs. For the Queen, Mrs Bush has increased it to five with a fish course of Dover sole added to the soup, lamb, cheese and 'Rose blossom' pudding. The First Lady explains that she has had a very thorough trial run. 'We invited a congressman and a senator to dinner, just twelve of us, to do a tasting. And we asked them to be perfectly frank, to say if they didn't think something was good. They actually thought everything was delicious.'

Besides a state banquet for 134, Cris is working on the small arrival lunch for the royal couple and a few members of the Bush family. The White House pastry chef, Bill Yosses, is particularly pleased with his dessert for this one – an edible watering can made of chocolate sorbet, raspberry meringue and mint granita. Nearby, chief florist Nancy Clark has a refrigerated vault full of fresh flowers of every shade. Her main ingredients will be white and pink roses, along with parrot tulips for the centrepiece at lunch.

The gift-buyers have been busy in the office of the Chief of Protocol. 'We try not to give anything edible or alive,' explains Tiffany Divis. At the First Lady's suggestion, the Queen will be given a bronze statuette called 'Desert Princess', while Prince Philip will receive a silver 'eagle' box. In addition, the couple will receive a leather-bound collection of souvenirs from previous visits.

The resident White House calligraphers are busy writing the placement cards in old English copperplate script. 'It's nicer by hand than by machine,' explains Anita McBride, the First Lady's Chief of Staff. Based in the East Wing of the White House – the President and his team occupy the West Wing – Anita runs a team of twenty-four, managing every aspect of Mrs Bush's public duties. For this visit, however, the First Lady has been leading operations herself. We even find her personally supervising a test run of different china settings. She has chosen President Johnson's china service for the luncheon because it features the flowers of different states. 'I thought Her Majesty would like flowers,' says Mrs Bush, adding that she has chosen former President Clinton's service (which has a White House motif) for dinner.

Over in the West Wing, Joe Hagin, the Deputy Chief of Staff, has had to extend the usual ticket numbers for the arrival ceremony on the South Lawn. More than 7,000 legislators, Government officials and their families want to greet the Queen. Joe has

happy memories of the 2003 trip to London and wants the same atmosphere here. 'The one thing we all commented on was how personal the royal family made us all feel and we were all surprised at how homey Buckingham Palace is,' he explains.

There might be a 'homey' feel on the inside, but the White House is at its very grandest outside on Monday morning as the royal motorcade heads for 1600 Pennsylvania Avenue (unlike Buckingham Palace, the White House has a street number). Honour guards from all the forces are spread across the lawn in front of a huge media platform. Before stepping outside, the President and Mrs Bush are taken into the White House Map Room for a military briefing on precisely where to stand. A soldier with a laser pen politely but firmly explains that they must move outdoors to the sound of the presidential anthem, 'Hail to the Chief', and then 'hold on your toemarks'.

And, finally, with a warm handshake, a 21-gun salute and a rattle of camera shutters, the 43rd President of the United States of America and the 40th Monarch since the Norman Conquest greet each other. After the anthems and the mandatory inspection of the troops, the two leaders return to the dais for what are charmingly described as 'remarks'. They are, by any standards, fully fledged speeches. The President delivers a glowing eulogy to shared values and the 'special relationship'; he praises British involvement in Iraq and Afghanistan and salutes the Queen's leadership 'during these times of danger and decision'. But it is his closing remarks which will lead the news bulletins. 'You've dined with ten Presidents,' he tells her. 'You helped our nation celebrate its bicentennial in 17…' Mr Bush pauses as he realises he has just aged his guest by a

Far left: President and Mrs Bush are briefed on their way to the arrival ceremony. Left: The President anticipates the royal visit.

couple of centuries. True, she has been around a long time. But she never met George Washington. '… in 1976,' the President continues. The Queen looks quietly amused. 'She gave me a look that only a mother could give a child,' the President continues, and laughter breaks out across the South Lawn. Was it a slip or a deliberate gag? Either way, it breaks the ice nicely.

Dressed in white jacket and black skirt, the Queen simply reiterates the messages of her previous two speeches, steers clear of Iraq and heralds her visit as a moment of justifiably happy reflection: 'It gives us the chance to look back at how the stories of our two countries have been inextricably woven together; it is the moment to take stock of our present friendship – rightly taking pleasure from its strengths, while never taking these for granted.'

There is hefty applause as the President leads her inside. Mrs Bush attempts to let the Duke of Edinburgh go first but he insists on ushering her through with the Panama hat he has been using to shield himself from the sun. The President steers them across to the White House visitors' book as Mrs Bush and the Queen both comment on the painful glare of the television lights outside. 'Blinding!' they both agree. In the Red Room, the gifts are exchanged. The Queen is delighted with her statuette and presents the President with a silver plate which has the Presidential Seal, the Queen's cypher and the Star of Texas engraved in gold. Mrs Bush receives an engraved gold and crystal clock.

Far left and left: The White House welcomes the Queen.

Upstairs, a Marine pianist is playing light jazz in the Yellow Oval Room as the small party sit down for a lunch of asparagus, sea bass, grapefruit and Bill Yosses's edible watering cans (or 'Spring Garden' as he has called them). Laura Bush kicks off the conversation on a gift theme and tells the Queen what has happened to all her previous presents to the American people. 'Your Majesty, another gift you gave to the White House are the candelabras over on the mantel, and they've been on that mantel since Jackie Kennedy,' she says. She has even learned their provenance: '1770, made in Birmingham by Matthew Bolton.' The Queen looks and nods knowingly, even if it has been fifty-six years since she presented them.

After lunch, the President escorts his guests over the road to Blair House, the 109-room complex for visiting heads of state, via a walkabout of several hundred extremely excited children. Beyond the police cordons, though, it is impossible to catch sight of anything more than the occasional motorcade. Many people have no idea why there is so much extra police activity around the White House. On being asked to name the 'famous British visitor' in town, most suggest either Tony Blair or pop star Elton John. They have all heard of the Queen, of course, but it hasn't occurred to many of them that she might actually be here.

If they watch the evening news shows, they will certainly find out. For now though, the Queen has just an hour before she is transported to the palatial Lutyens-designed

British Embassy on Massachusetts Avenue. 'It's a little bit of England,' says Amanda Downes, the British Ambassador's unflappable social secretary with seventeen years in the job. She makes a final inspection of the Embassy grounds, where 700 people are about to attend the royal garden party, and has one aim: 'perfection'. The marquee is gleaming, its tables piled high with scones (blackcurrant jam and Cornish cream), flapjacks, strawberries, meringues with hazelnut cream and chocolate tarts. The caterers have made 8,000 sandwiches – smoked salmon/cheese and tomato/cucumber etc – for 700 people. No one need go hungry. In some ways, this is a replica of a Buckingham Palace garden party but with two key differences. First, this one will be just a tenth of the size of the average do on the Palace lawns. Second, there will be something stronger than tea on offer. There is no alcohol at royal garden parties, but this occasion is very much a celebratory affair. The Ambassador will be serving Pol Roger champagne in addition to the Earl Grey.

Amanda changes into her smart yellow party dress, embellished by the MBE she received in 2005, and a hat which she cheerfully describes as a 'whopper'. She is not here to socialise, though, and gets working. The press are demanding a list of the celebrity

Below: 'Pristine for the Queen'. Below right: Setting 187 items on each table for the white tie banquet.

guests – actor Mickey Rooney, journalist Ben Bradlee and so on – while the Deputy Master of the Royal Household, Edward Griffiths, is trying to pinpoint a few guests in advance. The Duke of Edinburgh has specifically asked to meet a young cousin who is studying in Washington, and the British historian Professor Simon Schama.

A detachment from the Coldstream Guards has flown in from London to play music and decorate the premises. The band are playing Lionel Richie's 'Hello' as the Queen's convoy pulls up and Her Majesty emerges in pink. As she steps onto the terrace, the National Anthem is played and one poor bandsman fluffs the final note. The Queen appears to shoot him a look.

Everyone stands patiently in little groups as she moves around the garden. In one area, Amanda has formed what she calls an 'equestrian corner', which includes a couple of trainers, a jockey or two and Olympic eventer Nina Fout. There is no shortage of royal conversation here. Charlie Fenwick tells her that the greatest moment of his life was riding Ben Nevis to victory in the British Grand National in 1980. 'It's an achievement, isn't it?' the Queen replies. 'I was lucky to be in the right place at the right time,' says Charlie.

Elsewhere, Mickey Rooney is so pleased to meet the Queen that he gives her a deep,

theatrical bow and kisses her gloved hand. It's not in any protocol guide, but the Queen seems delighted by the gesture. There is not a cloud in the sky, and Amanda counts her blessings. This is about as perfect an event as a social secretary could ask for.

At the White House, the staff are laying the tables for the big state banquet. The media will soon be arriving for a preview and a few words with the First Lady. Each table of ten people will have a total of 187 items – knives, forks, the 'Kennedy' glasses – in addition to the food, so space is at a premium. Upstairs, the director of the White House Photo Office, Eric Draper, is already selecting some of the thirty-eight images he will place in a leather-bound picture album for the Queen at the end of this visit. Outside, hundreds of photographers have been admitted to witness the royal arrival and make a dash for the media platform. It is like watching a futuristic action thriller as an army of marauders charge the seat of power.

The guest list for the banquet is a blend of politics, big business, media and sport – but no big Hollywood names. The evening is hardly short of glamour, though. A last-minute addition is Calvin Borel, winner of the Kentucky Derby. 'I wouldn't have missed it for the world,' he says.

Everyone has made a supreme effort. Madeleine Pickens, wife of oil billionaire T. Boone Pickens, has such an elegant train that it is getting under her husband's feet. 'I tell you, that dress is driving me crazy,' he says. Asked if her dress is new for the occasion,

Far left: Lunch with the Bushes. Left: The candelabras given to the White House by Princess Elizabeth in 1951.

Tricia Lott, the wife of Senator Trent Lott, replies: 'About two hours old.'

There is no chance of any duplication with the First Lady. Mrs Bush is wearing an aquamarine Oscar de la Renta silk gown with a matching bolero which has been designed just for her. With fifty seconds to go before the royal convoy pulls up, she joins the President on the North Portico to greet the royal guests. Mr Bush actually looks comfortable enough in the dreaded white tie. The Queen is making the short journey from Blair House in an all-terrain Chevrolet SUV vehicle rather than the traditional flat limousine which brought her to the White House earlier. It is clearly her choice because, as she emerges, she jokes to Mr Bush that the other car had been too low to accommodate her hat.

Tonight's headwear is the fabulous Queen Mary tiara which, with the accompanying diamond festoon necklace, earrings and bracelet, lights up brilliantly in the ferocious salvo of camera flashes. The Queen is also wearing the blue sash and the star of the Order of the Garter over her Stewart Parvin dress with its full-beaded bodice and white chiffon skirt. In the State Dining Room, the Queen sits next to President Bush. Chief Justice John Roberts sits on her right and former First Lady Nancy Reagan sits on the President's left. The table also includes golfer Arnold Palmer and former Secretary of State George P. Shultz. The Duke of Edinburgh is at an adjacent table in between Mrs Bush and the Secretary of State, Dr Condoleezza Rice. As usual, everyone wants

Above: The Queen
and the Duke of
Edinburgh sign
the White House
visitors' book.

the speeches out of the way before dinner. 'Together, we are confronting global challenges such as poverty and disease and terrorism,' says the President. 'We're confident that Anglo-American friendship will endure for centuries to come.' He raises a glass to the 'valiant people of the United Kingdom', and everyone joins in.

The Queen's reply is a good deal more personal and direct than her previous speech. Her words are always delivered 'on advice' from ministers, but the Queen has her own input and someone has certainly decided that this banquet speech should go well beyond the usual niceties. It also serves as another reminder that she has been at the heart of the big historic events of the last eighty years. 'I grew up in the knowledge that the very survival of Britain was bound up in that vital wartime alliance forged by Winston Churchill and President Roosevelt,' she says. Turning to the present, there is no dodging the 'I'-word as she notes: 'Whether in Iraq or Afghanistan, climate change or the eradication of poverty, the international community is grappling with problems certainly no less complex than those faced by our twentieth-century forebears.' Her conclusion is simple: 'The Atlantic unites. Ours is a partnership always to be reckoned with. That is the lesson of my lifetime.'

She raises a glass of champagne to the President of the United States of America, but appears mildly bemused to find no one but him standing. For some reason, there is no indication to the other guests that they should rise from their chairs. So they don't.

Cris Comerford's spring pea soup arrives. Outside, Admiral Steve Rochon is delighted that all his staff have risen to the occasion and are actually enjoying wearing white tie. 'The carpenter, the plumbers, the electricians – they're proud of

Above: The Queen
visits NASA's Space
Flight Center in
Maryland.

it,' he says. 'They really clean up well. I'm impressed.'

After dinner, everyone retires to the East Room for entertainment led by the great violinist, Itzhak Perlman, himself a banquet guest. He begins on a light-hearted note, turning to the Queen and the President. 'Thank you for coming to our concert,' he jokes, before promising a selection of 'musical bon-bons'. He gives a passionate recital of works by Fritz Kreisler, Gershwin, Elgar and Franz Ries before the evening closes on a military note. The US Army Choir has the last word with 'The Battle Hymn of the Republic'.

MISSION ACCOMPLISHED

Having started her state visit honouring the settlers of the past, the Queen begins her final day with the explorers of the future. Among those in the greeting line at NASA's Goddard Space Flight Center in Maryland is British astronaut Nick Patrick, who says that meeting the Queen involves the same technique as flying the Space Shuttle – 'not making a mistake and remembering all the things you're supposed to do'. Some 250 miles up in the sky above California, three astronauts are introduced to the Queen by video link. The Duke of Edinburgh is intrigued by some of the practicalities of space travel. Shown a spacesuit by British astronaut Dr Piers Sellers, the Duke asks: 'What do you do about natural functions?' Piers explains that ten hours is normally the limit before a team effort is required to remove the suit from the astronaut back in the space station. 'It's a very good question,' he says later.

At the British Embassy, the big moment has come for head gardener, Jim Adams, who has arranged for the Queen to plant a hybrid British-American oak. If that is

not daunting enough, there are thousands of British expatriates in the garden to watch. 'I'm really nervous,' says softly spoken Jim. The Queen shovels some soil onto the roots. 'I hope it grows all right,' she tells Jim, who will henceforth be protecting this tree to the death. He is elated. 'It's very cool,' he says afterwards. 'Not a lot of gardeners get to do this. It's pretty cool!'

Jim has not been the only bag of nerves at the Embassy. In the drawing room, one small group is equally tense. The Queen is to perform a small investiture to reward three people who have done something notable for British-American relations. They include Charlotte Shultz, Chief of Protocol

Left and right: The White House state banquet.

for the Governor of California and wife of George Shultz. She has been appointed an honorary Commander of the Royal Victorian Order (CVO) for her help in organising numerous royal visits during a protocol career which spans forty-four years. She may be the ultimate authority on etiquette in California but one question has been exercising Charlotte for some time. Should she curtsy? American citizens, of course, are not expected to bow or curtsy. On the other hand, she is receiving a British honour. As they wait for the Queen to arrive, Edward Griffiths, the Deputy Master of the Household, explains that it is entirely up to Charlotte. She offers a little bob and everyone claps. So, that resolves the issue. It's a green light for genuflection. But Charlotte is still worried about the depth of the curtsy. Edward explains that he always advises restraint in such matters. 'The saying is that many a person has gone down but not come up,' he points out. Charlotte still has one more question: hat or no hat? She has brought one which matches her yellow outfit. But she does not want to wear it if the Queen is hatless.

Amanda Downes, the Ambassador's social secretary, comes to the rescue. She sneaks out into the gallery to get an advance sighting of the Queen and dashes back in making elaborate hand signals above her head. Charlotte instantly puts on her hat. 'Marvellous,' Commander Heber Ackland, the Queen's Equerry, assures her. As Charlotte explains later, 'I didn't want the Queen to feel uncomfortable that she was the only one in a hat so I helped her out.' Now, that's protocol.

Once the Queen has arrived, a military attaché reads out the citations. 'The Royal Victorian Order,' he declares. 'To be an Honorary Commander. Mrs Charlotte Maillard Shultz.' Charlotte steps forward, performs the perfect bob and receives her decoration. The Queen thanks her for all her help in welcoming the family down the years. 'It has been my wonderful pleasure,' says Charlotte. 'So many of them come now,' the Queen adds, almost apologetically. 'Keep them coming,' Charlotte tells her. How does she feel afterwards? 'I'll probably be dancing out of here.'

This is the busiest day of the entire tour with six separate engagements plus a transatlantic flight at the end of it. The royal couple move on to visit the Children's National Medical Center and then pay their respects at the World War II Memorial. Hundreds of veterans and British-born 'GI brides' have been invited too. Like the Queen, Betty Yendell served in Britain's Auxiliary Territorial Service in the war. Posted to Belgium, she met her future husband, Charles, and moved to the USA where she raised four children. But she has always kept her old ATS jacket and has brought it along to show the Queen. 'Oh, come on, breeze,' pleads Betty, sweltering in the heat. Just as the Queen reaches Betty's group, her friend, Joyce Kerr, does the talking and shy Betty is too polite to interrupt with her ATS jacket. The royal party duly moves on but Betty is quite content to have been so close. 'I'm so glad I was here,' she says. 'This is an honourable day to be here. It's VE [Victory in Europe] Day, which is really important to the British.'

At the British Embassy, the grand finale approaches. Amanda Downes checks that everyone is accounted for on the seating plan for the farewell banquet. She is rather envious of her opposite number at the White House. Amy Zantzinger has just acquired every social secretary's dream gadget – a digital seating planner. Amanda has to do it by hand. There will be 104 for dinner tonight, and it will be decidedly less formal in tone than the White House affair (it would be inappropriate to try to compete). Dress will be black tie, not white, there will be no tiaras and ladies need not wear long dresses. Lady Manning has decided that the tables will not be numbered. They will all be named after famous Derby-winning horses. So the Queen and President Bush, for example, will not be seated on 'Table 1' – they will be on 'Smarty Jones'.

A lucky handful of invitees from the White House banquet are about to enjoy their second royal dinner of the week, among them Nancy Reagan, who declares herself the Queen's 'biggest fan'. Waiting for the royal guests, the former First Lady says that her favourite encounter will always be her 1982 stay at Windsor when her late husband, Ronald Reagan, was President. 'It was family, it was informal,' she says. 'You get to know people much better in those circumstances.' She also has vivid memories of the Queen's 1983 visit to the Reagan ranch in California. The idea was for the Queen to see some of President Reagan's horses but the plan was scuppered by atrocious weather. 'It was pouring down, just pouring,' Nancy remembers. 'We never could get on a horse – or even see a horse. And Ronnie kept apologising and saying: "I'm so sorry. I'm so sorry." The Queen would say: "Don't worry. This is an adventure"!'

A harpist is playing in the garden as the Queen arrives in a dress of white tulle and

gold thread on Duchess satin, an ensemble designed by her own staff at the Palace. In keeping with the comparatively understated tone of the evening, she is wearing aquamarine jewellery rather than another selection from Queen Mary's diamond mine.

The Queen is at the main entrance to meet both Presidents Bush – 41 and 43 – plus their wives. All four have decided to come in the same low, flat limousine. Like the Queen, Barbara Bush is no fan of a vehicle which requires a lady to exit almost horizontally. 'That is the worst car!' says Mrs Bush senior after her son has helped her out of this rocket-proof bunker-on-wheels. 'Absolutely the worst.' The Duke of Edinburgh concurs. 'You came in that submarine?' he jokes. 'You get into it,' explains George Bush Senior, 'but it's hard to get out.'

The Queen leads them up the grand staircase for the official photograph at the top. Barbara Bush immediately tries to hide behind a door while her husband reverses down the stairs. They clearly view this as an occasion for their son and daughter-in-law, not the old guard. The Queen has other ideas. 'Don't go away!' she insists and a photograph is taken with both Bush generations.

Below: The black-tie 'return' banquet at the British Embassy.

This may be a less formal occasion but there is still the traditional greeting line. First in the queue is Nancy Reagan. Another former First Lady is here, too. Senator Hillary Clinton, who seems to be the only woman present in trousers, has a long chat with the Queen. Other guests include the former Chairman of the US Federal Reserve, Alan Greenspan, and the Mayor of Washington, Adrian Fenty. At the tail end of the glad-handing process, the Duke of Edinburgh is hugely amused when one woman fails to

recognise him and walks straight past. But when another guest tries to engage him in conversation for a little too long, he cheerfully gestures towards the door, saying, 'You're causing a traffic jam!'

When everyone is through – even the harpist turns up for a handshake – the guests sit down and the speeches begin. It is the Queen's turn to start tonight. 'I wondered whether I should start this toast saying: "When I was here in 1776," but I don't think I will,' she says with an impish giggle. The President can rest assured that she really was amused by his date-juggling act the day before. On a more serious note, she thanks her hosts for America's part in the quest for peace in Northern Ireland and for the universally warm welcome she has received. The Queen concludes with a toast – and an interesting choice of words. 'May I ask everyone to rise and drink a toast,' she begins, 'to President and Mrs Bush, to the future of our two countries and to the enduring friendship between Britain and the United States.' Normally, the Queen does not ask people to rise because it is assumed that they will. But after the previous evening, when the guests all remained seated, she is not taking any chances. All duly rise.

'Your Majesty, I can't top that one,' says the President in reply. Saluting the British-American friendship as 'one of the oldest and most enduring in history' and 'our shared sacrifices', he raises a toast: 'To our closest of friends, the British people.' As the guests tuck in to their wild Scottish smoked salmon, roast rib of veal and summer pudding, the diplomats in the room can surely reflect that diplomacy does not get much better than this. Both heads of state are happy. The afterglow is assured. Even the papers have been almost entirely positive. Indeed, many have been effusive. 'Capital Goes Gaga Over the Queen for a Day' says the front page of the *Washington Post*. 'On this side of the ocean, the Queen was making Americans go weak in the knees,' declares the *New York Times*.

'Thank you very much for so much kindness,' the Queen says to the President at the end of the evening as she wishes him goodnight. 'We've loved having you and so have the American people,' says Laura Bush. The Queen waves them off in their dreaded limousine, intrigued by President Bush's sleep pattern. 'He goes to bed very early,' she observes to Sir David Manning. 'Does he get up very early?' The ambassador assures her that the President is a morning person.

The Queen is interested for a reason. Within the hour, she is on her way to Andrews Air Force Base for the overnight flight home, still in her evening dress. She will change on the plane. There are 14 buglers and a 21-gun salute on the runway as Lady Manning performs a knee-scraper of a curtsy and Sir David bids farewell. Through the windows, we see the Monarch pulling off her gloves. Trip done. Mission accomplished. She doesn't even have a speech to deliver in the morning. Perhaps, on this last leg of her 8,000-mile journey, she might allow herself that in-flight movie.

ALL COUNTRIES GREAT AND SMALL

Even after more than fifty years on the Throne, there are some parts of the globe which the Queen has never seen – just as there are some countries which have never seen a British Monarch. If a state visit to an old destination like the USA can be regarded as historic, then a royal debut in somewhere like tiny Estonia is a national milestone.

To begin with, most of the tourists in Town Hall Square are too busy with their beers and their ice-creams to notice the smart posse of men and women pacing up and down the cobblestones and making copious notes. Minstrels in medieval fancy dress sing ancient tunes in front of young families guzzling pizzas and milkshakes. Such innocuous scenes would have been inconceivable fifteen years before, when this place was an outpost of the old Soviet empire. But since the dramatic collapse of the old Communist regime, this small Baltic nation has enjoyed a swift transformation into a flourishing western democracy.

Above: The Queen meets the President and First Lady of Lithuania at Holyroodhouse.

And that is why these over-dressed executives are standing in the middle of the square, perspiring gently. This is a top-level delegation from Buckingham Palace and the office of the President of Estonia. No British Monarch has ever set foot on Estonian soil but, three months from now, the Queen will be arriving here on a state visit. It will be the 132nd country she has visited during her reign. This square will be full to capacity. Emotions will be high – many people will be in tears. It is hard to overstate the symbolic importance of the Queen of Britain to 1.3 million people who have enjoyed freedom of speech, thought and movement for only fifteen years.

The British team are just as excited. 'She's the pinnacle,' says Louise Haywood. 'This is why we are here – to represent the Queen.' Her husband, Nigel, is Her Britannic Majesty's Ambassador to Estonia. This will be the most important twenty-four hours of his professional life. An Oxford graduate with a passion for fly fishing and languages, he has spent twenty-seven years in the Diplomatic Service representing his country all over the world.

'We're trying to produce an event over a couple of days that will be memorable and show-stopping,' Nigel explains. 'It's not just a visit that comes and goes. The trick is to get the visit to have a life beyond the two days it is happening.'

All over Tallinn, people are pinching themselves. Peter Knoll, manager of the Schlössle Hotel, has just heard that he is going to be in charge of catering for the grandest state banquet Estonia has ever seen. Michael Stenner, manager of the Three Sisters Hotel, has learned that he is accommodating the most important guest in his small hotel's history.

Estonia has never had a monarchy of its own, although it had a brief flirtation with the idea a decade ago, when a fringe political party invited Prince Edward to become King. Though touched by the offer, the Prince declined. 'We are in probably the most pro-British country I've ever been to in my life and I've been to quite a lot of countries,' says Nigel Haywood, pointing to Britain's support for Estonia in its darkest days. The trip will also take in the two adjacent young republics, Lithuania and Latvia.

In the meantime it has been decided that the Baltic tour will be even better if it is preceded by a get-to-know-you exercise. All three Baltic presidents are invited to Britain to meet the Queen in advance. President Valdas Adamkus of Lithuania tells her that she will be part of his country's 'history book'. 'Well that's very nice indeed,' replies the Queen. Like the Baltic presidents, journalists from all three Baltic nations have also come to Britain to learn more about the Queen. The Palace press team field the usual questions. Who does the Queen's cooking? What are her dogs called? But the Queen will not be the only remarkable visitor heading for the Baltics. The members of the Baltic press are about to discover the joys of another colourful institution: their British counterparts.

The Ratpack

If the Queen were to land on the Moon, it is a safe bet that there would be a few familiar faces already waiting for her behind a press barrier. The press – especially the 'ratpack' of 'royal-watchers' – is simply a fact of life for members of the Royal Family. Like the weather, it may vary but it is always there.

When the Queen came to the Throne, Winston Churchill was in Downing Street and an equally formidable figure was running the Buckingham Palace Press Office. Commander Richard Colville was a firm believer in the 'no comment' school of media management and regarded journalists and photographers as fractionally above the criminal classes in the human food chain.

No doubt, his views were shared by many inside the Palace, but they were hardly in the best interests of his employers. When faced with a promising story, Fleet Street reporters would not even bother consulting the 'Abominable No Man' as the Queen's press secretary was known. Things had changed little since 1894 when the Press Association, Britain's main domestic news agency, appointed the first Court Correspondent, George Morton Smith. Known as 'Royal' Smith, he was expected to write what he was told. The concept of the independent 'royal correspondent' was a long way off.

What Colville failed to spot was a growing public belief that the Royal Family did not do very much, a sentiment which stemmed from the fact that they were seldom seen doing very much. Subsequent press secretaries appreciated the need for a proper working relationship with the media. And however painful some of the stories and however much the Royal Family may profess not to read the papers, the Queen is always kept well briefed on all the major stories of the day. If they happen to involve her own relations, so be it.

The 'ratpack' are a small band of media working for the mainstream news organisations. They spend most of their professional life following the public activities of the Monarch and her family, whether these are sensational or routine. On an overseas tour, there will be around forty of them – reporters, photographers and film crews from Britain's national papers and networks. Also present will be the modern successor to 'Royal' Smith. Today's Press Association Court Correspondent, however, does not wear a morning coat. Laura Elston wears a skirt and writes her own material.

The most experienced members of the pack, like *Sun* photographer Arthur Edwards, will have followed the Queen round the world several times. He has even received an MBE. In his fifteen years of covering members of the Royal Family, the *Daily Telegraph* photographer Ian Jones has accompanied them to more than 100 countries. The Royal Family know most of the regulars and there is the very occasional spot of banter but, for the most part, the two parties simply get on with their respective jobs. The Monarch is not a politician. She does not give interviews. She is there to meet the people, not the same old press.

Above: Palace Press Secretary Penny Russell-Smith witnesses a ratpack stampede.

They may not endear themselves to the Royal Family but they will not be punished for what they say. Any attempt at censorship would be a public relations disaster. And the outgoing head of royal media relations, Penny Russell-Smith, knows it.

The seventeenth Palace Press Secretary since the post was created in 1837, she joined the Royal Household from the Ministry of Defence and is the first woman to occupy the post (her successor is also a woman – Samantha Cohen). A Cambridge-educated historian, Penny knows that it is best to be dead straight with the 'ratpack'. 'You don't spin the Queen,' as a former Press Secretary once said.

Today, Buckingham Palace employs eight press officers to handle media coverage of all the members of the Royal Family – except for the Prince and Wales and his family, who have their own team at Clarence House. It is a tiny operation by modern public-sector standards. The Palace Press Office, for example, is the same size as that of England's North West Regional Development Agency.

Ultimately, though, the media and the Monarchy do have one thing in common wherever they are: a sense of humour. When the Prince of Wales arrived in Sri Lanka in 1998, the formal ceremonial welcome at the airport went wrong from the start. The hot casings from the 21-gun salute set fire to the airport grass. As fire engines raced to the scene, a stray dog ran out in front of the royal party and started playing hide-and-seek amid the guard of honour. At this moment, the brass band struck up 'Liberty Bell', otherwise known as the theme to the comedy series *Monty Python's Flying Circus*. When the British and Sri Lankan media had recovered from their hysterics, they had their story on a plate. The Prince, on the other hand, had to keep a straight face. He later admitted that he had been biting his tongue so hard he nearly drew blood. Perhaps even the Abominable No Man might have seen the funny side.

CABIN FEVER

The US President has Air Force One. Similarly, every head of state of every G8 nation – France, Japan, Russia and so on – has a designated aircraft which goes with the job. Except one. The Queen is the only one without her own jet. But she still has to get to the Baltics and that means hiring a plane.

The going rate for an aircraft to cover this tour is £70,000. It must be cleared not only by the Queen, but also by her Treasurer, Sir Alan Reid. A former top accountant, Sir Alan knows the pitfalls of hiring planes. 'Sometimes, you have no choice but to hit the charter market because of the itinerary or security considerations or both,' he says. The plane for the Baltics will be an ordinary Airbus 320 from the British Airways fleet with just a few minor modifications carried out for royal purposes. The first and third rows of seats will be removed from the right-hand side of the plane to give the Queen and Prince Philip some extra legroom. While seats are removed, two extra items will be installed: a full-length mirror and a St Christopher's medallion. The Supreme Governor of the Church of England never forgets the Patron Saint of travellers when she is heading abroad.

A few weeks later, the Director of Royal Travel, Group Captain Tim Hewlett, draws up at BA's headquarters near London's Heathrow Airport. He is here to brief the crew who will be looking after the royal party and he is well aware that some of them may be a little nervous. This little trip across the Baltic Sea has been given its own secret codename: Operation Somerset. The chief stewardess (or 'cabin service director' in self-important airline jargon) will be Nettie Sayers, who has been pouring mile-high gin and

tonics for more than a quarter of a century and has looked after the Queen before.

The Queen will be flown by the man in charge of flight training for BA's Airbus fleet, Captain Dave Thomas. His crew will include a spare captain and one young officer whose principal task is to make sure that the Royal Standard is flown properly out of the cockpit window on arrival. 'It sounds like a menial job, but it would be very embarrassing to drop it in an engine,' he says.

Tim Hewlett kicks off his briefing, RAF-style, with some straightforward fundamentals: 'Whilst you can tell your family, it's not the sort of thing where you sit in the local pub and tell everyone the detail of Operation Somerset.'

The royal luggage will weigh between three and four tons. There will be a lot more than clothes in the hold. A travelling head of state has to bring her office with her. 'We do carry quite a lot of hand luggage and hanging space is always at a premium,' Tim explains. Empty seats will be used as extra space for strapping down hatboxes, briefcases, royal gifts, even wreaths. Tim informs the crew that the Queen and Prince Philip will not be eating on board but may want a drink. 'Can you remember how to mix a gin and Dubonnet, Nettie?' asks Tim. 'Seventy-thirty,' comes her reply. 'That's my girl,' says Tim, adding that the other royal passenger will prefer something more basic. 'It's bitter for the Duke. Boddingtons. It used to be Double Diamond but I think they've gone out of business.'

Staff, he explains, will be moving up and down the aisles, and the crew can expect some unusual sights during the tour. The royal passengers, for example, may decide to go walkabout. That, though, is nothing compared to the sight of the royal entourage undressing. On some legs of this tour, there will have to be a fast turnaround of suits, uniforms and even dresses in mid air.

'For the shy and retiring, you will find people going down the back and taking their trousers off,' says Tim. 'Please don't adjust your set. It's perfectly normal.' Some of the crew are trying very hard to keep a straight face. Tim reveals one or two further secrets of a happy royal flight. 'Newspapers and periodicals – a good selection, including the *Racing Post*, please.'

BALTIC BOUND

There isn't the remotest chance that this departure is going to be delayed as the Queen arrives at Heathrow Airport's Royal Suite on a mild October Monday afternoon. Not only has the Chief Executive of British Airways, Willie Walsh, turned up to greet his latest charter passenger, but so, too, has the man in charge of the airport. At 4 p.m., Captain Dave Thomas orders Nettie and her crew to shut the doors and Operation Somerset is under way. The first Sovereign in history is en route to Lithuania and the rest of the Baltic states.

The Royal Travel Agency

Tucked away down the side of what might be termed the Buckingham Palace accounts department is a long thin ground-floor office with the largest map in the entire building. It covers the entire globe and is so big that it has been wallpapered to the side of the room. Next to it is a more detailed map of the United Kingdom with orange and yellow stickers denoting civil and military runways for particular sorts of aircraft. There are models of planes, old photographs, stickers and souvenirs from every corner of the globe. This is the Palace's answer to the high street travel agent. Until 1995, it was called the Queen's Flight. These days, it is called the Royal Travel Office.

If any of the fourteen working members of the Royal Family want to travel somewhere and are not going by car, it will be arranged from here by the Director of Royal Travel, Group Captain Tim Hewlett and his team of two. Between them, they organise around 600 round trips each year. 'Whether the Princess Royal is going to visit a charity shop in Chipping Norton or Antarctica, it will come through us,' explains the retired fighter pilot.

Below: Welcoming the Queen to Lithuania.

The process starts with a note from the office of a member of the Royal Family saying that a particular set of engagements are planned for a particular date. Tim and his team will then produce a list of costed travel options.

For engagements at home, these will consist of car, rail and air choices. The Queen has imposed a general rule that no journey under fifty miles should involve air transport, so royal travellers must go by train – in which case Tim's office will make arrangements – or in their own vehicles. Above that distance, they can use the royal helicopter, a leased Sikorsky S76C, if it makes sense given the timings and locations of the various engagements.

Longer journeys may require a plane. Scheduled flights are fine if they fit in with the royal itinerary and do not involve the Queen (since 11 September 2001, she has not taken commercial flights). But royal tours often involve routes which don't fit with the open market. The Queen has no personal jet. She and her family share seven small Government planes with ministers and senior defence chiefs who have first call on their use. The fleet consists of two British Aerospace 146 aircraft – with room for 21 people and a fuel range of 1,700 miles – and five seven-seat HS125s which can travel 2,300 miles without refuelling. Although the unit is known as 32 (The Royal) Squadron, it spends 85 per cent of its time ferrying politicians and generals around the world. The Monarchy accounts for 15 per cent of its use.

Sometimes none of these planes is suitable or available. In that case, Tim will scour the charter market for something suitable. 'It is important to know who owns it.' No one wants the Queen inadvertently hiring a foreign mobster's getaway jet. If it's an overnight flight, Tim will try to charter a Boeing 777, the only model which can be easily reconfigured to accommodate a bed for the Queen.

The costs will be met by the Government which pays an annual sum for official royal travel called the Grant in Aid. In 2005–2006, the total was £5.5 million – around 14 per cent of the Monarchy's overall cost to the State. The Queen's Treasurer, Sir Alan Reid, must account for every penny. And every travel bill of more than £2,500 – be it for family or staff – must go before the Queen herself. Tim is also in charge of rail travel, but the biggest challenges usually involve the sea. Of all the requests he has received, few have rivalled getting the Princess Royal to and from the notoriously remote Atlantic island of St Helena by ship. 'We managed it, of course,' Tim says, turning to his huge map. 'Now, where is it again?'

In Estonia, Louise Haywood, the Ambassador's wife, has finally found something she is happy to wear to the state banquet. 'It's the only one I'll ever go to. When we went back to London for a few days, I thought: "I'll shop till I drop." I failed. Could I find a dress? No! So, I took a chance and someone's actually made me a dress here. I've gone for silk with a lace overlay with this slight frou-frou business at the bottom. I look very stately!' Louise is not going to compete in the jewellery stakes, though. 'We were told tiaras are not required by those who don't have them – which is just as well because I do not.' Peter Knoll and his team are preparing the dinner which will be served at the national banqueting venue, known as the Blackheads' House. Even now, the details are changing all the time. Peter is trying to find out what kind of handbag the Queen is going to bring to the banquet. 'The Estonian habit is that you don't put handbags on the floor because the money will drain away from you,' he explains. 'So, if it's not a small cocktail handbag, we must have a small footstool.'

His executive chef, Tõnis Sigur, is already preparing the basic ingredients for a dinner of Estonian mushrooms, local lamb and chocolate cake with kumquat ice cream. The wines will be a 2003 Pouilly Fume, a 2000 Château Cassagne claret and an apple wine from Estonia. The catering plans are equally advanced at the nearby Three Sisters Hotel, where the Queen will actually be staying. Within an hour of her arrival in Tallinn, she will be treated to a private lunch of grilled tuna, smoked duck fillet (well done) and sorbets. Given the banquet in prospect, she will not be expecting vast portions.

Manager Michael Stenner has thought of every scenario which might unfold during the most important night of his career. He has even sent the hotel engineers on an elevator management course.

In the main port of Tallinn, Her Majesty's Ship *Liverpool* has arrived to stage a military reception for the Queen. The entire ship's company are summoned for a full dress rehearsal. With the Queen still in Lithuania, Nigel Haywood has found a substitute monarch – his wife, Louise. She is thrilled to be Queen for the afternoon and plays the part to the full. 'Very nice to meet you, Commander,' Louise tells the ship's captain, Henry Duffy, as she is piped aboard. Come the visit itself, her role will not be entirely unlike that of the Queen. When Nigel is escorting Her Majesty, Louise must escort the Duke of Edinburgh. So, she is trying to find the old Duke of Edinburgh's Award badge she won as a girl in order to impress him.

Three days later, it is pinned to her lapel as the royal Airbus touches down on Estonian soil bang on 12.30pm. The Queen walks down onto the runway and is introduced to Louise, who performs a textbook curtsy. 'Nice to see you again,' says the Queen, remembering Louise's trip to the Palace when Nigel was appointed Ambassador. The Duke spots her Duke of Edinburgh's Award badge too and congratulates her on having kept it all these years. So far so good.

The Queen has reigned for over half a century and met hundreds of heads of state. Estonia's President Toomas Ilves is a new boy. It was just two weeks ago that he was elected as Estonia's head of state and he is learning fast. At the Presidential Palace, the Queen inspects the guard of honour, makes President Ilves an honorary Knight Grand Cross of the Order of the Bath and presents him with an engraved silver claret jug. In return, she receives the Order of the Cross of Terra Mariana and a tapestry entitled 'Maritime Nation'.

While the Queen has a rest after her tuna and duck lunch, the Duke of Edinburgh sets off to inspect an electronics factory where he meets the leading players in the British-Estonian industrial scene. He meets a headhunter who cheekily asks if the Duke might be looking for a job. 'At my age? You must be joking!' It's a vintage Duke of Edinburgh engagement, a combination of no-nonsense business talk, some interesting gadgets and a bit of banter to lighten the mood. A man called Jason introduces himself. 'I'm captain of the Estonian cricket team,' he says. 'We play on the ice from January to March. We are the lowest-ranked country in the world.' Once a keen cricketer himself, the Duke is intrigued. 'You haven't played against Afghanistan? They use hand grenades.'

The Queen squeezes in a concert and two receptions at the local modern art museum before it is time for the state banquet at the Blackheads' House. Inside, Peter Knoll's attention to detail is as obsessive as ever. He has not only made the staff rehearse the placing of the Queen's microphone but he has had another brainwave. 'In the main room behind the flowers, we are hiding a tissue box for the Queen just in case she sneezes.' He probably has a contingency plan to cover a plague of locusts or an alien invasion.

As ever, the gems are startling as the Queen steps out of the official Range Rover. She is wearing the Grand Duchess Vladimir Tiara, bought by Queen Mary in 1921 following the Grand Duchess's death. The Estonian public is delighted. This is the Queen as they expect her, a proper fairy-tale Monarch clad in white fur, white evening gloves and fabulous jewellery. As well as the tiara, the Queen is wearing Queen Mary's Kensington bow brooch and huge diamond triple-drop earrings. She has a silver handbag with a long strap which means that Peter Knoll will need a special stool for the royal bag. Before anyone can start on Tõnis Sigur's mushrooms, there will be the ritual speeches and Peter's microphone-placing ceremony is duly performed.

The themes have been the same all week but they are as heartfelt as ever. The sense of national rebirth after a long and painful struggle permeates the rhetoric. President Ilves traces the history of Anglo-Estonian relations from medieval times to the present. The Queen pays a tribute to all the Baltic states. 'I have seen three very different countries, but have seen one feature that you all share. It is that indomitable spirit, which was able to keep alive the flame of independence during the very worst of times.'

With the speeches out of the way, the atmosphere is convivial, even boisterous. The Queen and the Duke may be holding back on the wine but there are plenty who make the most of it and there is sustained applause as the royal party leave at 10.30. Peter Knoll can finally relax, although he is still finding fault with the evening. 'We had a little delay with the main course, but this is life,' he says. Louise has had the time of her life – although she has one small confession: 'I managed to knock over a chair which was a trifle embarrassing.' The Queen caught her eye but, mercifully, she was smiling.

The morning headlines could hardly be much better. The daily newspaper, the *Eesti*

Päevaleht, hails the Queen as 'the world's most desired guest' and her visit as 'a gift to the Estonian people'. Her day begins in Old Town Square in front of the largest crowd of the entire Baltic campaign, at least 10,000 of them, with many more turned away. Singing festivals are a national sport round here – occasions, it is said, when one half of Estonia comes to hear the other half sing. Nigel Haywood gulps as the 700 singers launch into a chant of 'Regilaul', an old Estonian salutation. There are no musical instruments. They aren't needed.

Penny Russell-Smith is having problems – not with the press but with the heavy-handed security teams. As the Queen moves down one line of well-wishers, the atmosphere suddenly sours. A security man starts shoving the BBC cameraman – who is filming on behalf of all the world's media – out of the way. 'Whoa! Whoa!' says Penny, trying to intervene. 'Queen's cameraman! Queen's cameraman!'

The security man either fails to understand or could not care less, and the cameraman is pushed over onto the cobbles. The official assumes that Penny is a troublemaker too. She may be a senior and trusted member of the Royal Household but this Estonian policeman says nothing. He chews his gum and bundles Penny out of the way like a protestor. 'Stop pushing me,' says Penny. 'I'm the Queen's Press Secretary. How dare you!' Just managing to keep her cool, she ploughs straight back in to the mêlée, unperturbed. 'Never mind,' she says matter-of-factly. 'They all got their pictures.'

The Queen takes her seat on stage as the choir pumps out epic tunes like 'Time of Awakening' and 'Litany To Thunder'. Finally comes a stirring old independence anthem called 'Can You Hear Me?' We certainly can.

The tour ends at HMS *Liverpool*, where the visit is timed to coincide with a flypast by aircraft from both countries. The Queen and President are in place and the anthems have been played. All eyes look to the skies for the formation of Royal Air Force Tornado jets. Nothing happens. Eventually, the second part of the flypast – three helicopters – chug overhead. While throats are cleared and watches examined, the unspoken question is: where is the RAF? Finally, the Tornado formation turns up to considerable relief.

After four days, three nations, twenty-four separate official engagements, several thousand handshakes and as many introductions, the royal couple bid farewell to President Ilves and the Baltic states.

The three nations have all seen modern history in human form. The Queen, in turn, has enjoyed visiting her 130th, 131st and 132nd nations.

For the Monarchy, this has been business as usual. Whether it is in America, in Estonia, on an ordinary British high street, at a school, in a hospital or on a Palace lawn, the job will remain the same, this year and the next: just keep on doing the same thing – differently.

THE LINE OF SUCCESSION
TO THE BRITISH THRONE

DESCENDANTS OF QUEEN ELIZABETH II

1   The Prince of Wales (b. 1948), eldest son of the Queen

2   Prince William of Wales (b. 1982), the Prince of Wales's elder son

3   Prince Henry of Wales (b. 1984), the Prince of Wales's younger son

4   The Duke of York (b. 1960), second son of the Queen (Prince Andrew)

5   Princess Beatrice of York (b. 1988), the Duke of York's elder daughter

6   Princess Eugenie of York (b. 1990), the Duke of York's younger daughter

7   The Earl of Wessex (b. 1964), the youngest son of the Queen (Prince Edward)

8   The Lady Louise Windsor (b. 2003), the Earl of Wessex's daughter

9   The Princess Royal (b. 1950), the Queen's daughter (Princess Anne)

10 Mr Peter Phillips (b. 1977), the Princess Royal's son

11 Miss Zara Phillips (b. 1981), the Princess Royal's daughter

DESCENDANTS OF KING GEORGE VI

12 Viscount Linley (b. 1961), grandson of King George VI through his daughter Princess Margaret

13 The Hon. Charles Armstrong-Jones (b. 1999), Viscount Linley's son

14 The Hon. Margarita Armstrong-Jones (b. 2002), Viscount Linley's daughter

15 The Lady Sarah Chatto (b. 1964), granddaughter of King George VI through his daughter Princess Margaret

16 Master Samuel Chatto (b. 1996), son of Lady Sarah Chatto

17 Master Arthur Chatto (b. 1999), son of Lady Sarah Chatto

Above: Rehearsing the Sovereign's Parade at Sandhurst. Above centre: The Palace by night.

DESCENDANTS OF KING GEORGE V

18   The Duke of Gloucester (b. 1944), grandson of King George V through his son Prince Henry, Duke of Gloucester

19   The Earl of Ulster (b. 1974), son of the Duke of Gloucester

20   The Lord Culloden (b. 2007), son of the Earl of Ulster

21   The Lady Davina Lewis (b. 1977), elder daughter of the Duke of Gloucester

22   The Lady Rose Windsor (b. 1980), younger daughter of the Duke of Gloucester

23   The Duke of Kent (b. 1935), grandson of King George V through his son Prince George, Duke of Kent

24   The Lady Marina-Charlotte Windsor (b. 1992), granddaughter of the Duke of Kent via his eldest son, the Earl of St Andrews (who lost his place in the line of succession after marrying a Roman Catholic)

25   The Lady Amelia Windsor (b. 1995), granddaughter of the Duke of Kent George and daughter of the Earl of St Andrews

26   The Lady Helen Taylor (b. 1964), daughter of the Duke of Kent

27   Master Columbus Taylor (b. 1994), son of Lady Helen Taylor

28   Master Cassius Taylor (b. 1996), son of Lady Helen Taylor

29   Miss Eloise Taylor (b. 2003), daughter of Lady Helen Taylor

30   Miss Estella Taylor (b. 2004), daughter of Lady Helen Taylor

31   The Lord Frederick Windsor (b. 1979), great-grandson of King George V and son of Prince Michael of Kent (who lost his place in the line of succession after marrying a Roman Catholic)

Above right: The Royal Family in the Centre Room at Buckingham Palace after Trooping the Colour.

32   The Lady Gabriella Windsor (b. 1981), daughter of Prince Michael of Kent

33   Princess Alexandra, the Hon. Lady Ogilvy (b. 1936), granddaughter of King George V through Prince George, Duke of Kent

34   Mr James Ogilvy (b. 1964), son of Princess Alexandra

35   Master Alexander Ogilvy (b. 1996), son of James Ogilvy

36   Miss Flora Ogilvy (b. 1994), daughter of James Ogilvy

37   Miss Marina Ogilvy (formerly Mrs Paul Mowatt), (b. 1966), daughter of Princess Alexandra

38   Master Christian Mowatt (b. 1993), son of Mrs Paul Mowatt

39   Miss Zenouska Mowatt (b. 1990), daughter of Mrs Paul Mowatt

40   The Earl of Harewood (b. 1923), son of Princess Mary, only daughter of King George V

41   Viscount Lascelles (b. 1950), son of the Earl of Harewood

42   The Hon. Alexander Lascelles (b. 1980), son of Viscount Lascelles

43   The Hon. Edward Lascelles (b. 1982), son of Viscount Lascelles

44   The Hon. James Lascelles (b. 1953), son of the Earl of Harewood

45   Mr Rowan Lascelles (b. 1977), son of James Lascelles

46   Mr Tewa Lascelles (b. 1985), son of James Lascelles

47   Miss Sophie Lascelles (b. 1973), daughter of James Lascelles

48   The Hon. Jeremy Lascelles (b. 1955), son of the Earl of Harewood

49   Mr Thomas Lascelles (b. 1982), son of Jeremy Lascelles

50   Miss Ellen Lascelles (b. 1984), daughter of Jeremy Lascelles

HONOURS –WHAT THEY MEAN
AND WHERE THEY GO

All honours, except Knight Bachelor, come with post-nominal letters which go after the holder's name. If the holder has more than one honour, then they must be listed in order of precedence. Here is the list of the main British honours worn today – along with their abbreviations – in the correct order of precedence.

Some of the old rank-based honours for the Armed Forces are no longer awarded and have been upgraded. For example, the Military Cross (MC) is awarded for 'exemplary gallantry' against the enemy. It used to be awarded only to officers, however, while other ranks received the Military Medal (MM). In 1993, the then Prime Minister, John Major, decided that such distinctions were outdated and the MC is now awarded to all instead.

Bt/Bart	Baronet
VC	Victoria Cross
GC	George Cross
KG/LG	Knight/Lady Companion of the Most Noble Order of the Garter
KT/LT	Knight/Lady Companion of the Most Ancient and Most Noble Order of the Thistle
PC	Privy Counsellor
GCB	Knight (or Dame) Grand Cross of the Most Honourable Order of the Bath
OM	Member of the Order of Merit
GCMG	Knight (or Dame) Grand Cross of the Most Distinguished Order of Saint Michael and Saint George
GCVO	Knight (or Dame) Grand Cross of the Royal Victorian Order
GBE	Knight (or Dame) Grand Cross of the Most Excellent Order of the British Empire
CH	Member of the Order of the Companions of Honour

KCB/DCB	Knight/Dame Commander of the Most Honourable Order of the Bath
KCMG/DCMG	Knight/Dame Commander of the Most Distinguished Order of Saint Michael and Saint George
KCVO/DCVO	Knight/Dame Commander of the Royal Victorian Order
KBE/DBE	Knight/Dame Commander of the Most Excellent Order of the British Empire
Knight Bachelor	Knight (no abbreviation)
CB	Companion of the Most Honourable Order of the Bath
CMG	Companion of the Most Distinguished Order of Saint Michael and Saint George
CVO	Commander of the Royal Victorian Order
CBE	Commander of the Most Excellent Order of the British Empire
DSO	Companion of the Distinguished Service Order
LVO	Lieutenant of the Royal Victorian Order
OBE	Officer of the Most Excellent Order of the British Empire
ISO	Companion of the Imperial Service Order
MVO	Member of the Royal Victorian Order
MBE	Member of the Most Excellent Order of the British Empire
CGC	Conspicuous Gallantry Cross
DSC	Distinguished Service Cross
MC	Military Cross
DFC	Distinguished Flying Cross
AFC	Air Force Cross
DCM	Distinguished Conduct Medal
CGM	Conspicuous Gallantry Medal
GM	George Medal
DSM	Distinguished Service Medal
MM	Military Medal
DFM	Distinguished Flying Medal
AFM	Air Force Medal
QGM	Queen's Gallantry Medal
BEM	British Empire Medal
TD	Territorial Efficiency Decoration
RD	Decoration for Officers of the Royal Naval Reserve
VRD	Decoration for Officers of the Royal Naval Volunteer Reserve
AE	Air Efficiency Award

INDEX